Twitch®

by Tee Morris

for
dummies®
A Wiley Brand

Twitch® For Dummies®

Published by: John Wiley & Sons, Inc., 111 River Street, Hoboken, NJ 07030-5774, www.wiley.com

Copyright © 2019 by John Wiley & Sons, Inc., Hoboken, New Jersey

Published simultaneously in Canada

For general information on our other products and services, please contact our Customer Care Department within the U.S. at 877-762-2974, outside the U.S. at 317-572-3993, or fax 317-572-4002. For technical support, please visit https://hub.wiley.com/community/support/dummies.

Wiley publishes in a variety of print and electronic formats and by print-on-demand. Some material included with standard print versions of this book may not be included in e-books or in print-on-demand. If this book refers to media such as a CD or DVD that is not included in the version you purchased, you may download this material at http://booksupport.wiley.com. For more information about Wiley products, visit www.wiley.com.

Library of Congress Control Number: 2018963624

ISBN 978-1-119-54026-7 (pbk); ISBN 978-1-119-54025-0 (ebk); ISBN 978-1-119-54029-8 (ebk)

Manufactured in the United States of America

C10006606_113018

Contents at a Glance

Table of Contents

Introduction

I f you play video games — regardless of your age, your platform, or your preference of FPS or MMO — you may have noticed there's this feature offered to share your gameplay. *"What is that?"* you might wonder before jumping into your game. Weeks later, that *"Share Your Gameplay"* option has been nagging at you. The only way you can quell this curiosity is to go online and do a little digging to discover this thing called *streaming*. Now, if you have been involved with online media for as long as I have (see Wiley Publishing's *Podcasting For Dummies* for all the details there), streaming in the early days of podcasting was emerging against many technological barriers, dependent on many factors ranging from computer processor speeds to Internet connections to host server capabilities. And if the stars aligned, you *might* get a video feed matching the quality of a convenience store security camera.

Then technology evolved. Computers not only performed faster, they performed more efficiently. And developers who created the hardware and software to stream also made the technology more accessible. Then came along a service called Justin. tv. Then Justin.tv evolved into its final form — Twitch.

I'm sure my own reaction was not too far from yours. *Twitch? Sounds serious. Have you consulted a physician?*

Twitch For Dummies offers you an explanation and a gateway, not into a strange medical affliction, but into an exciting, new entertainment platform that features video games and so much more. Beginning with the question at the forefront of your mind — *What is Twitch?* — this book takes you through the fastest-growing trend that is becoming a source of income for many. By the time you reach the end of this book, you will know how to stream, how to present, and how to effectively get your word out to audiences everywhere — and you can even have a bit of fun along the way.

About This Book

Twitch For Dummies should be these things to all who pick up and read it (whether straight through or by jumping around in the chapters):

>> A user-friendly guide in how to assemble a studio, produce, and stream video games, product demos, or self-help sessions

>> A terrific reference for choosing the right hardware and software to put together a professional-looking stream

>> The starting point for the person who knows nothing about video, audio, editing, recording, hosting streams, or how to turn a computer into a broadcasting studio

>> A handy go-to "think tank" for any beginning streamer who's hungry for new ideas on what goes into a good stream and fresh points of view

>> A really fun read

There will be plenty of answers in these pages, and if you find the answers too elementary, I will provide you plenty of points of reference to research. I don't claim to have all the solutions, quick fixes, and resolutions to all possible Twitch queries, but I will present to you the basic building blocks and first steps for beginning a stream. As with any *For Dummies* book, my responsibility is to offer you a foundation on which to build your Channel and grow.

I feel the need to also mention that I feature just a fraction of Twitch streamers that are online streaming their hearts out. You may not hear from your favorite Twitch streamer. In fact, you may hear from streamers that you may have never heard or seen before, and you may think *"Why didn't you talk to [insert favorite streamer here]?"* While you may not know these streamers, I do, and what I have learned from them I hope to pass along to you.

This book was written as a linear path from the conceptualization stages to the final production of your content. However, not everyone needs to read this book from page one. If you've already gotten your feet wet with the various aspects of streaming or Twitch itself, feel free to jump around from section to section and read the parts that you need. We provide plenty of guides back to other relevant chapters for when the going gets murky.

Icons Used in This Book

So you're trekking through the book, making some real progress with developing your podcast, when suddenly these little icons leap out, grab you by the throat, and wrestle you to the ground. (Who would have thought streaming was so action-packed, like a Daniel Craig *Bond* movie, huh?) What do all these little drawings mean? Glad you asked.

TIP

When I'm in the middle of a discussion and I suddenly have one of those *"Say, that reminds me . . ."* moments (which, in my own streams, happen often), I give you one of these tips. They're handy little extras that are good to know and might even make your podcast sound a little tighter than average.

REMEMBER

If the moment is more than a handy little nugget of information and closer to a *"Seriously, you can't forget this part!"* factoid, I mark it with a Remember icon. You're going to want to play close attention to these puppies.

WARNING

Sometimes I interrupt my own train of thought (again, something that happens often with me on stream) with a *"Time out, Sparky . . ."* moment. And this is where I ask for your undivided attention. The Warnings are exactly that: flashing lights, ah-ooga horns, dire portents. They're reminders not to try this at home because you'll definitely regret it.

Beyond the Book

You can find a little more helpful Twitch-related information on www.dummies.com, where you can peruse this book's Cheat Sheet. To get this handy resource, go to www.dummies.com and type *Twitch For Dummies Cheat Sheet* in the Search box.

In addition to the website hosted by the good people at www.dummies.com, this book comes with a companion *Twitch stream,* airing on Sunday afternoons. From your browser of choice, visit www.twitch.tv/theteemonster, and follow (or subscribe) to receive notifications when *Twitch For Dummies* author, yours truly, Tee Morris, goes live to take your questions. And maybe, on occasion, I may be joined online or in-studio by special guests, some you may read about in this book. Your questions are encouraged as I cover concepts in this book explored in greater detail, from Photoshop tutorials in creating overlays, to converting video content to audio, to managing the business of your Twitch stream.

Where to Go from Here

At this point, many *For Dummies* authors say something snappy, clever, or even a bit snarky. Chuck and I did so often throughout editions of *Podcasting For Dummies*, and I continue that tradition here. My best tongue-in-cheek material is saved for the pages inside, so here's a more serious approach . . .

If you want to hop around the book, that's your decision, but I suggest planting yourself in front of a computer and starting with Chapter 1. Together, we check out a few links, put together a Twitch Channel, and then we start working on that streaming persona. Along the way, I'm going to talk to other Twitch streamers and ask their advice, suggest other Twitch streams and their companion podcasts that can educate, inspire, and enlighten you. And through it all, we are going to work together to create engaging, original content.

Where do we go from here? Out into the Great Wide Open, my friends. So buckle up. It's going to be a heck of a ride.

1

Getting Your Game On

Set up your Twitch account and creating a complete profile.

Explore the Twitch platform by watching and following those who are already established on Twitch or are working to do so.

Put together a simple streaming setup using your gaming console.

Launch your Twitch Channel, critique your first week, and consider the options for you and the content you create.

IN THIS CHAPTER

» Finding out what streaming is

» Finding out what Twitch is

» Creating a Twitch account

» Following and subscribing to Twitch Channels

Chapter **1**

Welcome to the World of Twitch

ou ever look around and think *"How did I get here?"* I know, that's a pretty deep question to kick off a *For Dummies* book, but I have been doing this a lot lately. Technology, on the whole, is pretty awe-inspiring in how it evolves in such a short amount of time. When you find your niche, it is also amazing to see how things that were considered out-of-reach, if not impossible, are now suddenly tools of the trade, some of them a simple plug-and-play or a quick click of an "OK" button away.

Maybe that is how you are feeling right now with this copy of *Twitch For Dummies*. How did I get here? Maybe you've heard of Twitch before, and you may have quickly dismissed it because you're not a gamer. On the surface, Twitch may appear to be a gamer's haven only for those keyboard warriors with lightning-quick reflexes. Look a little deeper, beyond the *World of Warcraft* and *Fortnite* channels, and you will find streamers that have made impressions in society, raising money for charity, hosting tutorials, and even helping out others in creative or personal development endeavors. Not all Twitch Channels are so deep. Many of them are simply friends jumping online and having a good laugh, inviting you to join in on the experience.

Deciding Whether Twitch Is for You

Technically speaking, streaming is the distribution of specially encoded multimedia content, usually video (but it can include audio exclusively if you wanted to make the stream less robust) onto desktop computers, laptop computers, and mobile devices such as tablets and smartphones via broadband or wireless Internet connections. It's a bit like podcasting, something I've been doing since 2005. Now, if you are looking for a less technical definition of streaming, how about:

> Streaming allows you to broadcast or consume visual content on a global platform.

In a nutshell, you are doing what you would do when you're podcasting, only this time you're live, you're in real-time, and editing only happens after your stream is done and you want to convert it into the afore-mentioned podcast, a YouTube channel, or some other sort of consumable audio-video presentation.

While podcasting turns the tables on broadcast schedules, allowing the content consumer (or *subscriber*) to choose not only what to listen or watch, but also when; *streaming* does require — especially in the early stages of establishing a Twitch Channel — a reliable, set schedule. One of many things podcasting does share with Twitch is that your signal is not reliant on a transmitter or even a satellite for that matter. So long as you have a strong Internet connection and a device that is able to stream, you can host a Twitch Channel.

There are a lot of reasons you might want to launch a Twitch Channel, but the simplest reason to stream is that *it's just plain fun!* I've been streaming regularly since September 6, 2017, and through all the breaks, the changes, and the modest numbers I've seen, I am still having a blast, continuing to play video games with other gamers of varying backgrounds for worldwide audiences. It's a reoccurring reason people continue to stream, even when the hobby becomes something of a part- or full-time job. Even with channel hosts challenging themselves with new tricks and techniques in creating engaging and entertaining content, in the end it's just you, friends from parts known and unknown, and video games. Yes, Twitch is a lot of fun, as you can see in Figure 1-1.

But why would you want to put yourself — and yes, your questionable skills of aim — up for scrutiny from a global audience? There are a lot of reasons to set yourself up a platform on Twitch, each of these reasons come with their own rewards and benefits, and can really make a difference in your community, both online and in the real world.

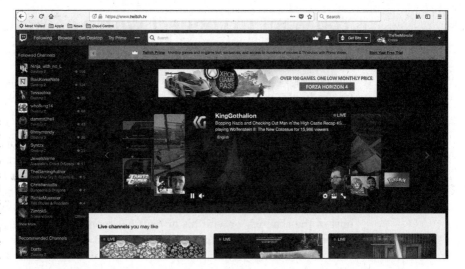

FIGURE 1-1:
Twitch, while known for gaming, also features creatives of all backgrounds sharing their passions on an interactive platform.

WHY TWITCH?

Streaming has been around for well over a decade, shortly after podcasting began to emerge as a form of consumable media. However, many of these early adopters were struggling with the ability to send out a strong, smooth video. With broadband becoming more and more prevalent, and devices both large and small able to process constant streams of data, Twitch's timing could not have been better. While other streaming services catered to special events and one-night performances, Twitch tapped into the billion-dollar industry of video games, allowing gamers of all skill levels to show people what they could do.

While Twitch blazed this trail in content streaming, other platforms have caught on and are making a play (pun *completely* intended) for the leaderboard. Twitter created Periscope, which laid the groundwork for Facebook to create Facebook Live. Facebook Live now offers Facebook Gaming, a platform similar to Twitch that offers viewers to interact with gamers, send "Cheers" (digital tips), and other kinds of transactions for the host. A new player on the market is Caffeine (`http://caffeine.tv`), emphasizing the social aspect of streaming rather than financial gain. Then there is YouTube Gaming (`https://gaming.youtube.com`) and Mixer (`https://mixer.com`), direct competitors to Twitch that offers both *Affiliate* and *Partner* opportunities. (More on Affiliate and Partner opportunities at Chapter 12.)

You have options, but for the purposes of this title, we are focusing on Twitch as this is where Tee finds himself entertaining fellow gamers coast-to-coast and around the world.

You want to connect with a community based on your passions or hobbies

The biggest draw to Twitch is this: finding people that enjoy what you enjoy, and establishing connections. It could simply be for social interaction, or it could be a desire for you to build a network for yourself. It could also be a desire to try and figure out what you can do to improve in a game, creative pursuit, or hobby. Are you wanting to get into cooking, and preparing healthier meals? What are the basic tools you would need to start costuming? Are you a photographer that struggles with Photoshop? Are you finding yourself stuck in a particularly tricky level of *Shadow of the Tomb Raider*? While you could go on and look up forums, YouTube videos, or other tutorials, Twitch grants you the opportunity to interact with the host of the channel, or with his or her Chat room, and ask questions. So Twitch can be an extremely immersive experience, and it can also be a real education. Add to that the community you meet, and soon you will find yourself connected with others all sharing your passion for the topic at hand.

TIP

The temptation to jump into the chat like an old friend may be a very tempting one, but it can do you a world of good to simply say "Good morning" and then sit back and listen to the conversation. Some hosts are very affable and congenial, quick to respond with a return greeting. Others may be late to respond on account of the activity they are engaged in. Some may not respond at all. Get a feel for what the relationship is between host and audience before engaging. Offer opinions if asked, but get to know the community before speaking as an old friend to the Chat.

You want to turn your subject of interest into a social experience

Okay, this may sound a little odd at first, and chances are, when you tell people about Twitch, they cock their heads to one side and ask you with all sincerity, *"Hold on, people watch you play video games?"* Phrased like that, even if you swap out video games with another pursuit such as costume crafting, scrapbooking, coding, or something else, it does sound unlikely, not to mention odd, that anyone would find that entertaining.

These people, most times, have never watched anything on Twitch.

Strange as it may sound, turning the subject of your Twitch Channel into something like an online talk show can not only benefit you in what you are pursuing (blasting a boss in order to progress to the next level, writing a particularly tough passage in order to progress in your novel, adding a certain spice to a dish you are making) but can also offer your audience something in return. This is reality television in its most raw form, and while you are opening the world up to your corner of it, the rewards can be amazing.

You want to generate excitement

As Twitch is live, there is nothing holding you back from nurturing anticipation over an upcoming release, event, or project you are involved with. This is, after all, your passion, and if you are sharing it on Twitch, the world can see just how excited you are about this. In a video games feed, it may be discussions over what was just announced at E3 (www.e3expo.com). In a Art feed, it may be an upcoming exhibition or new release about to hit bookshelves. In a Special Events or Just Chatting feed, it could be the purchase of a house or a moment from your first vacation overseas. The reason can be personal or pubic own nature, and Twitch offers you a platform to rally a community in what will be coming soon.

TIP

Promotion is fine and all, yes, and you want to generate the hype for your upcoming event or product release, but do not expect regular audiences or amazing community responses if this is all your channel does. If, one week, you're hosting a fashion show of geeky tee shirts and then the next week you are discussing with various guests the importance of life insurance, constant shilling does not necessarily make for good programming. When starting off as an individual, a lack of interest or critical pushback of just being another hype generator may occur. Make sure to find something your audience wants to engage with before you begin to promote.

You have a cause that needs attention

The Villalobos Rescue Shelter.

Mental health and wellness.

St. Jude's Children's Hospital.

Extra Life.

What these four things have in common? Twitch.

While it is easy to dismiss Twitch as just "a site where people watch other people play video games," there are streamers who are making the most of their platform and raising awareness, money, or in some instances both, for a cause they believe in. For example, the organizers of GuardianCon (http://guardiancon.co) — a video game and Twitch event held in Tampa, Florida — set out in 2017 to break their 2016 goal of $500,000 raised for St. Jude's Children's Hospital. They ended up raising just over $1,000,000. In 2018, they tripled that. To show support for rescue dogs like Layla, pictured in Figure 1-2, Aura hosts Gaming4Pits, an event raising awareness for rescue animals of all breeds; and each year Aura pushes the goal higher and higher.

FIGURE 1-2:
Twitch streamer
Aura raises
awareness and
money for the
Villalobos
Rescue Center.
His 2018 event,
Gaming4Pits,
raised over
$25,000 to
support rescue
dogs like Layla,
his Channel
mascot pictured
here.

Even if not hosting a charity stream, Twitch offers your channel a place to talk about issues that you feel need attention. In between her own stretches with *Destiny* and photo editing streams, Twitch broadcaster SheSnaps (http://twitch.tv/shesnaps) offers insights into mental health and depression, emphasizing her own journey with it and the importance of asking for help. This is a small sampling of what you can find out there on Twitch, and you may find this is the platform that best fits your needs.

WARNING

Before volunteering or giving to a charity stream, take a moment to find out what the charity is and the reputation of the organization. There are some unscrupulous types online, so it never hurts to be too careful. Additionally, charity streams will usually work with a third party to get donations to the recipients. If a stream is hosting a charity stream for, let's say, cancer research, but the donations are going to streamer claiming "I'll collect donations and then send them along to the charity . . ." be wary. This could be a scam.

You want to have a little fun

Then you have streamers that just enjoy a good laugh.

For some hosts, their Twitch Channel becomes a game show where the intent is to just have a good laugh. Other hosts reach out to their viewers and invite them to join in. And for some streamers, it's about offering a helping hand in accomplishing in-game tasks. Whatever the reason, the main point of the channel is to have a good time. Put on some tunes, chill, play, laugh. It's about helping others. It's about *community*, a word we will be saying often throughout this book.

TIP

One way to decide what kind of stream you want to host is to take a look at other streamers and see how they present their content. You can keep it simple, make a wish list of tricked out effects, or go full tilt into productions that could easily rival television studios. There is no "one way" to stream, but finding inspiration from other streamers is a great way to develop your own stream.

If Twitch is still the platform for you, and maybe you have an entirely different reason for hosting a channel from what we have listed here, then you are ready to set out on your own personal journey with streaming. You don't have to apply all the bells and whistles yet. There are quite a few Twitch streams that are sophisticated in their presentations, but those Twitch streamers have been at this for a few years. Some Twitch streamers find a basic look for them is all they need.

We all have to start somewhere. Twitch makes the starting process incredibly easy.

Creating a Twitch Account

There are two schools of thought when it comes to creating a Twitch Channel: There's the *"I need the latest and greatest studio gear, the fastest supercomputer on the market, and a full-on production set and crew in order to create a stream of broadcast industry quality that will make people flock to my channel!"* school of thought. And you also have the *"Huh... I've got on my PS4 an option to 'Broadcast Gameplay' and I've got a pretty decent headset. Why don't I give it a go?"* school of thought. Both are equally valid approaches to streaming, sure, and there are a lot of other disciplines and strategies in-between. The real questions are how far are you're willing to go, how far do you want to go, and will it be worth it — both financially and emotionally — to go that far?

These are the tough questions of Twitch, but allow me this moment to dispel a few misconceptions about streaming right off the bat: Streaming does not demand that you convert your basement into a broadcasting studio. You do not need a set, lighting equipment, or multiple cameras to stream. You do not have to invest thousands upon thousands of dollars to create the ultimate power stream. (I mean, you *could*, but why not crawl before running a sprint against Usain Bolt?) Streaming on Twitch is not rocket science. In fact, here's a quick rundown of how to launch a Twitch Channel:

1. Set up an account on Twitch with a preferred email account.

2. Find on your gaming console where you can broadcast your game.

3. Select something to play.

4. Start streaming on Twitch.

If you are thinking, *"Now hold on a minute — if streaming is that simple, then why is this book so thick?"* Well, yes, I did gloss over a few details, but streaming on Twitch *is* that simple. The details of putting together your own Twitch Channel start in Chapter 3 and wrap up in Chapter 8; then the rest of this book will walk you through all the geek-speak you need to begin building your audience and keeping them engaged, how to generate revenue, and what to do with all this content you are generating. Throughout all of this title, you will be given recommendations of other streamers and maybe even hear from them from time to time.

We got a lot to do, so let's get cracking.

Insert coins to begin: The basics

So, with that quick approach depicted above, you can have within moments a Twitch account activated and running, but that's all you would have. It would be an empty space with the most basic of contact info and no details to speak of. Right now, you're thinking *"Okay, so when do I start streaming?"* I'm going to have you pump the brakes and curb that enthusiasm of yours. Let's start from the beginning and then spend some quality time filling in the blanks and understanding this platform.

1. Go to http://twitch.tv **and select from the top-right side of your browser window the** *Sign Up* **option (see Figure 1-3).**

TIP

You can still watch Twitch streams without being signed up with the platform. However, if you want to take advantage of the Chat features, you will need an account.

2. Come up with a username for yourself on Twitch.

This is how you will appear in Chat. This can be a nickname you go by, a play on words, or your own name. There can be a lot of different ways you can approach the Username. Just make sure you are not violating any Terms of Service on creating it.

WARNING

When establishing a username for yourself, avoid picking something overly generic. Usernames like "Fortnitelover01" and "LeagueLegend2245" isn't going to stand out in a crowd and will lead to a branding change if your channel grows to something bigger. Additionally, if you are constantly changing your handle, it can become problematic with people finding you — and yes, trusting you — on Twitch. For more on this, see the sidebar "Branding 101: Your Username" appearing later in this chapter.

FIGURE 1-3:
Setting up a
Twitch Channel
only takes a
few minutes
and is free.

3. **Create a password.**

4. **Enter in your birthday.**

   Again, this is based on an honor system, but the birthday is there to verify your age and that it is within the Terms of Service as established by Twitch. For more on Twitch's TOS, visit www.twitch.tv/p/legal/terms-of-service.

5. **Enter a valid email.**

   This email is where all notifications and any news from Twitch are sent.

6. **After reviewing the Terms of Service and the Privacy Policy, click *Sign Up* to complete the application.**

Congratulations! Your Twitch account is now active. Technically, from here, you are ready to start streaming. You have a place on Twitch, but presently, the state of your Twitch account is a lot like the state of a Twitter account newly launched where the Profile Picture is the egg, the bio is blank, and the username is your Twitter handle. When you come across Twitter accounts like that, you can't avoid a hint of skepticism as to how genuine these accounts are.

So begins the work on completing the Twitch account and understanding the platform. These are details that, if you forge ahead without tending to them, you will find growth a challenge, ease of use a little elusive, and overall performance lacking. The sooner you sort them out, the better of a first impression you'll make. Maybe these details feel tedious, but they are the *"wax on, wax off . . ."* of Twitch. Completing these steps will grant you a deeper understanding of the platform.

New Twitch, who dis: Completing the Profile

Signed into Twitch with a newly minted account, you have a blank slate where you begin assembling a persona for yourself. The *Profile* is where you introduce yourself to the public, many times through a brief bio, maybe a few visual touches like a photo or a banner image. Think of the Profile as the interior decoration of your house. When people walk into your home, they will learn quickly what kind of personality you are. That's what we are going to build for you right now.

1. **Go to your Twitch account on** `http://twitch.tv` **and select from the top-right side of your browser window your Account Status' drop menu. seen in Figure 1-4. Select** *Settings* **(located near the bottom of the drop menu) to enter your Twitch account's Profile.**

    Your *Account Status* is always visible on the Twitch website. It tells you what is happening on your Channel and shares your activities with friends. You can also go "Invisible" or enable a "Dark Mode" scheme for the Twitch website.

2. **Find a good** *Profile Picture* **best representative of you. It can be anything (within reason), but it should be a simple image easily identified at a small size.**

    Twitch recognizes images in JPEG, PNG, and GIF formats. The dimensions of the image should not exceed 256x256 pixels or be larger than 10MB in file size.

TIP

    As with other social media platforms, the best profile pictures are simple, basic images. You want backgrounds that aren't too busy and photos that are taken in close up. So long as you can tell what the image is at a glance, you have a good Profile Picture.

3. **Upload for your** *Profile Banner* **an image that sets a tone or an atmosphere for your account and Twitch Channel page.**

    Twitch recognizes images in JPEG, PNG, and GIF formats. The dimensions of the image should not exceed 1230x380 pixels or be larger than 10MB in file size.

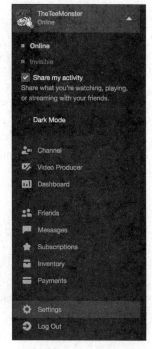

FIGURE 1-4:
Selecting the
Settings option
will take you to
the Profile option
of your Twitch
account. When
completed, it
should look
something like
Tee's, pictured
here.

4. **Scroll down to *Profile Settings* and either review or enter in your desired email.**

   Again, this email is where all notifications and any news from Twitch are sent.

5. **If needed, click on the pencil icon in the Username field to edit your Twitch handle.**

   This email is where all notifications and any news from Twitch are sent.

6. **In the Display Name field, edit your Username to appear the way you want it to appear.**

   For example, my username is "theteemonster" but "TheTeeMonster" is how I want it displayed.

7. **Scroll down to *Bio* and write up a brief biography of who you are.**

8. **Single-click the *Save Changes* button to accept your changes.**

The Profile section of your Settings is now complete, and when people visit your Channel, either online or through the Twitch app, they will see a completed profile as opposed to the default settings. It's always best to put your best foot forward, you know?

BRANDING 101: YOUR USERNAME

Rarely when you launch into a new online platform, or even social media for that matter, the notion of "branding" comes to mind. When I talk about branding, I am not referring to the kind of branding one would do with a cow as depicted in Westerns. Branding is, in a nutshell, your online identity. For example, my own screen name on Twitch is "TheTeeMonster" which is connected with my PSN account, TheTeeMonster. When I go live, notifications are sent out on Twitch and on my Twitter account, TeeMonster. Even before I go live, I drop promos about it on Twitter and my Instagram account, TheTeeMonster.

See what I'm doing here? This is branding. And it does matter.

By focusing on branding, you make it easier for people to find you, as well as identify you, on Twitch. While you may notice a variation on a theme (TheTeeMonster, TeeMonster, TheRealTeeMonster, etc.), there is a consistency there, and that consistency helps you strengthen your online identity as well as your online brand. Sometimes, you have to be clever. UK streamer "Munchie" couldn't get "Munchie" or even "RealMunchie" as a username, so he created the username "REALMUNCHIE" — with a lowercase "L" instead of an "I" at the end — to stay with his online brand. The end result: `http://twitch.tv/realmunchle`.

When establishing an online brand, you want it easy for people to find you online. That's why you may want to think a few steps ahead and find a name that could work across several platforms. There will be more about branding and other ways of promoting yourself positively in Chapter 13.

REMEMBER

If you decide that Twitch is not for you, go to Status ⇨ Settings ⇨ Disabling Your Twitch Account. You can follow the link offered to where you can shut your account down.

We have a few more details to take care of here, but you're off to the right start.

All in the details: Channel and videos settings

Once your Profile is complete, you can progress to the right of the Settings options. The Twitch Prime option, quickly described, is the option for you to connect your Twitch account with an Amazon Prime account. This is an on-going special deal for Twitch users where various perks and deals are offered if you do this. Continuing past this, you have *Channel and Videos* where you set specific details about your

Twitch Channel. While you now have an active *account*, that is not the same as having an active *Channel*. There is a subtle difference, and in Channel and Videos we will set parameters for our channel that helps you manage your Twitch Channel once content begins streaming.

REMEMBER

Twitch is always looking to improve their website and their User Interface (UI). That means some features highlighted here have moved from the "Settings" section to your "Dashboard" section. Throughout this exercise, we will be jumping between these two sections of Twitch.

1. **From your Account Status' drop menu, select *Dashboard* and then select the *Settings* > *Channel* option.**

2. **Upload or create a good Video Player Banner image (an example is shown in Figure 1-5) representative of your channel. It can be anything (within reason), but it should be representative of you or your channel.**

   The Video Player Banner is an image that works as your channel's placeholder when you are not streaming or hosting another streamer's Channel. Twitch recognizes images in JPEG, PNG, and GIF formats. The file size should not exceed 10MB.

TIP

   The Video Player Banner, as shown in Figure 1-5, can also serve as banners for special events coming to your Channel. When creating banners, don't be afraid to use them as promotional opportunities.

FIGURE 1-5:
When choosing a Video Player Banner, consider an image that informs people of your stream, whether it is your schedule or additional social links like Twitter and Instagram.

EYES UP GUARDIAN

BLIND GAMER PLAYS DESTINY 2
TWITCH STREAM WITH @THETEEMONSTER
COMING SOON!
TWITCH.TV/BLINDGAMERSTEVE & TWITCH.TV/THETEEMONSTER

3. **Scroll up to *Content Settings* and either select *Mature Content* or leave the switch in the *OFF* position.**

   Twitch's Terms of Service dictate that, if your channel is broadcasting sexual activity, nudity, threats, or extreme violence, and your Channel is not marked as "Mature," then Twitch can immediately and irrevocably terminate your account.

4. **Return to your Account Status' drop menu. Select *Settings* and then select the *Channel & Video* option.**

5. **Scroll down to *Chat Options* and either review or edit your settings.**

TIP

Many of these details in your Channel can also be managed by *Virtual Assistants* like Nightbot and Deepbot. To find out more about Virtual Assistants, jump ahead for an overview in Chapter 2 or a deep dive into how to set these online assistants up at Chapter 8.

A few details taken care of, and our account is beginning to take shape. Let's keep this streak alive, and complete the last few remaining settings for your Twitch account.

Controlling the signal: From privacy to connected third parties

Twitch, and social media on a whole, is all about sharing. That's the truth about all of these platforms: You reap what you put into them. So, garbage in? Garbage out. Quality talk? Quality stream. Twitch is an investment both on an emotional as well as a financial level. But what if there are details you don't want to share, or visitors to your Channel you don't want to share with? I would be the first to tell you: If you want to keep it private, keep it offline. *And there is nothing wrong with that.* There is no Prime Directive of Social Media saying you will be cast out if you do not share everything. And maybe you want to only be notified of certain details with your account activity, and connect with only certain third parties.

Here's the final steps needed in keeping control of your account. It's good to know what is running by default, and exactly what kind of control you have over your Twitch experience.

1. **In the Settings window, single-click the *Security and Privacy* option.**

2. **Under *Password* is where you change your password.**

3. **Activate *Two-Factor Authentication* for additional security with your Twitch account.**

Two-Factor Authentication is where, along with your password on Twitch, you enable an app like *Authy* (https://authy.com) to generate on your phone a security key. This is an additional layer of security in order to protect your account, something I and other streamers *strongly* recommend.

4. **Review Privacy settings to see if this is how you wish for people to reach out to you.**

    Whispers are direct messages between you and other members of Twitch. By default, anyone — be they Friends or not — can reach out to you and swap messages and URLs. If managing Whispers is not preferred, you can block that avenue of communications here.

5. **Single-click *Notifications* and review here all the different ways Twitch keeps you informed on what is happening in your account and on your channel.**

    Twitch has broken down the various ways you are notified of people going live, when Whispers arrive, and when special events launch, into the following categories:

    - On Twitch

    - By Email

    - On Mobile

    - Advanced

    These are all the different parameters you can set up for Twitch to send you notifications of when certain actions occur. When a channel you follow goes live, when special events begin, or when Friends whisper to you, Twitch will send notifications. The Advanced tab lists of every channel you follow. If you decide, after clearing out your Inbox, that you would rather not be notified in email when Channels you follow go live, you can disable those notifications here.

6. **Single-click *Connections* and review here the various third-party extensions and services that you have connected with your Twitch account.**

    These different connections — Amazon, Facebook, Twitter, and so on — are like plug-ins for social media platforms. They all, in some way, help your channel in notifying others when you go live, making the most out of your console's connection to Twitch, and much more. Think of these Connections as digital accessories to your Twitch Channel.

The Profile section of your Settings is now done. This may not seem like a lot, but when people visit your Channel, either online or through the Twitch app, they will see a *completed* profile as opposed to default settings. It's always best to put your best foot forward, you know?

Learning at the Feet of Masters: Following and Subscribing to Twitch Channels

This book is going to teach you a lot about streaming, and a lot about Twitch. When I was stepping into this community, though, there was no *Twitch For Dummies* as a guide. There were (and still are) online tutorials, and even Twitch streamers that tend to offer up help in getting your own Twitch Channel up and running. However, my own journey — the more people I talk to — tends to be similar to the majority of new and even experienced streamers. You stumble into Twitch and find yourself in a pretty interesting place, filled with a variety of personalities.

Along with this book, one of the best ways to really understand Twitch and understand the platform is to learn from watching others. Whether you are watching someone with a massive amount of audience or perhaps enjoying some time with streamers that are more popular with intimate crowds, a lot can be learned from just being part of the community.

But how do we join this community? It is so easy that it might surprise you.

Following on Twitch

Anyone can watch. You can easily just jump into a directory and start watching some Twitch streamers do what they do with their game of choice. Depending on how much the streamer has opened up or locked down their Twitch account, you may even be able to chat with the channel host.

So, let's say you find a channel (or recommended a channel which, yes, I'll be doing later in this chapter) and you want to support that streamer. The easiest way to do this is to give the Channel a follow.

1. **Go to** `http://twitch.tv` **and find a new channel to watch.**

   When you go the main page of Twitch, you will be presented with a variety of streamers and the games they play. The more Twitch programming you consume, the more your directory will change and adapt to your interests.

2. **Watch the streamer for a chunk of time. Give the stream thirty minutes at the very least, an hour at the most.**

It is always a good idea to give a stream a fair shake. You will probably know within a few minutes if the streamer you want to follow is either a streamer you connect with or is not running at your speed. If you decide to stick around for longer, engage with the Chat stream, see how that goes with you. At any new channel, though, give yourself some time to get to know the overall atmosphere of the Twitch Channel.

3. **Just above the Channel stream, you will see a white heart in a purple box (pictured in Figure 1-6). Single-click that purple heart to follow this streamer.**

   Following a channel is free and one way of showing your support for a streamer. By following a channel, you will receive notices on when a stream goes live. If you opt out of receiving notifications, live channels you follow will appear in the "Following" tab in the upper-left corner of your browser window.

4. **Wait a few minutes, and if the streamer received an alert, he or she will thank you for the follow.**

FIGURE 1-6: When you arrive to a new Twitch Channel, you have an option to *follow* a channel, located at the top of the stream window.

TIP

Whenever your audience shows any sort of support — follows, raids, subscriptions — it is considered good form to thank the people showing support. Usually you will receive alerts either from Twitch or from third-party services. For more on third party assistants like Streamlabs (`https://streamlabs.com`), jump ahead to Chapter 8.

STREAMERS OF ALL SIZES

The Twitch directory, early in your experience with the platform, will offer you a variety of games and streamers to choose from. What you may want to look at straight away in the featured thumbnail of these other streams is how many viewers that stream may have. It is easy to gravitate to the streamer with the larger numbers (larger numbers defined here as up to 10K of viewers watching in real time) and see how they are managing so much activity, but you will also see some streams with a modest amount of followers (20–30 viewers currently viewing). These smaller streamers could be worth your attention as they have more opportunities to interact with visitors. Large streams will, in many cases, find breaks in their gameplay to engage their Chat; but sometimes with larger streams, Chat will only be an option for subscribers. Also, the time to interact may be limited. Each streamer is different, but smaller streams tend to be more intimate, more interactive, and — for those new to Twitch — educational in how to manage Chat and keep connected with those visiting your Channel.

With something as simple as a follow, you have given support for a streamer that is tracked both by the Channel host and Twitch. These statistics help the Channel grow, and increases the reach of the streamer. Whenever this streamer goes live, you will receive an email notification. If you want to disable the incoming emails, you can always turn off Notifications when prompted after immediately following a streamer, or go to Settings ⇨ Notifications to disable the email alerts for this Channel.

Subscribing on Twitch

While a follow is the easiest and most cost-effective way to show support for a channel, a *subscription* is support for a Twitch Channel with a financial investment. Subscriptions are one way that streamers make money on Twitch.

Yes, Twitch can actually generate revenue for streamers, and for some on Twitch, streaming video games and hosting Chat is a full-time job.

Subscribing is a "higher level" of following as you agree to a monthly payment sent to Twitch, a portion of the payment sent to the streamer. In return, subscribers receive special benefits not available to people who just follow a stream. Subscribing to a stream is just as easy as following a streamer, but with a few extra perks.

Go to http://twitch.tv and either find a new channel to watch or visit one of the Channels you are following.

1. **Any Twitch Channel you follow, when live, will appear on the left-hand side of your browser window.**

2. **To the right of the *Follow* button, you should see a purple *Subscribe* button. Single-click the button to access a drop-menu of options.**

   When subscribing to a Twitch Channel, you have the option of subscribing at these levels:

   - Tier 1 ($4.99/month)
   - Tier 2 ($9.99/month)
   - Tier 3 ($24.99/month)

   These tiered subscriptions unlock a variety of *emotes,* small animated messages or images, that are only available to subscribers. These emotes are great representatives for streamers, and in many cases reflect the personality of the stream itself.

3. **Select a tier.**

   By default, you can select Tier 1 to subscribe, or single-click "More Paid Subscription Options" to select Tier 2 or Tier 3.

4. **Complete your payment either through PayPal, credit card, gift card, and so on.**

5. **Once your payment is processed, return to the stream you have just subscribed to.**

6. **Wait a few minutes, and if the streamer received an alert, he or she will in most cases thank you for the sub.**

7. **At the lower-right corner of your Chat window, you should see two icons.** The triangular one is for *Bits* (explained in more detail in Chapter 12) while the smiley face icon is your *Emotes.* Single-click that to access Channel and Twitch emotes.

REMEMBER

   While streamers offer their own emotes (exclusively for subscribers), Twitch offers to everyone with an active account a variety of generic emotes. You can use these emotes all over Twitch without subscribing or following anyone.

8. **Single-click the new emote from your newly-subscribed Channel to drop its code into your Chat field.**

9. **Single-click the purple *Chat* button to drop it into the Chat stream.**

Now, with following and subscribing (or *subbing*, as you may hear streamers and Chat refer to), you can not only show your support for streamers but also become part of the greater community and maybe pick up a few tips on how to stream, interact with regulars and newcomers, and multitask between the activity you are sharing and the Chat happening just to the right of you.

It is also worth mentioning that when you invest into a Channel with a subscription, bits, or even a follow, you are doing so because you want to. There is no expectation from either side (and if there is, these are issues that are best resolved someplace other than live-on-stream) that you always subscribe or throw bits your way. People show support for your stream because they want to, not because they have to. It is support like that which makes the relationship between supporter and streamer genuine.

Something to think about.

Other Twitch Resources

If you are reading this book, thank you. Seriously. As a writer, I can say without question that tech books are the hardest thing to write as changes can occur overnight. Terms of Service can be amended. UI's can be upgraded or rearranged, as they already have been between writing and editing this chapter. You name it, the book might end up dated on Release Day. That doesn't mean there are not some evergreen nuggets in this book. I have a few suggestions for you to investigate while going through this book. These resources are listed here as additional founts of knowledge and experience that will only help you in becoming a better streamer:

>> **Twitch Help:** While I will be drawing a parallel between podcasting and streaming, one thing I did not have was https://help.twitch.tv/, the official Help Center section of Twitch. This title is comprehensive when it comes to streaming, but in the case of a sudden change at Twitch.tv, the Twitch Help Center will be your best and most reliable location online for answers. You can also find here a list of commands for you, your moderators, and your Chat to take advantage of during your stream. There are also some cases where Twitch.tv will offer up etiquette and tips on how to improve the stream quality. If anyone online knows anything about Twitch, it's Twitch.tv.

>> **Meetup.com:** When you set yourself up on https://meetup.com and perform a search for 'Twitch' you might be surprised to find others in your area streaming a variety of games as well. Broaden the search to Console Gaming or even eSports (if you are the competitive sort) and you will find a whole new network to tap into, many of these streamers more than happy to

help you out. Meetup.com is a great place to organize anything from a meetup at a coffee shop to a group of 200 in a rented hall to get together for an impromptu brainstorming session. If you don't spot anything in your area, why not set up a Twitch Meetup and see who responds — it's free.

» **Other Twitch streamers:** If you take a look at Twitch pages, you may see one consistent field popping up — the streamer's rig. The host's stream machine can sometimes appear in the Chat as it is the most common, often asked question from those new to the channel: *What are you using to stream?* In the same manner as podcasters who love to talk about their setup and recommend gear to anyone who asks, Twitch streamers don't mind sharing what tools of the trade they are using. From the gaming chair to the mouse in hand, ask your favorite Twitch streamer what they think is a solid set-up. Compare what other Twitch streamers are using, and then mix and match. From here, you can start building your own rig and maybe even pick up a few tips in real time on improving your stream.

» **Special events:** In the same vein as Twitch streamers sharing their rigs on their respective Channel pages, conventions dedicated to streaming are also great places to pick up tips, tricks, and ideas on how to improve your streaming rig, your stream on a whole, or your business building around your stream. *TwitchCon* (http://twitchcon.com) is exactly what it sound like: a weekend where thousands of Twitch streamers and fans of Twitch streamers gather to talk about Twitch. VidCon (http://vidcon.com) is similar to TwitchCon but covers more than just Twitch. Mixer, YouTube, Vimeo, and other video content creators are highlighted here. Then there is GuardianCon (http://guardiancon.co), originally a convention dedicated to celebrating Bungie's award-winning video game, *Destiny* (http://bungie.net), GuardianCon has evolved into the East Coast's premier event, featuring top streamers like Ninja, Dr. Lupo, Datto, Geek Chick, and SheSnaps. Similar to VidCon, GuardianCon features streamers from Twitch, YouTube, Mixer, and others.

» **Stream coaches (like Ashnichrist):** Who is Ashnichrist? Recommended to me by several streamers, Ashnichrist (http://twitch.tv/ashnichrist) is a streamer focused on coaching others in the art of streaming. How do you make content when you are feeling sick? Where do you begin with your own stream, in the presentation or with all the bells and whistles set to go? How do you make drop-in's and overlays? All these things are covered on Ashnichrist's stream, and she streams her advice on Twitch, on YouTube, and via podcasts. She is like many other Steam Coaches who have converted their streams from gaming to self-help and streaming tips. If you make it through this book from cover-to-cover, find Ashnichrist (or any streaming coaches that you find a connection with) on Twitch. These passionate streamers may just pick up where I left off.

Chapter **2**

Building a Streamer's Studio

lright, that first chapter has brought you up to speed to some degree on to what streaming is, what Twitch is, and how to join the community. All you need now is to start building your streaming studio. This studio can come in a variety of shapes, sizes, and price tags; and Twitch is like any creative endeavor you pursue: It's an investment, based on how passionate you feel. If hopping on Twitch is something to pass the time, then keep your setup simple. A modest setup with little to no investment — the biggest purchase being the gaming console itself — is not only reasonable, it is common. If, on the other hand, you find yourself tapping into a hidden talent of improvisation and inspiration, you might want to upgrade.

That's a word I like a lot. Upgrade. *Mmmmmm. . . .*

I'm sorry. Where was I? Oh, right, *the basics.* Crawl before we run the Boston Marathon, and all that.

This is the real charm with streaming. Whether you are doing a simple point-and-stream set-up like REALMUNCHIE (`http://twitch.tv/realmunchie`) or create a virtual studio complete with game show-inspired effects like James Werk (`http://twitch.tv/jameswerk`), both approaches are valid. In the long run, it doesn't matter whether your streaming studio is a smartphone with a Bluetooth-ready headset or a studio that looks like the cockpit of Star Lord's *Milano*. What matters is the streamer's dedication and drive to entertain and engage their Chat.

So which approach works best for what you have in mind? That's what we take a look at in this chapter, discussing the options, advantages, and disadvantages of each setup.

Where Are You Streaming From?

In Chapter 1, I said you can't stream without a Twitch account, and that is true. However, even if you got the Twitch account, you aren't streaming yet. You're going to need a stream machine to make the magic happen from, so exactly what is the plan? What platform are you planning to stream from?

This, depending on what kind of investment and what kind of streamer you want to be, will be your first major chunk of change you are about to drop. No, it's not as monumental as buying a house or a car, but it is a decision that will put you on a path. Before running out and buying up the first console that's on sale at your local GameStop, you will want to consider the following criteria concerning your streaming setup:

>> **What's your budget?** You want the most affordable studio gear that will help you create the stream you want to create. In many cases, especially with cheap headsets and discount computer gear, you get what you pay for in quality of construction and range of capabilities; but a budget matters. Find out what you can afford and if it will help you accomplish what you want to do in streaming.

>> **What platform do you want for your games?** There are three popular platforms for you to choose from: Sony PlayStation, Microsoft Xbox, and the Personal Computer. There are other platforms out there that people are streaming, raging from mobile devices to the Nintendo Switch, but the Big Three covered in detail in this book are the PS4 (including the Pro), Xbox One (including the X), and the PC. If you know you have friends on one particular platform, that may decide where you go. Weigh the pros and cons of all three, and then choose wisely.

WARNING

There may be a temptation for you to go all in, maximize your potential audience interaction, and invest in multiple platforms. Some streamers like the bearded wonder from Wales, The Bonj (http://twitch.tv/thebonj) or the always effervescent Tiddlywinks (http://twitch.tv/tiddly), to start their week on the PlayStation, then play on the PC midway though, and enter the weekend playing on an Xbox. Keep in mind, both Bonj and Tiddly are streamers who have the time and the talent to go from one platform to another without little to no effort. If you are not that confident in your skills on a certain platform, don't make an investment into multiple platforms unless you are unquestionably savage on all of them. Stick with where you are most comfortable.

Speaking of comfort . . .

>> **Where are you planning to stream?** This may not seem to be a big deal, but an important one nonetheless. Where is this stream actually going to happen? From the couch (as in Figure 2-1)? Sure, not a problem (so long as you are able to give yourself proper support). Will it be in a proper office or studio? That works, too. Wherever you decide to stream from, remember you can always relocate (with some effort) your setup. Just be aware of what is around you, especially if you are streaming with a video camera. What are you revealing about you and your house? Is your setup tidy or a complete train wreck? Is your environment inherently loud or noisy? Are you okay with that? Find where you think will be the best place for your stream and then stake your claim. This is where you are going to get your game on!

FIGURE 2-1: For some beginning streamers, the show begins on the couch.

The easiest way to get streaming is to simply go into the console and start streaming. It is not out of the ordinary for streamers to dive deep into their consoles and find the options for streaming. So, in the early chapters of this book, we will focus on streaming with the two leading gaming consoles on the market.

Let's take a closer look at those two leading consoles and how to get them set up and ready for streaming.

PlayStation 4

First introduced to the world at the end of 1994 (just in time for Christmas, kids) the *Sony PlayStation* is one of the leading console gaming systems in the world. In 2006, Sony launched the PlayStation Network (PSN), an online network of gamers looking for and establishing online communities around different games, and of consumers looking for new digital media. The idea of PSN was to encourage multiplayer gaming on the platform. Since its launch over a decade ago, over 110 million users have been registered in the network with over 70 million users actively raiding tombs, traversing the underworld, conquering outer space, and earning the coveted "Play of the Game" title.

REMEMBER

Along with a PlayStation console, you will also need a PlayStation account established. This grants you access to the PlayStation network (as seen Figure 2-2)and is free. *PlayStation Plus* is a premium service, providing access to exclusive content, complimentary games, discounts on games, and early access to highly anticipated releases. PlayStation Plus also grants you the ability to chat with other PSN members. PlayStation Plus' counterpart on Xbox is called *Xbox Live*. On the PC, there are a variety of online networks like this, but arguably *BattleNet* (`http://battle.net`) from Blizzard Entertainment (`http://blizzard.com`) remains the most popular. The network is tied into many games developed by Blizzard and other game developers. Whichever platform you game on, these accounts should be active and running before you start streaming.

FIGURE 2-2:
The Sony PlayStation Network, your one-stop shop for online media.

Once you get your PlayStation out of its box, a few other cables, accessories, and details should be on hand:

>> **LAN Cable.** This is something of a running joke on my podcast, *Happy Hour from the Tower* (http://happyhourfromthetower.com) as my upgrade from a PS4 to a PSPro called for that which I didn't have. Now, at random points of the show I will ask, *"Do you need a LAN cable? Willa LAN cable fix that? Because I have a LAN cable!"* A LAN cable is a direct, hard wire connection between consoles, or between your console and the Internet. If you are transferring data from one PSN to another, you will want this on hand. If not, it is still a good idea to have one on hand in case you decide to go with a hard wire connection to your Internet as *direct* connections to one's modem provides faster internet speeds, important in getting better resolution and framerates for your stream.

>> **HDMI Cable.** The HDMI cable provides connection between your console and your monitor. This connection is all you need for high-quality audio and video. While you may have a cable included with your PSN, depending on your studio setup, the complimentary HDMI cable may not be long enough to reach your console. Check the length of the cable and see if it fits your need.

>> **Internet Access.** I don't just refer to a laptop that's connected to the Internet in case the enclosed documentation is not coming through for you. I'm also referring to your network name and password. You will need to get your console on to your network once it is all up and running.

With your patience checking your expectations and excitement at the door, it is all now a matter of setting up your PlayStation.

1. **Power down all your equipment.**

   If you are setting up your PlayStation as part of an entertainment or gaming center, you are going to want to make sure to avoid any sudden power surges. Check to see that all electronics are turned off.

2. **Look on the back of you PS4 for the HDMI port near the top-left. Go on and plug your HDMI cable into that port.**

3. **Take the other end of your HDMI cable and plug it into an available HDMI port of your display device.**

   Your display can range from anything to a computer monitor to a flat screen television to a wall-mounted wide screen. It all depends on the kind of studio you are making.

4. **Plug the power cable into the AC IN port located to the lower-left of the PS4.**

5. Plug the power cable into any electrical outlet.

6. If you are intending to connect to the Internet through a hard-wire connection, plug the LAN cable into the port just right of the HDMI cable.

7. Plug the other end of the LAN cable into an available port on your router.

   When it comes to streaming and the best quality stream, a direct connection between console and Internet is best.

TIP

8. Connect the DualShock 4 controller to one of the available USB ports located at the front of your PS4.

   Your PS4 should come with at least one controller and a USB cable that will charge up your controller. Use this as a hard connection to your console.

9. Turn your monitor on and press the PS button (the button with the PSN logo) to turn on your PS4.

   A single beep should sound, and then the PS4 should have a blue light appear across its face. The light will slowly pulse and turn white. You should see an introduction screen appear on your monitor.

10. Press the X button and follow the initial set-up steps on your screen, which should include:

    - Selecting your language

    - Setting up your Internet Connection (Ethernet or Wireless)

    - Set your current date and time

    - Read and accept your User Agreement

    - Sign into PlayStation Plus (if you have setup an account)

And that's it! You're ready to "git gud" on the PSN!

Xbox One X

Microsoft, on seeing the success of console gaming, entered the industry with their own offering: the Xbox. Running a 733 MHz Intel Pentium III processor and the first console to feature a built-in hard disk, Microsoft's Xbox would make itself a force to be recognized in gaming. Currently, we have the Xbox One X, which you can see if Figure 2-3.

THE UNKNOWN WOES OF
WIDESCREEN GAMING

Bigger is better. At least that's what home theatre systems promise us. When we go for the latest and greatest gear for entertainment, we go all in. We are bringing home the theatre experience, complete with lighting thanks to the Hue, sound thanks to Yahmaha, and — of course — the flat screen, wall-mounted, widescreen window of awesome. And if you think the 4K edition of *Thor: Ragnarök* looks mind-bendingly good on that 60-inch screen, just wait until you load up *Destiny 2: Forsaken* on there!

But before you do . . .

What you may not know is that your eyes are working a little harder, taking in anywhere between 50–70 inches of digital real estate as opposed to computer monitors more than half that size. Add to this, if you are working with a large, wall-mounted flat-screen television, casting from your couch will mean that you are not keeping the best posture. And how the remainder of your setup is arranged around you, things are not going to be optimal. If you really want to game and only game, the Panavision approach to video games works fine. If you want to stream, though, it's possible, but can be awkward. Streaming can be an exhausting pursuit, but more so when you're working harder than you need to.

FIGURE 2-3:
The Xbox One X,
the latest console
model from
Microsoft

In November 2002, Microsoft launched Xbox Live, an online gaming service similar to PSN. Xbox Live granted subscribers access to new content and connect other players online. Coming to fruition four years before PSN, Xbox Live and Microsoft were early adopters of the online gaming movement, and the Xbox continues to be a major player in the gaming community with popular franchises like *Halo* and *Gears of War*. So let's go on and set ourselves up with an Xbox One X.

1. **Power down all your equipment.**

    If you are setting up your Xbox as part of an entertainment or gaming center, you are going to want to make sure to avoid any sudden power surges. Check to see that all electronics are turned off.

2. **Look on the back of you Xbox for the HDMI port labeled specifically for the TV. (It should be the left of the two available HDMI ports.) Go on and plug your HDMI cable into that port.**

3. **Take the other end of your HDMI cable and plug it into an available HDMI port of your display device.**

    Your display can range from anything to a computer monitor to a flat screen television to a wall-mounted wide screen. It all depends on the kind of studio you are making, but take a look at the side bar above about the up's and down's of using a widescreen home theatre to stream from.

TIP

Microsoft recommends an *HDMI Premium Certified Cable* if the provided cable is not an adequate length. If you need a cable longer than 50 feet, find a cable that is *Active High-Speed HDMI Cable* certified.

4. **Plug the power cable into the AC IN port, the farthest left of connection ports.**

5. **Plug the power cable into any electrical outlet.**

6. **If you are intending to connect to the Internet through a hard-wire connection, plug the LAN cable into the port to the far right.**

7. **Plug the other end of the LAN cable into an available port on your router.**

REMEMBER

When it comes to streaming and the best quality stream, a direct connection between console and Internet is best. (We will repeat this throughout the book.)

8. **Turn your monitor on and press the *Xbox* button (the button with the Xbox logo) to turn on your Xbox.**

9. **Press the *A* button and then follow the initial set-up steps on your screen, which should include:**

   - Selecting your language and language variety (Is it "color" or "colour" where you are from?)

   - Setting up your display settings

   - Setting up your Internet Connection (Ethernet or Wireless)

   - Setting up your location

   - Updating your console's system software, if necessary

   - Setting up your Xbox Live account (and note the "Branding" callout in Chapter One)

   - Read and accept your Privacy and Account Settings

   - Set your current date and time

   - Set your Power Preferences

   - Set your Updates preferences

   - Sign into your Xbox One X

Now that you have gone through this detailed setup of your Xbox, you are all set and ready to game. Good luck and game on!

Non-Essentials . . . That Are Essential

You have a gaming console ready to go. All that stands between you and that first stream is the command to "Start Broadcasting" and go live.

But check your budget, and it turns out you've got room for a few more add-on's for your steaming studio. No, you don't *need* them straight away, but they would be good to have in place. If not now, then maybe another month or two down the road, once you figure out if streaming really is for you or not.

Or maybe you want to dive in with both feet? You want that extra polish on your newly-launched stream on your inaugural stream, so why not drop a little more cash for these accessories?

Video cameras

Once considered a luxury but now standard fare on most laptops, video cameras have considerably come down in cost while stepping up in their quality. For as low as $10USD, you can add video to your steam and put a face with a screen name. Granted, at $10, the camera in question will only capture at a lower resolution while a $50 camera, like Logitech's C920 shown in Figure 2-4, could capture at a full HD 1080p resolution.

FIGURE 2-4: The Logitech C920 webcam, priced at just under $50, offers streamers full 1080p video, built-in microphones with automatic noise reduction, and automatic low-light correction.

Our featured gaming consoles have their own proprietary cameras — the PlayStation Eye and the Xbox Kinect — offering optimal performance for their platforms. When making the jump to PCs (which we talk about in Chapter 6), your options open up. Again, depending on your budget, you can decide if you want go with something economic or a model that offers a few more features under the hood. Regardless of what make or model you chose for your console, you will want to make sure the video camera is compatible. In the end, it should be a simple matter of plug-and-play; and your stream is granted an extra attribute of video.

Audio gear

Audio design has really come a long way in game development. It can be jarring when you are ripped out of video game, television show, or movie when audio repeats itself. (A good example being this one, stock scream that somehow finds its way in every *Star Wars* film.) This is why entire teams are assembled in video games to make audio unique and distinct as well as realistic. If your opponent is coming in from the left, you will hear sounds coming from the left. Someone trying to sneak behind you from the right? Audio designers work with other game development teams to make the sound creep from your right headphone to your left.

This is why, when it comes to audio quality, that mono earbud from PlayStation only offers so much.

Imagine how different *Destiny, Tomb Raider*, and *Fortnite* was for me when I graduated to an actual gaming headset? This was an unexpected advantage with quality headphones as some games go so far to have audio transfer from one speaker to another, so if an enemy is closing from the left, you hear them coming from the left. *Closed-ear headphones* are worth the investment and can start as low as $25. When it comes to headsets, it is always best to try them out before purchasing. I know I was sold on the Corsair Void Pro Wireless Headset (shown in Figure 2-5) when the store pumped in actual gameplay audio from *Overwatch*. Quite an impressive headset for the price.

FIGURE 2-5:
The Corsair Void Pro Headset offers audio quality and ergonomic comfort, all while remaining connected wirelessly to your gaming system.

Audio gear isn't just limited to gaming headsets. Perhaps you want a completely separate microphone for your stream while the headset's mic is dedicated to your team? Thanks to the popularity of podcasting, *USB Studio Condenser* microphones, like Blue's Snowball iCE ($50) and Yeti Pro ($270), are common additions to a streaming studio. Thanks to USB microphones, streamers can now record studio quality audio a direct connection to the computer or console.

Green screen

Sometimes called "privacy screens" the green screen is exactly what you're thinking: a backdrop of a lime green color that, when well-lit, removes the background from your video, leaving only you visible. You may notice that some streamers take advantage of the green screen while others ditch the screen and leave the background visible. Is there a standard?

The "standard" is truly up to you. The main reason for a green screen would be to reveal more of the game, less of the streamer taking up on-screen real estate. You may decide that you don't want to share with your audience your studio décor. People can learn a lot about a personality based on their living space, and some streamers prefer to keep that to themselves. And while green screens are usually associated with streaming from PC's (which I go into in Chapter 6), both PlayStations and Xboxes can remove a green screen from video with the right settings selected.

If you do invest into a green screen, know you're going to have to experiment with lighting, space, and comfort. There are many benefits to employing a green screen into your studio setup, but it is an extra step that will come with a learning curve to it. Green screens are not a standard, and if you can create a backdrop that isn't distracting to your stream, then stream without. If you are concerned with how much of the game is visible, then make the investment into a green screen and work through that learning curve.

Deck switchers

Ever listen to a radio show or podcast and catch how seamless broadcasters drop in audio clips, segue to "Intermission" or "Be Right Back" video loops, or jump from one camera clip to another? This is accomplished through a *deck switcher*. Deck switchers, like the Elgato Stream Deck shown in Figure 2-6, allow you the ability to switch from video source to video source with the tap of a key. This is a nice bit of luxury to have when you are wanting to take a quick break from stream, whether it's a "bio-break" or maybe a refill of your coffee. Instead of shuffling through screen or running a hot key sequence, you tap one button on the Elgato Stream Deck and your looped video is playing.

FIGURE 2-6:
The Elgato
Stream Deck,
priced at just
under $150USD,
gives you
professional
control over
multiple video
sources.

Virtual assistants

Streamlabs. Nightbot. Deepbot. All of these online services (many of them free) are *virtual assistants* geared to help you maximize your stream and even manage it. Whether it is setting up a comprehensive look and feel on your Twitch stream, or simply policing your feed to make sure you remain troll-free, virtual assistants are here to make your stream easier to manage.

There are a few virtual assistants to choose from, but in this title, I focus on *Nightbot* (http://nightbot.tv) as it is the virtual assistant I rely on. When you authorize Nightbot to access your Twitch account, you are giving it permission to run *commands* — quick, automated messages — for you. What kind of automated messages? Well, how about a message reminding your Chat where they can find you on social media outside of Twitch?

Let's go on and set up an automated command that we will time to happen at certain intervals.

1. **In your browser, go to** http://nightbot.tv **and select** *Sign Up* **from the homepage.**

2. **Follow the Sign Up procedures which includes authorizing your Twitch account to Nightbot. If you are prompted for Two-Step Authorization (and you really should!), have Authy ready and enter in the number generated in order to connect Nightbot with your Twitch account.**

3. **In your menu to the left of the browser window, select *Timers* from the list of options.**

The various options listed here are various tasks that Nightbot can help you manage during your Twitch stream, ranging from Commands (that you or your moderators can launch manually, to Spam Protection against potential trolls, to integration of your custom commands into *Discord*, a chat engine we will discuss later in Chapters 7 and 13.

4. **Single-click the blue button labeled *Add* to the top-right of the screen.**

5. **From the Add Timer window, shown in Figure 2-7 , you will want to give your command a name. Call this one: "Social Media"**

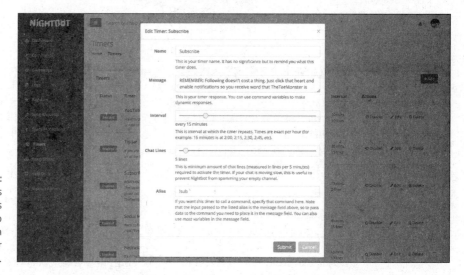

FIGURE 2-7:
Nightbot's "Timers" allows you the ability to launch custom messages for your Chat stream.

6. **In the Message field, type in the following: "Want to find me online? Visit**
`http://yourwebsite.com` - `http://www.facebook.com/myFBpage` -
`http://www.twitter.com/myTwitter` - `http://www.instagram.com/`
`myInstagram."`

Current limits to messages you can post suggest up to 500 characters, but it is a good idea not to make any message in Twitch too long. Keep it brief and to the point, as do many of the messages that appear in Chat.

7. **For the Interval, set up the time period you will want your custom message to appear.**

In this particular instance, the "Social Media" message will appear in your Chat window every 40 minutes.

8. The *Chat Lines* setting is a second timer where, instead of time, the amount of activity in your Chat window is measured. When the number of lines is reached, the custom message appears.

   In this particular instance, the *Social Media* message will appear in your Chat window every 15 minutes. This option is good for when activity on your channel is slow.

9. In the last option, use "!social" as the "Alias" for this command.

   Commands are automated messages that can be sent with a quick keyword, usually preceded by an exclamation point. For the "Alias" option here, we have assigned the message containing our social links the *"!social"* command.

10. Click the *Submit* button to save this command.

Virtual assistants take a lot of headaches away from moderating channels and posting answers to many repeat questions you may get while you are streaming. *Where can I find you on Twitter? Do you have a Discord channel? What's your streaming rig?* You can keep your Chat in the know while never relinquishing your controller with their help. Your Chat Moderators will also be granted access to your virtual assistant and can help in creating, editing, and managing the various commands that they, you, and your Chat may have access to during your stream.

Like in any creative endeavor, you are going to come across new and exciting apps, gadgets, and third-party services, or pick up suggestions from other Twitch streamers, that are designed to make your stream more efficient, easier to manage, and a better experience for you and your Chat. With this chapter, you should have a fantastic starting point for your stream. In the next chapter, we take a look at your Twitch Channel over at Twitch.tv. This is the first impression you're going to make with potential followers and subscribers as a Twitch streamer. We want to make sure it's a positive one.

Chapter **3**

Making First Impressions

S o we quickly touched base with setting up a Twitch account in Chapter 1, and you're probably realizing there's a good amount you should know before you fire up that Stream Machine of yours. Yeah, maybe you've been to other Twitch Channels and seen others just jumping into the deep end. No one says you can't. First impressions, though, are a truly delicate thing. They are long-lasting if you put the right foot forward, and pretty easy to screw up if you don't have a care. When people come by your channel at http://twitch.tv, what do you want people to know about you? What do you want people to know about this stream? When your channel starts to grow — with some luck, some hard work, and a little bit of fun, it will happen — do you have a plan in place to sustain your numbers? And what if you're not stressed out about the numbers, what is your investment into all of this?

These sound a lot like the questions we ask in Chapter 1, don't they? Well, Twitch could easily be considered the Artichoke of the Interwebs. Keep peeling back those layers, and you find out there's more than you thought. . . . But you need to proceed with caution and know what you're doing, lest those prickly spines get caught under your fingernails.

Ouch.

Creating a Complete Twitch Channel

If you've jumped ahead on account of the Table of Contents and what's in Chapter 3 . . . no, wait, let me guess: You're one of those gamers who, on hearing of exclusive gear, runs to the nearest in-game vendor, buys it, dons it on your character, and then tweets an image of your fashionista avatar with *"Eh, that wasn't so hard."* as its accompanying message, aren't you?

Sorry. Triggered.

If you have made it here starting from the intro, then you know what? You're my favorite. But seriously, if you've jumped ahead to this chapter, then backtrack to Chapter 1 where we talk about setting up your Twitch account. The basics of your account are established, sure. Your *Channel* is still an idea in the making. The account grants you access to those streaming content through the Chat function but if you are entering the Twitch arena as a content maker, your Channel beings here.

Creating an Info Panel

When people click on to your name to visit (and hopefully, follow) you, your Channel should tell them something about you, about your stream, and about your approach to the platform. *Info Panels* are blocks of real estate on your Twitch Channel that allow for you to tell visitors to your page something about you, your content, and how to connect with you away from Twitch. This grid serves as your ambassador when you are offline.

1. **Scroll past the screen where your feed would appear and click on the switch that reads *Edit Panels* and then click on the *Add a Panel* area.**

   For this exercise, we will set up an "About Me" page, using my own information as stand-in text in order to teach you some of the nuances of what Info Panels can do.

2. **In the Panel Title field, type "About Me" for your bio title.**

TIP

   A good amount of Twitch Streamers create custom graphics to reflect an established theme of their Channel. These graphics add a touch of flair and design to your Channel. There are also artists available for hire (or maybe some eager fans in your stream) who will apply their talents to your page. As I discuss in Chapter 16, knowledge of Photoshop goes a long way on Twitch.

3. **In the Description field add in the following text:**

   "Hey, everyone. Welcome to the official Twitch stream for Tee Morris (a/k/a TheTeeMonster) and the Happy Hour from the Tower podcast. I am an award-winning writer of Steampunk and non-fiction. Being a

productive writer, though, is hard when you're gaming. And I love Destiny. And Fortnite. And . . . I'm starting to venture into other games on my RADAR. No, I'm not the best gamer, but I do love video games. So stick around and have some fun."

What you put into the Description field can be as brief or as in-depth as you like, but you should not make it a deep dive into who you are, what your astrological sign is, who is your favorite boy band, whether or not you like Piña Coladas, or why getting caught in the rain is your jam. Maybe three or four points to let people know something about you. Something simple as a takeaway for your audience. This should be the approach for all the Info Panel Description fields.

4. **Go back to the bio and edit the phrase "Happy Hour from the Tower" to read as follows:**

   [*Happy Hour from the Tower* podcast](`http://happyhourfromthe tower.com`).

   Twitch offers some ability to apply *Markdown* (a coding language, seen in Figure 3-1) into your Info Panels to add in basic formatting and active hyperlinks into your Info Panels. By placing asterisk marks around a phrase, you apply *italics*. Placing a word or phrase within brackets designates that word or phrase as a *hyperlink*. To set a *destination* for your hyperlink, place a full URL within a set of parenthesis.

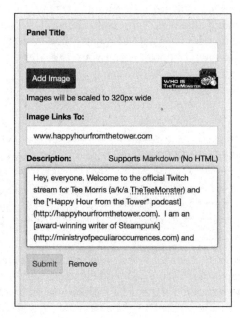

FIGURE 3-1:
Twitch uses its own flavor of markup language called "Markdown" to allow you the ability to format text and apply hyperlinks on your Twitch Channel.

5. **Edit the phrase "award-winning writer of Steampunk and non-fiction."
   to read as follows:**

   [award-winning writer of Steampunk](http://ministryofpeculiaroc
   currencies.com) **and [non-fiction]**(http://podcastingfordummies.com).

6. **Edit the phrase "No, I'm not the best gamer," to read as follows:**

   No, I'm not the **best** gamer,

   If you surround a word with a pair of asterisks, you *bold* a word using Twitch's
   markup language.

7. **Click the *Submit* button.**

   Now take a step back and look at your first Info Panel. This is one of those
   "Wash. Rinse. Repeat." things you'll be doing in the building and developing of
   your Channel. It takes a chunk of time to sit down and get your page laid out to
   the way you want it to look, but this is how you represent you and your
   Channel in between your streams.

So now that you know how to make Info Panels . . .

Deciding what Info Panels you should create

Across the Twitch platform, there are a few common threads that you can apply to
your own up-and-coming Channel. These Info Panels I suggest as a starting
point, and if you come up with ones not listed here, then by all means, go on and
create your own. This is your Channel. Make it yours. You got this.

But if you are looking for a few ideas, I suggest that your Info Panels should
cover . . .

>> **Streamer's bio.** We did this one already but it might surprise you how many
streamers don't share a bio on their page. I believe it's a great way to get
additional background on the streamer hosting this Channel. As mentioned
above, this is not *War & Peace* or *Les Misérables* that you are writing. This is a
brief *"Who is . . ."* and your audience is more accustomed to Twitter than they
are to blog posts. So let people know who you are, what it is you do, and what
people might expect if they hang out on your stream.

>> **Streaming schedule.** There's a real mixed opinion about streaming sched-
ules. For some people, they just fire up the stream machine and go! For
others, it's a special occasion that they go out of their way to promote. The
good thing about streaming schedules (for an example, see Figure 3-2) is you

are making a promise to your loyal and potential audiences when they can find you online. Think of it as your favorite TV show just going live when it did. How would you catch it, unless you keep a schedule? Of course they will get the Twitch notifications when you go live, but a schedule also serves as a routine for you and helps you find a rhythm for streaming content.

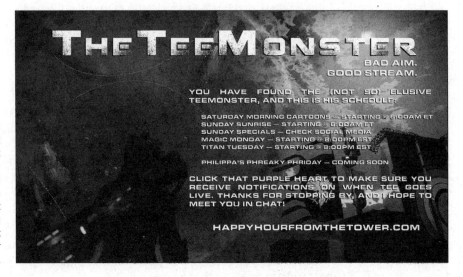

FIGURE 3-2:
Streaming schedules not only help you maintain a schedule with your viewers, but can also help you build up a set routine for your streaming.

>> **Rules for Chat.** It's never a bad idea to make it clear that you have a zero tolerance for certain things. This is, after all, your stream. Your stream, your rules. Skip around from Channel to Channel, and you will find that a good amount of streamers adhere to a few simple tips on creating the best kind of Chat:

1. Have fun.

2. Stay positive.

3. Don't be a jerk.

There are other rules you can probably think of for your own Channel, and if a follower or subscriber can't abide by them, then okay. No real loss. This is your scene, so set the stage the way you want it to be. Not just for you, but for your Chat as well.

>> **Social media links.** Are you online? Got a podcast? Then go on and list your various social media links here. While you can list all of your various social links in one Info Panel, I have found that separate panels for individual platforms — especially if you decide to create custom art for your

stream — work best. So decide what other social media platforms related to you and your stream you want to share with your Twitch stream, and point people in that direction.

>> **Contact.** Yes, technically people can contact you through your Social Media links. People can also contact you directly through Twitch itself. In this particular case, the Contact panel would be a direct contact between you and those visiting your Twitch Channel. Most of the time, the contacts listed here are more for professional queries, but maybe the odd fan letter or voicemail option will appear. That can happen, but that is the approach with a Contact panel on a Twitch Channel.

>> **Amazon Wish List.** Maybe this isn't your thing, but go on and create your ultimate streaming studio as an Amazon Wish List; and then set up an Info Panel sending people to it. The generosity of others just may surprise you. I have donated accessories to other streamers, and streamers have stories of other viewers contributing to their dream setups on account of shared Wish Lists. The Twitch Community has a lot going for it, and having your Wish List on your Channel also gives you and your Channel goals to strive for that you can reference anytime.

From here, you can decide what other Info Panels you need to represent your Channel in the best way. With studio updates and changes in your Twitch stream, you will add, edit and delete Info Panels. All this is part of the evolution of your Channel and you as a Twitch streamer.

Editing and deleting Info Panels

Creating Info Panels is the hardest part because you're trying to deduce what you want to share and how you want to convey your message without sounding verbose but not so terse that you come across as vague. Once the panels are created, editing and deleting are a cinch:

1. **Scroll past the screen where your feed would appear and click on the _Edit Panels_ switch to get your Channel Page into Edit mode.**

2. **In About Me's Description field, edit the text to read:**

   "Hey, everyone. Welcome to the official Twitch stream for Tee Morris (a/k/a TheTeeMonster) and the [*Happy Hour from the Tower* podcast](http://happyhourfromthetower.com). I am an [award-winning writer of Steampunk] (http://ministryofpeculiaroccurrences.com) and [non-fiction](http://podcastingfordummies.com). Being a productive writer, though, is hard when you're gaming. And I love Destiny. And Fortnite. **And Tomb Raider. And Detroit: Become Human.** And . . . I'm starting to venture into other games **on my RADAR.** No, I'm not the **best** gamer, but I do *love* video games. So stick around and have some fun."

As you find, editing the text is easy. Just like working on a word processor or simple text editor.

3. **Single-click the *Submit* button to accept the changes.**

   There is, at the time of writing this book, no universal "Accept All Changes" command for the Info Panels. They all are accepted one panel at a time.

4. **Click and hold your mouse on the gray area of one Info Panel, and then drag the panel into the direction where you would like your panel to reside.**

   If you want to change the arrangement of the Info Panels, it's a simple click-and-drag method (pictured in Figure 3-3), where you can move panels in any direction. You will see other Info Panels adjust automatically as you do so.

TIP

When you begin moving panels around, the reshuffling of your other panels may completely throw the order you're wanting. This may mean toggling back and forth the "Edit Panels" switch to see what the layout looks likes and how you need to compensate. There's a bit of fiddling and some trial-and-error in this process. Just know that Info Panel arrangement is more about patience and determination rather than design.

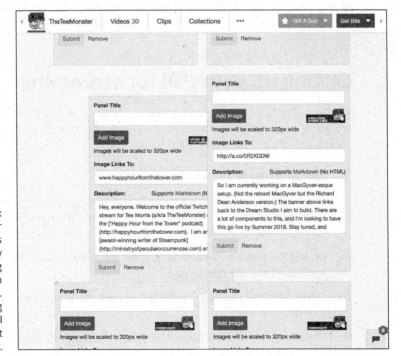

FIGURE 3-3: To adjust your Info Panels layout, simply click-and-drag a panel in any direction. Remaining panels will adjust accordingly.

5. **To remove a panel from the page, find the Info Panel you want to delete and single-click the _Remove_ option at the lower-right of the Info Panel.**

6. **Toggle the _Edit Panels_ switch back to the _Off_ position, and then review your Channel layout.**

With your Info Panels all set, your Channel is almost ready. Yes, _almost_. We have set up our Twitch account, filled in all the important details we need to make the right impression with people new to our Channel and our stream, and have a sharp channel ready to show off. What we need to do is connect our consoles, and then we make our first stream happen.

So, best foot forward. Let's get cracking.

Streaming Off Your Console

The first stream is always the trickiest because you are going live with your gaming skill and your personality. You want to make sure you are ready and able to kick off your stream with style and confidence. Both of those attributes will take you far in streaming.

So for now, let's set up our consoles for streaming. Once we get those up and running we will get to the actual process of streaming and present to the world our first stream.

Setting up your PS4 for streaming

We have the basic studio set up and we have completed our profile. Now we are going to get our consoles synced up with our Twitch, starting with my own console-of-choice, the PlayStation 4.

1. **Launch the game you wish to stream.**

   For many of the screen captures, I will be streaming from the game _Destiny 2_. It does not have to be _Destiny_, _Fortnite_, or _God of War_. The game should be the game you want to stream.

2. **On the PS4 DualShock controller, press the _Share_ button, located to the top left off the directional pad.**

3. **From the menu sliding from the left of your monitor, select the _Broadcast Gameplay_ option.**

4. **Streaming services will appear on your screen. Select _Twitch_.**

5. PSN will access the `http://twitch.tv` **Login/Sign Up screen. Enter your username and password here.**

6. **Once logged in, your Broadcast Page (shown in Figure 3-4) appears. Review to make sure you are include video from the PlayStation camera (if installed) and audio from your microphone.**

There is another option where you can include Chat Comments in your PSN display. Make sure that is turned off.

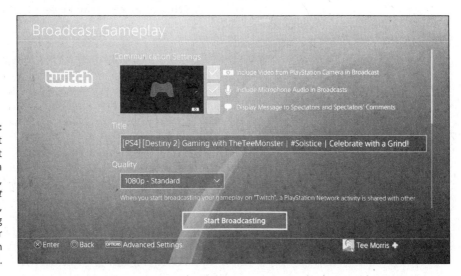

FIGURE 3-4: When you select "Broadcast Gameplay" from the "Share" menu, the *Broadcast Page* appears, displaying settings for streaming from the PSN.

7. **Scroll down to review the title of your stream. Select the field with your stream's title (right joystick) and press the *X* key to edit the title.**

TIP

To edit and type a title on the PS4 using the DUALSHOCK controller can be a little awkward and may take some getting used to. You can either introduce a USB keyboard to your console setup, or go into your Twitch Dashboard online and set up a title for your stream.

8. **Scroll down to look at the resolution of your gameplay.**

Depending on your Internet connection and the make of your game, resolution may vary. For higher speed connections and recently released games, your game will broadcast at 1080p resolution.

9. **Continue to scroll down to Social Links to Facebook and Twitter. Select both platforms for you to notify followers in your networks that you are going live on PSN.**

While there are notifications sent out on Twitch, sending out a message on Facebook and Twitter can help boost your signal or attract new viewers to your stream.

10. **Under the Twitter and Facebook options is the Comment window, the message you would like to send out with the announcement of your stream. You can either leave the default message of "Check out my stream . . ." or create a custom message accompanying a link to your Twitch Channel by pressing the X button.**

    The Comment you go with here is the message shared on Facebook and Twitter.

11. **At the bottom of the screen, select the *Start Broadcasting* button. You're taken to a final option to either change your audio settings or start your broadcast.**

Once you launch into your stream, you are live with your game. Now it is time to play your game, interact with your audience, and have fun.

This is how we stream from a PlayStation, but what about an Xbox One? If you "bleed green" as some Xbox gamers attest, the steps you follow are not too far from those of us who bleed blue.

Setting up your Xbox One for streaming

Now let's get that Xbox of yours set up to streaming. You will note that the steps are similar to the PS4 but with one exception: While the PlayStation has a built-in streaming capability, the Xbox requires an additional software install and a few more steps. At the end of this set-up, though, you will be up and streaming.

1. **Start your Xbox One console.**

2. **From the menu located above the Xbox home screen, navigate to *Apps*.**

    At the Xbox home screen, you can browse through Games, Movies and TV, and Music, all made available though Xbox. The *Apps* directory are additional downloads that allows your console to go above and beyond media entertainment.

3. **Look under the *Apps for Gamers* section for the Twitch app. If you cannot find Twitch, you can always navigate to the top-right of your screen and select the *Search* icon (the magnifying glass) and search for Twitch.**

    You can also download apps at the official Xbox website at www.xbox.com/en-US/entertainment/xbox-one/live-apps.

TIP

4. **Once you find Twitch, select the *Get* option to download and install Twitch on to your Xbox.**

5. **Before launching the Twitch app, go online and make sure you are logged into your Twitch account. Once confirmed, launch the Twitch app.**

6. **Select *Login*. Then go online to `twitch.tv/activate` to enter a 6-digit code that appears on your Xbox app. This code will link your Twitch account to your Xbox Live account.**

   This is a one-time set-up, so you should only have to go through this two-fisted approach of Xbox and online device (desktop, laptop, or mobile device) to Twitch is not a regular thing.

7. **Access your Profile by pressing the *Xbox* button on the controller and selecting your profile picture. Then pressing the *A* button on your controller. Make sure the *Appear Online* option is chosen.**

   If you appear offline, your ability to stream from the Xbox is disabled.

8. **Still in the Profile, go to your Privacy settings and set up your account as follows:**

   - "See if you are online" option: set to *Everybody*

   - "Broadcast Gameplay" option: set to *Allow*

9. **Return to the Xbox home screen by pressing the *Xbox* button on the controller. From the Preferences, make sure the *Allow Broadcasts . . .* option is selected.**

REMEMBER

   You may also see settings and options in this section of your menu for the Kinect. This is a camera specifically designed for the Xbox. Originally designed for Kinect-style games (where your body is the controller), the Kinect also works as a camera for your stream.

10. **On launching the Twitch app, Twitch will start a test to recommend the best bitrate for your stream. You can either agree to the suggested bitrate, or go with something lower or higher, or request a new test for a new recommendation.**

    Bitrates in streaming is the amount of data your router is managing while you stream. This setting is going to dictate how smooth (or how choppy) your stream appears. The higher the bitrate, the better your stream plays.

11. **Once all network settings have been confirmed, a panel should appear, shown in Figure 3-5, asking for placement of Kinect video and settings for Microphone. Select the *Enable Microphone* option so that your audience can hear you.**

    Set your microphone level at this step. Make sure that your voice is not constantly peaking into the meter's red zone.

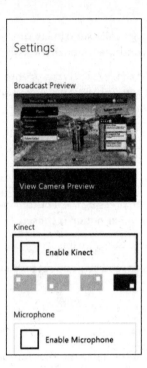

FIGURE 3-5:
When preparing your Xbox One for streaming, you will come up to a panel that sets preferences for audio and video. These preferences include video placement and audio levels.

12. With audio levels set, you can then choose to have your Chat on screen, or you can go with a full screen view with Chat minimized.

TIP

Instead of limiting the real estate of your game on a monitor, I recommend you have Twitch running on another device, like a laptop, desktop, or mobile device. Monitor Chat on a second device while you stream and interact with your audience on mic. By keeping your Chat on a second device, it is easier to manage. I will go deeper into other ways of managing Chat in Chapter 8.

13. The next option is the Broadcast Title window. Select the field where you would enter in the title of your stream or the game you are planning to stream.

14. Select *Start Broadcast* to begin your stream.

Take a deep breath and get your game on, because once you hit "Start Broadcast," you go live! It's you, your Xbox, and your game. Go forth and be awesome.

The Twitch Channel is up and running. Your console is set up. If you are following my steps from beginning to end, you're streaming at this very moment.

And I hate to break it to you, but as much as *I* would love it, reading *Twitch For Dummies* as a stream might not be the most engaging of content.

BEYOND THE DYNAMIC DUO: STREAMING ON OTHER SYSTEMS

As we are focusing on Sony and Microsoft, you may be reading this wondering, *"What about my Nintendo Switch?"* which is a legitimate concern. What about gaming on iOS? Or how about going on a retro platform like Atari 2600? (Yes, people have streamed from the classic Atari.) How do you stream off these other platforms?

This book, as mentioned before, will be focusing on three platforms. At first, we will be covering the PlayStation and Xbox. When it comes to the PC, however, streaming takes on a very different strategy and approach when you're using a personal computer (PC). When streaming directly from a PS4 or an Xbox, you are reliant on the console. The PC, however, broadcasts from whatever is the source of video. If you can hook up the console or gaming device to your PC, and if the PC can see the device, then you can stream it. You may have to get creative in how you hook up that alternative console to your streaming machine, but yes, there is a place on Twitch for your Nintendo Switch . . . and other preferred platforms. Jump ahead to Chapter 6 to get a few more details on how to hook up a console to a PC.

Whether you jumped in with both feet after setting up your console, or if you took a breath and said, *"Maaaybe I should wait before I hit that 'Broadcast' button,"* then let's take a moment to break down and figure out how a stream goes. There is an approach. There is a science. Nothing's wrong with jumping into the stream, letting the current take you where it flows . . .

. . . but there is something to be said about knowing how to work the keel and having a sense of direction.

Chapter **4**

And We're Live! (Wait, We're *LIVE?!*)

When you're standing at the starting line of a run — be it a 100m sprint or a 13K half-marathon — the adrenaline is flowing. You see that distance ahead of you, and all you have to do is reach the finish line. You could be looking to win this race. You could be looking to score a personal best. Wherever you are or whatever you have in that headspace, the finish line calls to you, and in that final stretch, you may have to dig deep to reach it.

Streaming, however, has a funny kind of finish line. When you see it coming, there's a little voice that whispers to you *"Just one more game . . ."* because you really don't *want* the stream to end. You're having a good time either gaming on your own or gaming with friends. When you have a lively Chat, it is even tougher to stop, but all good things must come to an end. *Star Trek: The Next Generation*'s Q taught me that.

Just because you end a stream, though, doesn't mean you cannot stream again. You can always come back when you're ready, or you stick with your schedule and pop on as promised. Still, it's always tough to find that point when you say, *"Okay, I'm done,"* but you also want to make sure you're not burning yourself out.

That's why a little planning would benefit you.

Streaming Your First Gameplay

With your gaming system set up, your Twitch Channel complete and thorough, and your game selected, it's time to start streaming. Take a deep breath and then follow these steps:

1. **BEFORE YOU STREAM, jot down a few notes on what you want to do.**

   Maybe you think you got this without a problem, but if you are not used to performing live or working with an audience, then you may want to have an idea of what you want to do in game as well as what you might want to say to people who come by and check out your stream.

   All this — the final check on your gaming setup, jotting down notes, and setting up your recording area — is called *preshow prep*.

2. **Start up your game.**

3. **Tap the *Share* button on your PS4 Dualshock Controller located to the upper right of your "Directional Pad" (also called the "D-Pad") to access the Options menu (see Figure 4-1). From the menu, select *Broadcast Gameplay* to initialize your console's streaming features. From the options listed on the PS4, select *Twitch* to grant your console access to your Twitch account and dashboard.**

   For the Xbox One, tap the *Xbox* button located at the top center of your controller to access the Twitch app. Once launched, click the *Broadcast* button.

   As my console is a PS4, many screen captures will be coming from a PlayStation interface. Whenever possible, Xbox directions will be provided.

REMEMBER

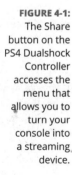

FIGURE 4-1:
The Share button on the PS4 Dualshock Controller accesses the menu that allows you to turn your console into a streaming device.

4. **From the options listed on PS4 and Xbox, give your Twitch stream a title.**

5. **For the PS4, after naming your stream, scroll down to the social options and select Facebook, Twitter, or both to publicize that you are going live.**

6. **For the PS4 and Xbox, select the *Start Broadcasting* option to begin streaming.**

   For PS4, there is one more page of options offering you to do one final adjusting of your audio and video settings. You can either double-check your settings here or go live with selecting "Start Broadcasting" again.

And with that, you are live. Game on!

Now I don't want you to overthink this, but with the game going, the stream running, and the world watching, you are on. This is nothing to take lightly. Everything you do and say is heading out into the great wide world.

How do you make it happen?

OMG! I'm live! What do I do now?!

Being a podcaster, you would think streaming is a walk in the park for me. Well, with podcasting, I have the luxury of editing, removing awkward pauses, and cutting anything that might have sounded witty in the moment but on playback comes across as crass or inappropriate. Streaming is a very different animal. Everything you think and do goes pouring out into the ether. You're live, and you're trying to play a video game all while adding some sort of value with your voice — and your image, if you are on camera — added to the stream. It would be reasonable to think, *"Well, people are going to be there to watch my channel for the game . . . ,"* but people are also coming to the channel to see what kind of gamer you are as well as what kind of personality you have. What are *you* going to bring to your channel? How will you stand out in the directory? *ARE YOU NOT ENTERTAINED?!*

Expectations, whether you think they are there or not, are omnipresent; and it is up to you to do a little more than just play a game.

Any ideas what you want to do?

> **Invite friends to your feed.** If you know you have friends online, send out a call for them to join you. It's always easier to talk when you have people you know on mic with you, chatting about in-game activity or real-life going's on. Having that back-and-forth banter will create a pleasant atmosphere that will

encourage your Chat to participate. So bring in some people you know to serve as icebreakers, and then watch as your Chat becomes part of your trusted circle.

Hanging with friends is a lot of fun. Making time for gamers new to your feed is cool, too. Just remember: It's *your* stream. You are the host, you are the Fireteam leader, you are large and in charge. This is your show. Sometimes, new friends (and old) and gamers from all parts can try and hijack your stream. Sometimes, it's unintentional. Other times, it becomes a battle of wills. So remember: your stream, your rules, your call.

>> **Have something to talk about.** Did you catch a movie the other night? Are you trying out something new in your daily regime? What new cuisine are you sampling? Whatever is happening in your life, provided you are comfortable with it, could serve as a spring board for you and Chat to start conversation. Your feed becomes a sounding board for your own perspectives. In turn, Chat comes along with you, agreeing or disagreeing with your take on things. This can be a springboard of conversation.

>> **Talk about Twitch:** As you are streaming, you will discover there is a lot to learn with all this: audience interaction, technical issues, multitasking between game and Chat, game progress. Your audience is genuinely curious about what you do and how you make it happen, so feel free to talk about your Twitch experience. It makes for good conversation.

What is key in making a stream engaging and interactive is you, the host, talking to the Chat and keeping the conversation going. This can be easy if you kick off your stream with a healthy-sized audience. This can be hard when you are streaming to the void. Regardless of the size of your audience, you are on. If you don't look like you are enjoying your stream, there is a good chance your audience will not stick around. Enjoy your game and your time with Chat.

Twitch is a different experience for everyone. There will be streamers that will choose not to interact with their Chat. It's just the host and the game, and in some cases the host does not even appear on camera. This book offers not hard-and-fast rules but suggestions for making your stream more entertaining for your Chat and for you. If you're okay with your Twitch channel consisting of only game audio, then game on and have fun.

Wrapping up your stream

You've been gaming for a good chunk of the day. You're feeling hunger pangs, or maybe your significant other is giving you *"the look"* — and you know what I mean by *"the look"* — so you need to go and wrap up your stream.

I HAVE . . . PART . . . OF A PLAN!

When you talk with other streamers, a good amount of them started streaming by simply hitting the "Broadcast" button and going for it. That approach can only be described as brave, if not a little fearless. Launching into a stream without a plan may unearth in your hidden talent for improvisation. Speaking as an improv actor and comedian (many years with ComedySportz of Washington D.C.), though, allow me to let you in on a secret to improvisational comedy: Even when it is coming off the "top of our heads," we have a plan of attack. The games you see and the spontaneous jokes we fire off do happen off the cuff and from the hip, but not without some practice. For example, if you are improvising Shakespeare, at least one character will say "But soft . . ." or "Forsooth and anon . . ." while another may suddenly spout "What, ho, sirrah . . ." within simple dialog. With enough planning and preparation, an actor may come out with a rhyming couplet, but that comes with a plan.

You can approach your stream as a blank slate, but you are taking a risk of floundering and flopping. Keep that edgy, spontaneous approach with zero planning, but before hitting broadcast, 12 percent of a plan can actually go far. (It did for Peter Quill and the Guardians of the Galaxy.) Have at least one idea of what you want to do with your plan and then take a leap. You might discover that improv is your jam.

Sure, you can just stop the stream, turn off your console, and call it a day. Some streams do just that. I find that approach, while simple and efficient, a little distant. You're spending time and energy with your audience, dealing with your game triumphs and pitfalls. They are getting to know you, and maybe even rooting for you to enjoy a moment's triumph. You are creating a bond with your audience, and when you're done, you're just going to . . . get up and leave?

It's your call in the end, but going for something a little more personal only makes that connection with your Chat stronger. It also makes folks want more from you and your channel.

When you are ready to finish up your stream:

1. **If you know your stream is coming to a close, let your stream know with the *"I've got one more game in me . . ."* and continue to play.**

2. **At the end of your game, ask your Chat to stick around for a few more minutes.**

   One way of introducing yourself to another stream, without being rude or inconsiderate to its host, is to host a *raid*. A raid is where you lead your audience to another stream, and you drop in with your viewers all while hosting the other streamer's broadcast on your channel. In Chapter 13, we will talk about raiding and hosting channels.

3. **Create a raid message for your Chat to copy (see Figure 4-2). Type the following line in your Chat window:**

twitchRaid twitchRaid TwitchUnity TwitchUnity YOU ARE BEING RAIDED!!! TwitchUnity TwitchUnity twitchRaid twitchRaid

Then single-click the *Chat* button, and tell your Chat to copy that line of text.

While you can create a new message every time for a raid, you can create a *command* that can easily reproduce a raid message. Chapter 8 will cover third-party software that allow you to automate parts of your stream.

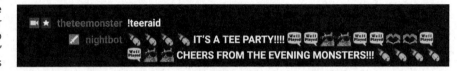

4. **Let your Chat audience know who you are going to raid and maybe even a few fun facts about the streamer in general.**

TIP

When sending your audience to a new stream, it's a good idea to consider to whom you are entrusting your audience. What are they streaming? What kind of personality is this streamer? Do you think this stream is a good association with your own stream? While it is always good to send your audience to another streamer who is in your Game Directory, it's always good to know something about that streamer. Nothing wrong with sharing the love to someone just starting out streaming. Just be aware that the stream could be a completely different experience from you.

5. **Type into the Chat field `/raid [username]` and then give a closing message to your Chat.**

The best closing script usually thanks people for watching. *"Thank you, everyone, for watching. Your support helps this channel grow. Let's go raid this awesome streamer. See you all next game."*

6. **Single-click the *Chat* button to begin the raid.**

A countdown clock appears. Once the time ends, your audience is taken to the other stream.

7. Go to the *Share* button on your PS4 Dualshock Controller to access the Options menu. From the menu, select *Broadcast Gameplay* and follow steps provided to stop your broadcast.

    For the Xbox One, tap twice the *Xbox* button located at the top center of your controller to access the Twitch app. Follow the steps provided to stop your broadcast.

From here, your gaming session is free and clear. You are done until the next stream.

Post-Show Production: What to Do After a Stream

Congratulations on a solid first stream! You've just taken that first big step, and you may have launched with an audience expecting to see you, or you may have organically picked up a few new viewers on this inaugural stream. Don't doubt for a moment that it was a success. How do I know your first stream was a success? You just streamed. Any first stream beginning and ending on your terms is a successful stream.

Now that the stream is over, what do you do until the next stream? Actually, there's a few things you can do that will not only provide your audience with content but also give you a chance to promote you and your stream.

Take a bow: Social media shout-outs

When you are done with a stream, you experience this euphoric rush, especially if your Chat were going back and forth not just with you but with one another. Add to that a really good game and your head is practically spinning with joy. It's hard to bring that to a full stop and just let that go.

That's why you see streamers taking to social media with a final word or a look back on a stream that was well done. Social media offers a platform of promotion, it's true, but for streamers it is a genuine connection with their audience. The ability to send out notifications on Facebook and Twitter on the PS4 is just an example of how important letting people know when you are about to go on, and it is equally important for when the stream ends to share with your community how much fun you thought that stream was for you.

Such was the case for SheSnaps (shown in Figure 4-3 and found at `http://twitch.tv/shesnaps`), who on July 9, 2018, was featured on GuardianCon's Charity marathon stream for St. Jude's Children's Hospital. Her own goal was to raise $5,000 on her channel, but when SheSnaps appeared in the Charity Marathon, her predecessors and GuardianCon had brought their goal of $1.5 million tantalizingly close. SheSnaps launched her stream and lit up Twitch with personal stories of her sister battling cancer, of the importance of St. Jude's, and of how easy it would be to donate. She didn't stop, and in the end not only led a push for the $1.5 million goal, but raised during her time on stream $15,000.

Immediately following an emotional, inspiring stream, SheSnaps fired off a selfie and posted the following on Instagram:

> "Over $15k raised in four hours for St. Jude - you guys are INCREDIBLE. SNAP PACK BEST PACK! Thank you so much!"

FIGURE 4-3: After raising $15,000 for GuardianCon's St. Jude's charity marathon, pushing the stream beyond the goal of $1.5 million, SheSnaps posted one more thank you on Instagram.

Streamers also find Twitter, now with their character limitations increased, a fantastic place for a final thank you to the audience. It was once considered a challenging platform to say anything of depth, but with the right strategy, you can accomplish a lot with a single tweet.

1. Following your Twitch stream, log into your Twitter account.

Having Twitter is not an essential app with streaming, but you will find that Twitter is a powerful instrument in your streaming toolbox.

2. **If you are on your Twitter mobile app, tap the quill icon in the top right corner of your smart device. If you are on your desktop or laptop app, single-click the *Tweet* button in the top-right corner of the browser window. Compose the following tweet:**

   "Woah! I just gave my first ever stream. Had a blast playing @DestinyThe Game with everyone, and I ended with a raid on @TeeMonster. I think I like streaming on @Twitch. Thanks for joining me. #PS4 #gaming #consolegamer

   Your "thank you" tweet may not be exactly what I've got here, but here's what you should look for in your tweets: tags of other streamers that were directly involved with your stream, the games you played (if possible), and a "thank you" for your Chat.

3. **Find an image related to your game or a GIF from Giphy and attach it to your tweet.**

   Tweets with images or GIFs earn more traffic and engagement than text-only tweets.

4. **Review your tweet for grammar and spelling and then single-click the *Tweet* button.**

Social media platforms are excellent ways to build your community, expand your network, and enjoy that connection with your Chat well beyond the end of your stream. Watch how other streamers tap into social media platforms, and take advantage of that reach.

After your thank yous, you should start thinking about your next stream, and your next stream may not need you behind the controller. Your next stream may very well be a severe case of déjà vu.

Reruns: The ICYMI Stream

Twitch provides you the ability to take the stream you just created and turn it into a *rerun*. A rerun is exactly what you think it is: a reply of stream (or multiple streams, after you have been streaming on a regular basis) that happened. You can take several past streams and run them in sequence so that you can continue to stream while you are away from your studio. It's a great way to give people an opportunity to see what they have missed and provides content on your stream when you aren't around.

1. **Go to your Channel at `http://twitch.tv` and access the drop menu for your account, located at the top-right corner of the browser window.**

2. **Select the *Dashboard* option from your account's drop menu.**

   The *Dashboard* is your Channel's Mission Control, granting you access to a variety of controls over your channel and your Twitch account. This is a little different from the Account Settings we worked with in Chapter 1. Unlike the Account Settings, which you occasionally access if you need to make a change to your account, the Dashboard grants you access to details of your Twitch Channel and its content on a regular basis. You can create or edit titles for individual streams, create highlights from your stream, and even download past streams for yourself.

3. **In the upper-right corner of your Dashboard, you should see a Video Broadcast panel. Select the *Reruns* option.**

4. **Next to Rerun Queue, you will see an + *Add Video* option. Single click *Add Video* to access a drop menu of your available past streams, shown in Figure 4-4.**

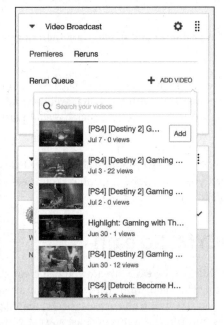

FIGURE 4-4: From the "+ Add Video" option of the Reruns panel, you can select as many available clips as you like and create programming for your Twitch Channel.

5. **Hover your cursor over the previous stream you want to rerun, and single-click the *Add* button next to the clip.**

6. **Once you have your stream (or streams) selected, single-click the *Start Rerun* button.**

   You should see a notification that the rerun is starting. The Video Preview window will also change from your Video Player Banner to a live preview of your rerun.

Reruns have mixed reactions from streamers. It is instant content and another way you can be seen, and that can be a good thing. If you are a morning streamer — say you usually go live at 6 a.m. — take your day's content and run it twelve hours later. In this case, your rerun would play at 6 p.m. You might catch a few new viewers who will join you next time for a live stream. A rerun is a great way to breathe new life into previous streams.

On the downside, reruns can create confusion for people new to a stream. They may think you're live, only to find out their Chat comments are being sent out into the void, no answer in sight. It can also be unclear as to when you are actually live (hence, the importance of having a schedule posted somewhere).

Most broadcasters will announce when they are going to do a rerun, and tend to reserve reruns for special or evergreen content like talk shows and live podcasts. Your mileage may vary, but have a strategy with reruns.

Repurposing content as a rerun isn't the only option before you. You have other ways of grabbing viewers' attention, and Twitch makes this process extremely easy. Read on.

YouTube: Your content, on demand

You might be surprised to learn that YouTube (http://youtube.com) is an invaluable service that you should take advantage of when building your Twitch Channel. While it's true that *YouTube Gaming* (https://gaming.youtube.com) is a direct competitor of Twitch, but YouTube is one of your best friends when combined with Twitch.

Twitch offers you a place for your content, and depending on the amount of time you stream, that could mean hours upon hours of content. Twitch, in order to keep their own storage demands in check, limits how long previous streams are archived on their platform. If you are using Twitch for free, your past streams remain on your Channel for two weeks before they are deleted. If you subscribe to Twitch Prime (which means linking your Amazon Prime account with Twitch), your videos stay on your Channel page for 60 days before being deleted. YouTube, however, allows you to archive your streams on their servers, presently with no limitations. All you need to do this is link your YouTube account with Twitch.

1. **Go to your YouTube channel at** http://youtube.com **and log in.**

2. **In a separate tab or window, go back to your Channel at** http://twitch.tv **and single-click on your account's drop menu, located at the top-right of the browser window.**

3. From the drop menu, select the *Settings* option.

4. Single-click the *Connections* options in your Settings menu.

5. Scroll down until you find the *YouTube* option offered. Single-click on the *Connect* button to the right.

6. Follow the login procedure and verification steps to connect your Twitch account with your YouTube account.

7. Return to your Channel at http://twitch.tv and single-click on your account's drop menu.

8. From the drop menu, select the *Video Producer* option.

Your *Video Producer* (shown in Figure 4-5) is where you take previous streams (available for only two weeks) and edit them with various titles and tags, create *highlights* (which always remain on your Twitch Channel), or download for later viewing and/or editing.

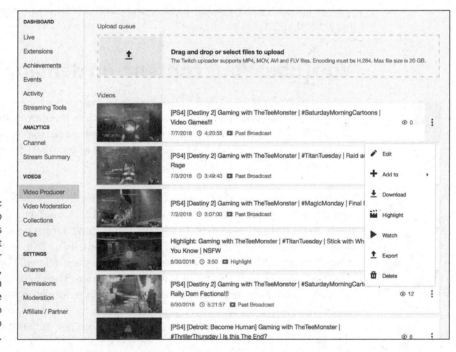

FIGURE 4-5: Twitch's *Video Producer* offers you different options for your previous streams, ranging from capturing favorite moments to exporting to YouTube.

9. Find your most recent stream and single-click the three vertical dots (the Options menu) located to the right of the clip.

10. Select *Export* from the Options menu.

11. **In the Export to YouTube window, you can edit the following parameters of your stream:**

- **Title:** The title of your stream when it uploads to YouTube.

- **Description:** A summary of the content in this stream. It should be brief, no more than a few lines of what is happening.

- **Tags:** These are *keywords* that best describe your stream, and assist in helping people find your streams on YouTube. I suggest between 10-20 tags total that best describe your content.

- **Visibility:** Do you want your clip to be viewable by all, or only by invitation? Decide here. (Most, if not all, times, you will want your streams to be Public.)

- **Length:** Twitch will take your stream and divide it up into 15-minute segments, making the stream more palatable for YouTube. This is a judgment call as to whether or not you want to manage in your YouTube account one large clip or several smaller clips.

After editing these parameters, single click the *Start Export* button to begin your export from Twitch to YouTube.

12. **Once your video has been accepted and processed, you will receive email notification that your video has been successfully uploaded to YouTube.**

WARNING

Your video may be rejected by YouTube with no reason given. First thing to check is your title. In many cases, the title of your stream may be too long for YouTube, so you may want to shorten it. Another item to review would be your tags. You may have too many tags in place for your clip. If you are still having problems with your export, you may want to review your YouTube channel settings to see if you have any time limitations. When in doubt, consult `http://help.twitch.tv/` for assistance.

With your streams now archived on YouTube, how you organize them is all up to you. For myself, I have broken up my own stream into multiple playlists:

- » 2017 TheTeeMonster's Streams from Twitch

- » 2018 TheTeeMonster's Streams from Twitch

- » A Guardian's Greatest Hits (and Misses)

- » Podcast Episodes

- » In Real Life: Twitch in the Real World

As my streams vary in content and theme, I try and keep my Playlists focused on a single topic. The "Guardian's Greatest Hits" is a collection of highlights. The "Podcast Episodes" playlist features the different podcasts I produce for *Happy Hour from the Tower* or *The Shared Desk*. Your own organization methods are strictly up to you. Take advantage of YouTube as your archive tool. You never know when you might want or need to return to some of your first month streams, if for anything, just to see how far you have come as a streamer.

Creating a highlight

In my introduction of the Video Producer, you may have caught a mention of creating *highlights* on Twitch as an option. What exactly is a highlight? While Twitch does not shoulder the burden of hours of content, it does encourage streamers to grab their best moments from a stream and create independent clips that you can keep on your Twitch channel, export to your YouTube channel, or both.

1. Go to your Channel at `http://twitch.tv` and single-click on your account's drop menu, located at the top-right of the browser window.

2. From the drop menu, select the *Video Producer* option.

3. Find your most recent stream and single-click the Options menu located to the right of the clip. Select *Highlight* from the Options menu.

4. As you can see in Figure 4-6, the new window that opens features your stream along with the title and directory from where your stream came from. Along the bottom is a graphic representation of your stream and a yellow ruler where you can adjust the Start and End points. This is where you create your highlight from.

5. If you recall a spot in your stream that was particularly outstanding (and that is defined strictly by the stream host, mind you!), click-and-drag the left end of the yellow timeline ruler to a few seconds before that moment.

   For this exercise, I will be using a moment in this stream where I am raided by *Destiny* streamer JSniperton (`http://twitch.tv/jsniperton`), which starts at 1:55:55 in this stream's Timeline.

6. If your stream's playback has paused, go on and click on the *Play* icon to resume playback. Scroll down in your Highlight window to see the *Use Current Video Time* button. Continue playback until reach the end of the moment you wish to capture, and then single-click the *Use Current Video Time* button located to the right of the *End Time* readout.

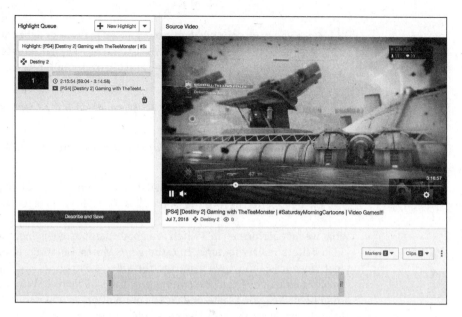

FIGURE 4-6:
The *Highlight* option is where you can create from one stream a favorite moment or a collection of favorite moments.

7. **In the window to the right of *End Time*, round up the number to the nearest ten second mark or to an end point with no dialogue, as shown in Figure 4-7, and then hit the Enter key to accept changes.**

   When I reached a solid "End" to JSniperton's raid, the clock read 2:02:36. I clicked into the End Time window and changed it to read 2:02:40. When you enter in a time signature, Twitch will play the final few seconds to show you how your video ends. Adjust accordingly if needed.

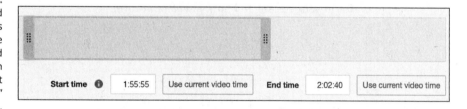

FIGURE 4-7:
Start Time and *End Time* points can either be designated manually or with the "Use current video time" options.

8. **Scroll up to the top of the Highlight window and single-click the + *New Highlight* button to add this clip into the Highlight Queue.**

   You have just created your first highlight, but it is currently queued up in case you wish to capture more moments from a stream. This is a batch process built into Twitch's Highlight option.

9. **Repeat Steps 5–8 to isolate more highlights from this stream.**

10. Once you have your highlights designated in the Highlight Queue, single-click the *Describe and Save* button. The Highlight Creator allows you to individually title, describe, and tag each clip. Single-click on the clips queued up to edit.

11. Once you have edited your highlights, single-click the *Create Highlights* button.

12. Single-click the *Go to Video Producer* button to return to the Video Producer.

Your highlights are now in the Video Producer and can be edited further, can be exported to YouTube, or downloaded on to your computer.

What we just performed in Twitch is a good example of *logging*, the process where video editors review footage, find the gems worth isolating, and make a note of what video it is and where it falls in the video's Timeline. Highlights courtesy of Twitch should not be confused, though, with *highlight reels.* When putting together a highlight reel, you create one video compilation as opposed to a series of small clips which you create with Twitch's Video Producer. We go into detail on logging, editing gameplay, and creating highlight reels in Chapter 11, where I cover the basics of video editing on a Mac and PC.

With your first stream under your belt, you should take pride in what you have accomplished. Achievement unlocked! You're streaming. That first stream was probably far from perfect, maybe raw around the edges with gaps in the interaction between you and your Chat. Maybe you'll want to get another stream or two under your belt, or maybe you want to make some time to look at your first stream critically. There is always room for improvement, even for streamers who have been at this full time for years. When doing so, think about what you need to look for in your stream and how you can improve.

Chapter 5

Improving Your Stream: Being Your Own Harshest Critic

Let's set the stage here: you have streamed a few times, you feel like you are finding a groove, and now you've returned here for a few more tips. (Welcome back!) After a few gaming sessions, you may be working on that balance between you, your game, and your Chat. Maybe you have managed to keep a schedule you have set for yourself, such a schedule that scientists could calibrate astronomical instruments by it; but it has felt somewhat difficult finding viewers. The numbers just . . . aren't there.

First, you have to accept a cold, hard reality about this adventure that is Twitch: You are in it for the long game. The numbers are not going to be there in the first week. They will probably not be there in the first *month*. At the time of writing this book, my numbers fluctuate (the reasons stated later in this chapter), and I've been at this for over a *year*. Disappointing viewer numbers are a common reason why so many new streamers abandon Twitch within months of launching a channel. Why bother? Because creating and maintaining an audience is a long game, and while some streamers defy logic and launch to impressive numbers, it doesn't mean you will follow suit. Building an audience is hard enough work. You are setting out to build a community which is a very different animal.

And now for the second thing you have to accept: Try not to think of the numbers. True, as Lieutenant Worf so eloquently put it, *"If winning does not matter, then why keep score?"* You want the numbers to go up, of course, but if you spend your stream preoccupied with numbers, you will be even more distracted than usual. If you are willing to be critical about your stream — constructively critical, I should add — then you can make a few improvements or changes to your stream that should help improve your numbers. (You know, those numbers that you really shouldn't be paying attention to in the first place.)

Your first week of streaming is not — repeat, not — going to raise you to the same level as that of Datto (`http://twitch.tv/datto`), KingRichard (`http://twitch.tv/kingrichard`), or SchviftyFive (`http://twitch.tv/schviftyfive`). Much like the wicked skills that these streamers show in their games, they work at their presentation skills, their timing, and their on-camera personas. If you want to even head in their direction, you're going to have to look at your own stream and ask tough questions of yourself. Yes, George Benson and Whitney Houston did say the greatest love of all is learning to love yourself, but neither of them were streamers, now were they?

Being critical of your own stream, what you are streaming, and how you are streaming is really difficult. It's a hard look at how you are starting off and what direction you are headed. It would be nice to think that straight out of the box you could have both the on-screen charisma and talent of top tier streamers; but there is a strong possibility that you and your stream needs work. This means to ask tough questions such as what kind of streamer you want to be or what you need to do to be a better streamer.

And in some cases, that might mean looking at the game you are streaming, or even ask why you are streaming video games in the first place.

G, PG, PG-13, or R: What's the Rating?

True confession: When I game and I see myself going *backwards* in my skill and ability to play, I get salty. *Salty,* when heard in gaming circles, means you get harsh, bitter, or raw. When I get salty, I tend to curse. Like a sailor. Like a drunk sailor. Like a drunk sailor with a nonexistent temper fuse. Yeah, my vocabulary would be the kind that would make Deadpool blush.

This isn't a brag. It's a bad behavior that I am working to refine.

Much like a podcast, Twitch went online with no rules about adult language. There are rules about adult *content*, but language? Go ahead and spout George Carlin's list (the *amended* one) of words he can't say on television. It can be pretty liberating being able to swear without a care . . .

. . . but this is not the same as no repercussions. Since the beginning of the Twitch Unity Movement (`http://bit.ly/twitch-unity`) on May 12, 2017, there has been an effort to hold people accountable for salty language. Other problems can occur for you and your stream when your language and conversations stray out of PG-13 territory.

>> **Front Page Feature:** There are many occasions where Twitch will reach out to new and engaging personalities on their network and say, "We would like to feature you on the front page." This means that for a designated time, when people go to the homepage, you will be one of those select few featured. That sounds cool, but that time featured may be severely cut if you're dropping the F-bomb like it's going out of style. If you're going to represent Twitch, then Twitch will want you to clean up your act. Something to consider.

>> **Charity Affiliations:** As you have read, one of the more popular charities that is affiliated with Twitch is St Jude's Children's Hospital. Think about that for a moment. You're on your stream, an opponent gets an unexpected upper-hand on you, and you scream, "[CENSORED]! You mother-[CENSORED]! Bet you [CENSORED] like a little [CENSORED] while you're [CENSORED] a [CENSORED] [CENSORED]!!! Oh hey, Chat, we're still raising money for the kids of St. Jude's, so dig deep and donate the link in Chat . . . unless you're cheap [CENSORED]-ers." Yeah, that sort of talk may not go over well with a *children's* hospital. It may not go over well with many charities, and charity streams as we talk about in Chapter 15 are a good way to introduce yourself to the larger Twitch Community.

>> **Sponsors:** I cover in Chapter 12 the business of sponsors, those vendors who look at your stream, look at your followers, and think, *"There's an opportunity here."* The double-edged sword of sponsorship is that you are accepting either a stream of revenue or some sort of financial investment in your stream. This means, depending on how deep on an investment your sponsor makes, the sponsor now has a say in how things work on your stream. Certain subject matter and favorite vocabulary may not be tolerated. Even before you start seeking out a sponsor, your demeanor on the stream may affect your chances in finding a backer.

Your mileage may vary; and while some streamers are able to bend the understood rules to a point where they don't break but strain under the stress, categorizing your stream as "Mature Content" or "Open to General Audiences" can affect how marketable your stream is to outside parties.

What about these General Audiences? How does the Twitch Community on a whole view *working blue,* a distinction in the stand-up comedy industry for adult-only acts, when streaming? In the end, depending on your concern over the factors mentioned above, you are the host of the stream, and it's for you to decide if you want to enjoy the dance between PG-13 and R or simply go all in and not worry about how you come across. If people don't like the way you carry yourself, then maybe your stream isn't for them.

Then there's the option of self-moderation, working blue when and where it's appropriate. SheSnaps, in her recent 2018 GuardianCon charity stream, cleaned up her own stream, avoiding mature content while she represented St. Jude's. ZGphoto tries to clean up his language when he deems certain days as "Disney Days" for song requests. "It feels weird dropping F-bombs," he says, "when you have *Moana* or *Frozen* playing in the background." It all depends on how you want your stream to be represented and perceived.

Setting the Mature Content option

If you decide that you want to hold nothing back, you will need to take care of one particular detail on your account:

1. Go to http://twitch.tv and access **Settings** from your **Account** drop menu located in the top-right corner of the browser.

2. In the Settings window, single-click the *Channel and Videos* option.

3. Scroll down to the *Content Settings* and — provided you know you would prefer to work in the raw — switch the *Mature Content* option to the *ON* position (see Figure 5-1).

As I said back in Chapter 1, Twitch's Terms of Service dictate that, if your channel is broadcasting sexual activity, nudity, threats, or extreme violence (in-game activity included), and your Channel is not marked as "Mature" then Twitch can immediately and irrevocably terminate your account.

The parameters of "Adult Content"

When it comes to "adult content" (that step beyond "mature content" where it's no longer about the language) and what falls into that category, where exactly are the limits? Does that mean content in the game, from the streamer, or both?

Twitch is more than aware this could be considered a gray area and they explain at http://bit.ly/sexual-content exactly what their policy is. Concerning the game itself, Twitch states:

Games featuring nudity, pornography, sex, or sexual violence as a core focus or feature, and gameplay modified to feature these elements are entirely prohibited. Occurrences of in-game nudity are permitted, so long as you do not make them a primary focus of your content and only spend as much time as needed in the area to make progress. Games rated Adults Only (AO) by the ESRB are not permitted in gameplay-oriented broadcasts or complete or unedited format on Twitch.

While some games may go for extreme violence (*Bioshock, Tomb Raider, God of War*) or sexual situations (*Castle Wolfenstein: The New Colossus, The Order: 1886*), other games focus less on adult content as a story telling device and more as the focus of the game. This is why Twitch maintains a list of games prohibited for streaming on their service. If you are concerned about whether or not your game would be allowed on Twitch, a visit to http://bit.ly/prohibited-games will answer that question. Also at this URL, you can access the online documentation if you feel there is a game that warrants a review.

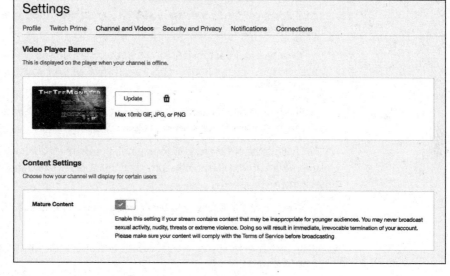

FIGURE 5-1: From the Content Settings option, you are making a pledge, based on an honor system, that you are either going to keep it clean or party like a rock star.

Popularity Versus Pleasure: What You Are Streaming?

Along with looking at how you are streaming, you might want to take a closer look at what you are streaming. Yes, there are hundreds on hundreds of games currently streaming on Twitch. Some of these featured games are just newly released. Some may have been a hot title a few years ago. Some may even be a throwback to the classics.

But what are their directories like?

We're going to look at the kind of video games that you can stream, and talk about both the benefits and the pitfalls of what you could stream on Twitch.

Before we turn that critical eye back to our own stream, let's visit the Directory, briefly touched on in Chapter 1, and poke around there a bit.

1. **Go to** http://twitch.tv **and log in with your account credentials, if you haven't already.**

2. **In the top section of your Twitch Directory, you'll find a carousel of streams to choose from. Click on the right or left arrow on either side of the carousel to rotate through the featured streams.**

    The featured streams on the Twitch carousel are the top performing Channels. Programming range from tournaments to special reveals to popular streamers running live in a game of choice.

3. **Scroll down to _Live Channels You May Like_ and take a look at who is presently streaming.**

    Live Channels looks at previous streams you have followed or watched, and, based on those analytics, offers up several streamers for you that match your profile.

4. **Scroll down to review games you have previously watched that are presently streaming, as shown in Figure 5-2.**

    Twitch looks at your viewing history — not by streamers but by the games that streamers featured — and offer up other streamers all playing games that fit your interests.

5. **Scroll down to the _Games You May Like_ section to enter specific game directories.**

    Again, Twitch looks at your recent viewing and offers you direct access to these game directories.

TIP

Take another look at Figure 5-2. To the left of the Twitch Directory is a listing of your Followed Channels (the ones currently live highlighted), followed by Recommended Channels, and finally Online Friends. This side menu is just one more way to discover new streamers or new games. Through this sidebar, I've found some terrific streamers like OneActual (http://twitch.tv/oneactual) and ZGphoto (http://twitch.tv/zgphoto). Keep an eye on it for recommendations as it is always present, even when you are viewing your own or other channels.

FIGURE 5-2:
Twitch looks at your viewing history and puts together a new list of streamers featuring games you enjoy for you to review.

Now that you have a comfortable grasp of Twitch's Directory, let's return to our own feed and look a bit closer at what we are streaming.

Streaming popular games

Fortnite. Hearthstone (pictured in Figure 5-3). *League of Legends. Player Unknown Battlegrounds* (also known as *PUB-G*). You see these games dominating the top slots of Twitch's Directory. There doesn't appear to be any sort of connection with these games, or at least it appears that way until you take a closer look at the games off-stream. The four games I mentioned earlier are all games that follow or are recognized by professional tournament leagues, or *eSports,* a multi-billion dollar industry we talk about in Chapter 15.

You might want to roll your eyes at the notion of "professional video game athletes," but you would be rolling your eyes at a professional sport that is a multi-billion dollar industry. Along with individuals streaming these popular games, Twitch also hosts tournament play happening across the country and around the world.

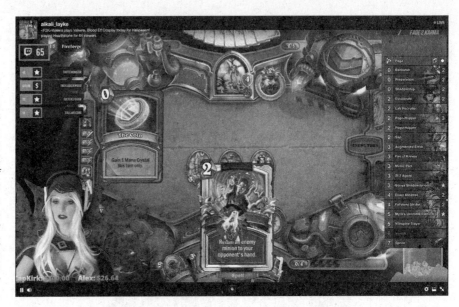

FIGURE 5-3:
Hearthstone, pictured here with cosplayer and multi-legend player Alkali Layke (dressed as *World of Warcaft's* Valeera Sanguinar), is one of many games finding success in the multi-billion dollar industry of eSports.

And you want to host a stream in this directory.

>> **Pro:** Anytime you jump into the directory for one of the top games in the Twitch directory, you are targeting an audience that is hungry for this content. Twitch viewers actively jump into directories for *Fortnite, Overwatch, Rocket League,* and others as they want to see how others play.

>> **Pro:** Twitch audiences may visit these popular game stream in the hope that hosts will open their streams to Chat and invite them to squad up for a few rounds. These games invite a crowd by default, and depending on the host's trust in his or her Chat, are opportunities to learn a few new tips.

>> **Con:** The inherent problem with streaming popular games? Popularity. Yes, you are streaming the popular strategy game *League of Legends,* but depending on the time of day and what is happening in Twitch, hundreds or thousands of others are streaming it. And if any of the eSports teams are streaming these games, either in competition or just for fun, audiences will flock to those streams without question. Popularity is a double-edged sword, and it may yield mixed if not disappointing results.

THE ALL BLACKS: FROM RUGBY PITCH TO GREASY GROVE

The New Zealand All Blacks are a team of history, of renown, and of excellence. If you play rugby, you know the All Blacks. If you ever do a search on YouTube for "Haka" then you know the All Blacks. If you don't know the All Blacks, then go to Amazon and look up *All or Nothing: The New Zealand All Blacks*, a behind-the-scenes documentary of this World Champion team. When you watch that series, you'll know the All Blacks.

What you might not know about the All Blacks is that they are on Twitch, and they game. And as able as they are with a rugby ball, they are quite able in *Fortnite*.

With a Chat admin offering light color commentary, the All Blacks and Silver Ferns — that's the New Zealand National Women's rugby team — squad up and run Battle Royale rounds. During game play, All Blacks and Silver Ferns swap stories about other teammates and their gaming prowess, and they might even engage in some playful trash talking if the situation warrants as much. While there's a lot of impressive plays from the Kiwis, don't worry yourself too much that the All Blacks or Silver Ferns are going to trade their National Team jerseys for those of an eSports team. They know where their talents are best applied.

Streaming games you enjoy

What about streaming games not necessarily in the Top Ten or even Top Twenty of the Twitch Directory, but streaming a game that you are driven to play? These games can run the gambit from turn-based strategy games, to epic adventure games, to MMO-style games: *Destiny, Sea of Thieves, Horizon Zero Dawn*, or the juggernaut that is *World of Warcraft*. On drops of *downloadable content* (or *DLC*), or the release of a new version of the game, these titles may rally for top slots in the directory, so they share the potential for stream growth as you would find with popular games.

>> **Pro:** With titles like *Destiny* (versions 1 and 2), *Horizon Zero Dawn*, and *Sea of Thieves*, there is a *grind* aspect to the game. A grind in gaming terms is a stretch or a challenge in the game that involves a lot of repetition and tests a gamer's drive and determination in order to earn a treasure at the end of said grind. During these moments, gamers find opportunities to connect with their Chat, jumping into conversations, kicking off a new topic, and eliciting a response from them. Grinds are great for streamers as it is easy to multitask during these long stretches.

>> **Pro:** Twitch audiences are pretty intuitive and can tell when a streamer is enjoying themselves. If you are playing a game that you really enjoy, it is obvious. And if you are having fun, Chat will want to take part in that fun as well. While my own stream numbers fluctuate, I can say that some of my best, consistent numbers came when I was playing the 2013 reboot of the classic adventure heroine, Lara Croft, in *Tomb Raider*. Chat celebrated my "A-ha!" moments with me, and even reacted with me on some of my more tense, action-filled moments.

>> **Con:** If a game is particularly engaging for you, you run a risk of forgetting that the world is watching. When I was streaming *Detroit: Become Human*, a choose-your-own-adventure-style of game, I had forgotten that I was streaming . . . for over half an hour. I blinked and suddenly realized, *"Oh yeah, people are watching,"* but even after touching base with Chat, I slipped into silent running once again because the storytelling in this game is just that good. While these games are excellent for you in your own gaming experience, it may not be the best kind of game to stream if you are so immersed that you forget about your Chat.

Streaming retro games

It's hard to define *retro* games, as a game can be five years old and considered "retro" by some gamers. For this book, I define retro games as being a game that reaches back to the early days. Titles like *Tetris, Super Mario Brothers*, and — if you can hook up that old ColecoVision — *Zaxxon* come to mind. These were the games that started as coin-operated video games and then arrived into homes coast-to-coast and around the world. These titles may be harder to stream on account of the hardware needed to make the stream happen, but there is an audience for these games.

>> **Pro:** Summed up in a single word: nostalgia. Watching modern day audiences playing classics from the early days is just plain fun. As many of these games were built around a grind, the ability to multitask and connect with your Chat is quite easy. It can also be fun to watch players skilled with modern games struggle and noodle through what should be "simple" games but turn out being something of a challenge. At the core of this is an appreciation, if not a romantic look, at the games that came before.

>> **Pro:** Playing retro games may not be high in the Twitch Directory, but on account of their iconic nature, people may actively seek out these titles. Retro games sometimes fall between popular games and those titles you enjoy playing, and it is that novelty and reputation in being throwbacks to video game history that make searches for these games worth mentioning.

>> **Con:** As mentioned earlier, it's not software that is a problem but hardware. Obviously, older games and the consoles they were built for were not necessarily built or optimized for streaming. So you are going to be streaming off a PC (which we will explore in Chapter 6), implementing hardware that you may have to seek out on eBay and other websites specializing in jury-rigging old consoles with new computers and making them work. So be prepared for some extra mechanical challenges ahead of you.

>> **Con:** The retro directory is a *collective* directory. This means instead of looking for a specific retro game in its own category, games like *Metroid, Mario Brothers, Excite Bike,* and *Megaman* are all found in one directory. If viewers are looking for a specific game, viewers have to work through the entire directory hoping to come across the retro game they are interested in watching.

Beyond Consoles: Streaming without Video Games

Sometimes, things you love to do can throw you for a loop, and you find yourself making tough decisions about them. With streaming, you may have a hard choice with Twitch: When it comes to video games, your performance is an equivalent to a dog's breakfast.

Accepting the fact that video games are just not your thing is not an absolute. You can always return to playing video games, but your stream seems to lack the enthusiasm to join you as it is just too painful for people to watch you struggle with the controls . . . or the basic skills needed to shoot . . . or your hesitation that causes you to have a main character die. Repeatedly. Presently, video games just aren't your jam.

But you love to stream.

Perhaps your love of streaming is better expressed in an alternative approach to Twitch. Photography, cross-stitching, sculpting, art, live recordings. All of these options await for you to take advantage of and act upon in new and creative directories that are completely detached from gaming consoles.

REMEMBER

Something you should notice about these non-gaming streams: These streamers are not using consoles. While streaming is possible through both PlayStation and Xbox, the streaming capabilities have limited settings. Your inset video is the most simple and basic of set-up's. To free yourself of the console is going to require you to make an upgrade to a PC, covered in Chapter 6. Which solution best suits you and your budget rests in how deep you want to travel down that rabbit hole.

Streaming in the real world

In September 2018, Twitch announced on their blog at `http://bit.ly/category-change` that the popular IRL and Creative categories were being reorganized as they were considered difficult to navigate. As of writing this title, the non-video game directories Twitch offers are the following:

>> Art

>> ASMR

>> Beauty & Body Art

>> Food & Drink

>> Just Chatting

>> Makers & Crafting

>> Music & Performing Arts

>> Science & Technology

>> Sports & Fitness

>> Special Events

>> Tabletop RPG

>> Talk Shows & Podcasts

>> Travel & Outdoors

With the release of the Twitch app (pictured in Figure 5-4), streaming no longer has to happen from a console or a PC, and when it comes to a broad spectrum of topics, IRL and Creative once covered a lot of ground. Now, if you have something on your mind or something to share, you have multiple directories offering you and your stream a home. From relationship advice to visits at popular tourist attractions to streams on mental health, these directories offer Twitch audiences all kinds of content. Many of these stream hosts are not — repeat, *not* — experts in a particular field, but they are speaking from the heart. The final decision as to the worth of their words rests with you, and it may take a few streams for you to decide if the host is connecting with you.

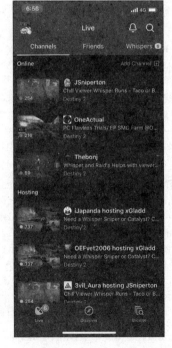

FIGURE 5-4:
The Twitch
Mobile App,
available for both
iPhone and
Android
smartphones,
puts an entire
streaming studio
into the palm of
your hand.

There is a lot of pressure to deliver if your stream becomes a stream dedicated to financial investments, legal advice, make-up tips, or relationships. Before giving a stream like this a go, ask yourself:

>> **What am I passionate about?** Are you yourself struggling with diagnosed depression? Have you picked yourself up from a financial pit, and feel like you

have a good way to approach money, spending, and budget management? Do you consider yourself good with job interviews? What about do-it-yourself projects around the house? There is probably a topic you are passionate about, whether it's hobby-related or setting a course for yourself professionally. Focus on that.

>> **What resources can I offer people?** So you want to do a stream on home improvement? Awesome. The project you've got set up as your first stream: swapping out a sink from a powder room. Okay, great. During the stream, though, someone in Chat asks a question about plumbing and how to clear out a particularly clogged U-bend. This is when you should have on hand online resources that might reach beyond your know-how. If the topic is on mental health, streamers will say, *"The first thing you do is talk to a doctor. Talk to a certified mental health physician."* When questions go into a legal matter, the streamer will say, *"I am not a lawyer, but you should talk to a lawyer specializing in. . . ."* Have a go-to list of resources — not other streamers, but legitimate resources — that you trust and in turn your Community can trust.

>> **What are my credentials?** In another idea, you decide to cover collectibles: baseball cards, autographs, movie tie-in toys; historical documents. Whatever the fandom, this is what you are going to talk about. What is it in your background that gives you a expertise in this subject? Have you been collecting autographs for a decade? Two decades? Are you knowledgeable on how to spot a fake? Do you know how to identify solid authentication for collectibles? Here, you are putting yourself forward as an expert, and it's up to you to back up the talk with some serious walk.

>> **How many cameras do I need?** This is dependent on exactly what kind of Creative stream you are intending to do and how much coverage you think you will need. Some Creative stream employ two (or more) cameras, with the Twitch Channel divided into multiple panes where each window is a different look at the same project. The advantage of streams like this is maximum coverage. In the case of artist Dawn McTigue (`http://twitch.tv/dawnmctigue`), she has one camera on her while her main camera is a top-angle view of the work-in-progress. Of course, your stream machine will need to have enough ports available to support multiple cameras, a situation that a USB Hub can remedy.

WARNING

Before going live with multiple cameras, test your connections and assure that everything is working properly. It is not out-of-the-ordinary for software and drivers to conflict with one another.

>> **How strong is my Internet connection?** What if you decide to take your love of travel to the next level with a Just Chatting stream? This is pretty ambitious as you're taking your feed on the go with the Twitch mobile app, shown in Figure 5-4. The mobile app turns your phone into a hand-held stream machine and allows you to stream free of your studio. Exciting as this may sound, streaming from the Twitch app is reliant on the strength of your Internet connection. A bar or two of signal is not going to yield the best quality video or audio, and if you are on Wi-Fi instead of cellular data, your signal will be tested by the amount of users on the stream and the quality of the router you're working on. The option is available, but do know the quality of your stream may be affected.

Your stream becomes something of an open workshop for you and your work. Acknowledge Chat whenever you can.

Sharing your creative pursuits

Before taking your creative pursuits to one of Twitch's creative directories, you need to remember that your stream in inviting others to be a part of your creative process. People visiting your stream will want to help, and there is nothing wrong with that. It's when the people in Chat believe they know more than you do — regardless if they do or not — or try to make the work-in-progress their own, constantly questioning what you do. As I have said again and again, this is *your* stream. If some visitors to your Chat cannot respect your experience, then it may be time to issue a warning or two. Respect should be earned, but there is a level of etiquette that should be followed. Set that limit, welcome feedback, but remain in control of your Channel.

Works-in-progress are exactly that: works-in-progress. Some days, the ideas will come easily. Other days, it may be a struggle. Inviting and interacting with an audience can add to that stress of the creative process. Be ready to contend with that.

Twitch's creative directories host a lot of different personalities, including cosplayers, crafters, musicians, and coders, some of whom we talk with in Chapter 15. This is the corner of Twitch where if you want to teach people Photoshop by doing, where you want to tease your next costuming wonder, or where you want to showcase your favorite computer language. Take a look at these new directories, and see if you find a better fit for you and your streaming interests.

2

Creating Your Broadcasting Studio

Stream from a PC and explore the various pros and cons of working console-free with your stream.

Setting schedules and taking advantage of social media platforms in order to promote your stream.

Add automation and community management to your stream by introducing moderators, using online services like Nightbot, and looking at details of where and how you are streaming.

Upgrade your stream with overlays, and audio & video accessories.

Chapter **6**

Streaming without Constraints: Streaming from a PC

So far, we are working within the parameters of a gaming console. You are streaming from your PlayStation or Xbox, and going live with your game could not be easier. Push this option on your controller, select that option on your screen, and then type in a message. Select another option and then you are live. No fuss, no muss. It's you and your skill (or lack thereof) to share with the world.

Venture out to other streams, though, and you come to discover that you have barely cracked open Pandora's Box of Streaming. You see a world where the Channel host is not merely tucked neatly away in one corner of the screen but seemingly superimposed with the game behind him or her. You see a surrounding frame for your gamer, displaying in real time different things about the stream, ranging from the most recent follows to the Top Tip of the Day. When followers subscribe to the channel, a sudden fanfare plays followed by a clever animation celebrating the new arrival. Your gaming console does not allow for this stuff, so how is it all happening?

These multitude of nuances are only the beginning as you see other streamers broadcasting themselves *full screen* with a custom backdrop or even an *animated* screen behind them, and they are sharing advice or some other creative pursuit. Let that sink in: Streamers are on Twitch and *they aren't playing video games!* What madness is this?! And how are they doing this with a console?

That's the truth of it. They're not. These streamers are working without a net.

As shown in Figure 6-1, *a personal computer* or *PC* is what you need to be able to go beyond what PlayStation and Xbox currently offer you. Streaming with a PC doesn't just change the playing field; it changes the game from beginning to end. Creatively, a whole new realm of possibilities is offered.

FIGURE 6-1:
Personal computers (PCs) like this Origin PC Neuron are optimized to take your gaming and streaming to entirely higher levels.

Time to strap in, my friends. We are about to experience a very different approach to Twitch!

Looking under the Hood: What a PC Needs

When you stream from a console, there are some benefits. You can send out notifications, it's plug-and-play, and a lot of the technical details are taken care of, making this whole streaming thing a piece of cake.

When you stream from a PC, things get a little harder. You need to know what you are putting into a machine and why it's there. Can you stream from an off-the-shelf PC laptop? Sure, you can. However, if you are turning your PC into an all-in-one streaming studio, you're going to need upgrades, something laptops are not essentially known for being easy to do. So a tower model might be a better option.

What goes inside that tower? Well now, where do we begin?

The computer processor (CPU)

When pricing out computers, you might notice a dramatic rise and fall in sticker price. If you were curious as to the why's behind this, take a look at the *processor*, which is responsible for making your computer . . . well, compute. It receives, retrieves, interprets, and sends information to all parts of the *motherboard* where it resides. When shopping for a stream machine, the processor is usually the first place people start, but what should you look for in such a crucial piece of hardware?

Clock speed

With processors, you will find some numbers measured in gigahertz (GHz). Sounds really impressive but, so what? *Clock speed* is a measurement of how many instructions — everything a processor does — it can accurately handle in 1 second. So if a processor handles one single instruction every second, its clock speed of 1Hz.

Instead of you doing the math, I'll do it for you. My Origin PC has a clock speed of 3.7 GHz, meaning it can carry out 3.7 *billion* instructions per second. This means my machine can handle all the data being thrown at it to not only play a video game smoothly but stream it to the public.

Cores

While we want our computer to be able to handle all this data, we would also like it to be able to multitask. I don't want to just stream from a PC or play a game from a PC. I want to play the game on PC *while* I stream, and I want it to look as good as it possibly can be. This is why you want to have a computer with multiple *cores*. The way to look at cores is to look at that 3.7 billion instructions per second being processed by my Neuron. That would be the extent of it if the processor was a simple, single core. If my Neuron came with a *dual*-core processor, it could potentially, with each core processing simultaneously, perform two instructions a second. The more cores a processor has, the more it can do.

My Neuron does not have a single- or dual-core processor. It has six cores.

Yah, brah. I'm good.

Cooling systems

Whatever computer you are going to use or invest in for your Twitch studio, your PC will be impressive in what it can do at 3.7 GHz or *faster*. You know what else is impressive? The amount of heat these processors will create. Considering the amount of data needed to stream video alone, your computer is working hard to make your stream everything it can be. This means your computer will generate a lot of heat, and that can do a lot of damage to the processor and motherboard, so you want to keep your computer cool.

Air cooling

Computer manufacturers usually install *air cooling* arrays of different kinds inside computers. These internal fans are no different than oscillating fans in the summertime. They push air over hard drives to keep them cool, and they even expel heat if it detects temperatures rising inside your tower. If your computer rarely needs to start up its fans, they can last for a long time.

When you upgrade graphics cards for your computer, you might notice the cards are built with their own fans. Combined with ones already in your computer, fans can keep your PC's internal temperature under control.

Fans are cost-effective, and there are even upgrades for better, more efficient fans if you desire a quieter stream machine, but there are downsides. Fans create noise beyond your control. You also may have to contend with heat sinks on machines optimized for gaming and streaming. (Read that as machines that could double as Terminators on account of their processors, RAM, and other add-ons.) You can keep the costs down on your computer using air to keep your processor cool, but it can be somewhat frustrating competing against the wall of sound created by internal fans.

Liquid cooling

Modest PC towers are kept cool using air cooling systems, but when you are working with video in real time and graphics-intensive video games, you need something more that fans. You have liquid cooling systems, like the one shown in Figure 6-2, installed.

Let's address the neatest thing about liquid cooling systems: The tubes coolant travels through are usually lit under some kind of bright color. Sometimes, there are bubbles involved, too. That's just rad.

Okay, now for the practical: Liquid cooling systems allow you to cool *specific* components, namely the components you need to make the stream happen. Liquid cooling systems also make *overclocking* your processor safer. When you overclock a CPU, you are setting your processor to run at speeds higher than the "official" speed grade. Liquid cooling is also much quieter than air cooling systems, and tend to be more compact than fan arrays.

FIGURE 6-2: Liquid cooling systems are radiators for PC, providing constant cooling of your computer and its interior components quietly and efficiently.

So why doesn't everyone have a liquid cooling system in their PC's? The cost, for one reason. These systems aren't cheap, and when it comes to upgrading one's machine, the cost of a quality liquid cooler tends to lose out to other components like additional RAM, external peripherals, and — surprise — fans. There is also the installation and maintenance of your liquid cooling system. Even with previous experience installing fan arrays, liquid coolers will be a new test in confidence and stamina. Of course, you will want to be assured all tubing and fittings are secure lest your system springs a leak all over the tower's interior. Manufacturers, unless they themselves are building your stream machine, won't take responsibility for any liquid-damaged components. Double-check your warranty to make sure you know what to do in a worst-case scenario.

Random Access Memory (RAM)

"Maybe I need more RAM?"

"A RAM upgrade will fix that."

"This program really goes through my RAM . . ."

When your computer begins to slow down, or things just stop moving as fast as you know they should be moving, the first thing that usually gets upgraded is *RAM* or *Random Access Memory*. RAM has a simple job: Provide quick read and write access to a storage device. This is why, when we upgrade RAM, we suddenly notice everything moving faster. RAM temporarily holds on to any data you are accessing and then loads it once a command calls for it. This tends to run faster than if the data is running directly off of a hard drive.

TIP

It is always a good idea to have double the RAM that the application or game you wish to run requires. That way, you have the ability to multitask a bit more. As RAM comes in different speeds, make sure you are getting the right kind of RAM, and find out if it is being sold in a matched pair or a set of four.

Graphics card

If you don't hear people talking about upgrading their RAM, you may hear people say this:

"I need a new card if I want to get over this major lag in game."

"Since upgrading my GPU, Destiny 2 has been crispy!"

When you hear people talking like this, they are referring to *graphics cards*. Specifically, they are talking about *dedicated* graphics cards. A dedicated graphics card is its own device, complete with its own fan and onboard RAM, and processes graphics of any kind for the devices plugged into it. These are the upgrades that help you run a game like *Tom Clancy's The Division*, *Shadow of the Tomb Raider*, or *Marvel's Spider-Man*, with power, speed, and crisp resolution.

Graphics cards (also called video cards) like the NVIDIA GeForce GTX pictured in Figure 6-3, are built to get better performance from your in-game graphics. This happens on account of internal hardware and dedicated RAM optimized for processing video; so not only will your video games love upgrades like this, programs like Photoshop, Premiere, and After Effects will also benefit. This improved performance also includes additional video ports be they Display Port or HDMI.

FIGURE 6-3:
Dedicated graphics cards like this NVIDIA GeForce GTX 1080 boost performance and give your video extra polish.

A REFRESHER ON REFRESH RATES

You got your computer with one sick graphics card installed. You should be all ready and set to go, right? Well, not quite. You've got to have somewhere to send your signal, and that means you got to have a monitor connected. When monitor shopping, you will see one monitor at $167 and another at $315. They are both 27" and both are curved monitors, giving you a pretty neat "surround" effect when playing. So what's the different, apart from price? This would seem to be a no-brainer.

The first thing you want to look at is the *refresh rate,* measured in Hz. The refresh rate of a monitor is the number of times per second a display refreshes its image. The lower the number, the greater chance of lag (stutter) appearing, so you will want to look at something with a higher refresh rate. This is when you will notice that the $167 model has a refresh rate of 60Hz while the $315 model sports a refresh rate of 120Hz.

One more thing to consider with your monitor is the native resolution. Again, the $167 model has a native resolution of 1920 x 1280, which is as high as the screen resolution can go. This means your monitor will be rendering impressive results but nothing along the lines of the $315 model, which offers a resolution of 2560 x 1440. Little details like this will definitely improve both your stream and how audiences see your content.

Capture card

Wait a minute, you're thinking, *I already have this*.

No. You have a *graphics* card, not a *capture* card.

The graphics card is for you and your PC-native video games. If you are streaming directly from the PC, then you have everything that you need. If, however, you are wanting to stream a PlayStation, Xbox, or some other console game, then you will need a *capture card*. With a capture card installed, either internally or externally, you are still streaming from your PC, but your gameplay is from a console. The capture card works like an input data receiver and keeps your stream lag free, assisting in producing high quality video — something we all want in a stream, right?

If you are streaming directly from a PC and streaming only PC games, then a capture card becomes something of a redundancy unless you are streaming from a second PC, and then the second PC becomes your "console" device. A capture card like the Elgato Game Capture HD60 Pro is going to help you get the most out of the gaming and the streaming PCs you are working with.

TIP

Streamers continue an ongoing debate about whether or not a two PC setup is truly necessary or not. It will depend on the make and model of the PC, the hardware and peripherals I am highlighting here, and what your budget allows. Streaming and gaming from one machine is not only possible but perfectly acceptable.

Power supply

When putting together a rad, dream stream machine, you might try to cut corners to stay in budget. Perhaps you don't want to double the RAM of your computer. If your graphics card offers optical audio, then you can go without a bigger, better internal audio card. Whether you are building the PC on your own or going through a vendor, you will try and find every which way to make that dollar of yours stretch farther.

One item you really should not skimp on, though, is your *power supply*.

"Thanks, Captain Obvious." But before you mock me on this suggestion, it just might surprise you on how many try to save a few bucks with 500-watt power supply against the higher-priced 650-watt power supply. Without the right power supply, your computer may not be able to run any of the components optimized for gaming or streaming. Don't skimp on the power supply to save a few bucks. You're going to want that juice on tap.

TIP

Some computer vendors will allow you to buy a computer *BTO*, or *built-to-order*. In situations like this, the vendor's marketplace may not allow you to buy a lower wattage power supply if your customization cannot run it properly. It is just an additional layer of precaution that the computer vendor offers in order to make sure you have a machine that works.

So, once you have your PC put together and you have it up and running in your studio, it is time to hook up your console of choice to your PC.

Game On, Again: Setting Up Your Console

As you know by now, I am on a PlayStation, but this hook up is good for any console: Xbox, Nintendo, whatever. If there is an HDMI connection (or a connection that can be adapted to HDMI), your console is PC-ready. What you need cable-wise for this connection, outside of the power cable for your devices, includes the following:

➤ HDMI cable

➤ Digital optical audio cable

That should be all you need to make this connection between console and PC happen. Now just follow these steps:

1. **Make sure your PC and console are both powered down.**

2. **Plug in your console and then plug in an HDMI cable to your console's HDMI port.**

   If the console you wish to plug in does not have an HDMI cable, do a little research on plug adapters to see if this is even an option.

3. **Plug the HDMI cable into the IN port of your PC's capture card.**

4. **Connect the digital optical audio cable to the console's appropriate output.**

   Both PlayStation and Xbox have digital optical audio outlets. Some other consoles (the PlayStation Classic, for example) may not have this option.

5. **Connect the other end of the digital optical audio cable to the PC's graphics Card.**

6. **Power up the PC.**

7. **Power up your console.**

Your console and PC are connected, your first step in leveling up your Twitch stream. Here we go . . .

YOU CAN'T STREAM FROM A MAC. WELL, THAT'S NOT *ENTIRELY* TRUE.

During my research into streaming, my buddy Matt informed me *"You are going to need a PC if you want to stream."* I was disappointed to hear this as I have been dyed-in-the-wool Mac user for decades. I've been very happy with being on the "other side" of the computer argument, but there are several reasons why this is true . . .

. . . and one reason why it is false: Because it is.

When I found that OBS came in a version for the Apple OS, I decided to give it a try. Not only did it run without fail, I was able to effectively stream from my Mac. First, I used a solo camera, then went with three cameras and a Skype connection (which did test the limits of my computer's graphics card). Oh, and did I mention that my 8-core Mac Pro tower is *eleven years old?* 32 GB RAM, a video card with 4GB RAM, and a 3.1GHz processor, and I can stream talk shows with the best of them, as seen in this shot of me and my wife, Pip Ballantine, recording our podcast live on Twitch! Pretty proud of that.

Where Matt was correct in that I could not stream from a Mac is that most of the newer MacBooks and Mac towers (the ones that look cylindrical and are whisper silent) are built-to-order with no options for upgrades. With a PC, even a BTO model, you can still swap out components and upgrade when necessary. Another problem is that most dedicated video and capture cards are optimized for PC, as well as many peripherals like a high-end gaming mouse or keyboard. Finally, there is *Streamlabs OBS,* which is covered in this chapter. Streamlabs OBS offers many creative options for you and your stream. *SLOBS* only runs on Windows.

So yes, you can stream from a Mac. An older Mac Tower, to be precise. But if you want to take your stream to new heights, consider a PC for your stream machine.

Now with a stream machine in place, peripherals both internal and external all up and running, you are ready to take that next step. You've been working directly from your console of choice. Now it's time to visually raise the bar for yourself and maybe for your fellow streamers.

Let's tumble down the creative rabbit hole that is *Streamlabs OBS.*

Streamlabs OBS: Where Creativity and Interactivity Happen

Open Broadcaster Software, or *OBS* (http://obsproject.com), is software you as a broadcaster will grow very familiar with over time. OBS is an open source application that turns your computer and any audio-video components associated with it into a broadcast studio. It, along with other software like *XSplit* and *Bandicam*, is incredibly quick to set up and easy to use, and as it is open source, there are many developers online who are anxious to make their own impression on the OBS community with extensions and add-ons that aim to improve and enhance a streamer's experience.

OBS is also something of a blank slate. After installing and launching the application, you are staring at blank screens. Pretty much, your imagination is all that you need to get things going. If this is what you want to do, then I got good news: In Chapter 9, we go over how to incorporate your own *overlay*, an image (or, for the filmmakers, looped *video*) that gives your stream a little bit of pizazz. You see overlays everywhere in Twitch, and they play directly into a channel's branding.

But maybe your budget isn't ready to hire anyone to create overlays for you, and in that D.I.Y. spirit, you would rather teach yourself how to create overlays, but time and resources do not allow. This is why *Streamlabs OBS* (`http://streamlabs.com`) is, without question, the best friend of the new and veteran streamer. While OBS is a blank canvas, Streamlabs OBS (or *SLOBS*, as some streamers call it) comes out-of-the-box with a variety of bells and whistles just waiting to be implemented. Streamlabs integrates with your OBS a wide array of *widgets* (small applications that add functionality to your stream) as well as a *dashboard* that tracks everything from follows to subscriptions to donations.

Incorporating a template

Along with all of the many add-ons you can implement, Streamlabs also offers up *overlay templates* that range in themes, moods, applications, and colors. With just a few clicks, your stream is transformed from the basics to breathtaking. And if you have the processing power to back it, your overlays and widgets can be animated, adding an even more dynamic look to your Channel.

REMEMBER

OBS and Streamlabs OBS are not the same application. While Streamlabs did develop from OBS, the latest version of OBS has different features and functionality from Streamlabs.

But what you will find the best attribute of Streamlabs is how insanely easy it is to get cracking with it.

1. Go to `http://streamlabs.com` and single-click the *Login* button in the upper-right corner of the browser.

2. You will be asked to login with Twitch, YouTube, or some other streaming service. Login in with Twitch.

   Depending on whether or not you ask Twitch to remember Streamlabs or not, you may be prompted to perform a full login of username and password, and enter in your generated authorization code. Otherwise, Twitch will automatically sync with Streamlabs and take you to the Dashboard.

3. From the upper-left of your browser, single-click the *Download Beta Streamlabs OBS* button.

4. Once downloaded onto your PC, launch Streamlabs OBS.

   This application is no longer the website but the standalone Streamlabs, which syncs with the website, as well.

5. **In the top-left section of the Streamlabs OBS application, single-click the** *Themes* **option.**

6. **Find a theme for your stream either by searching through the various templates offered, or by using the** *Scene Theme Category* **located on the left-hand side (see Figure 6-4). Click a template's preview image to see a full-screen preview of it.**

   Streamlabs offer Scene Theme Category filters that narrow down search parameters to templates matching your mood. If you are known for streaming adventure or FPS games, or if you are hosting a talk show, filters make the decision process a little easier.

FIGURE 6-4: The Themes section of Streamlabs OBS offer you a variety of moods, looks, and atmospheres for your stream. All of these options are customizable, too.

7. **Once you find a theme you like, click the** *Install Overlay* **button on the top, right-hand side of the preview.**

   For this section, I am using the "Alpha Sections" template. You can use this template, if available, and follow along with me; or find one that appeals to your own interests.

You now have a template in place. What you need to do now is populate this look with all your incoming video and audio sources in order to get your stream up and running. This is something OBS, both Streamlabs and the original software application, makes incredibly easy. It comes down to series of clicks and knowing where your resources are.

Adding a console in your template

1. **Click on the *Editor* option in the upper-left section of Streamlabs OBS.**

   If you have multiple templates loaded into your version of Streamlabs, they can all be accessed from the lower-left menu that will show the current active template.

2. **The template, if it has a "Starting Soon" scene, will begin with an introduction screen. As shown in Figure 6-5, under the name of the template, you will see other items or scenes listed.**

   Scenes are the various stages of your stream. From introduction images to intermission placards, scenes should follow a progress for your Twitch channel.

FIGURE 6-5: Scenes are different segments of your stream, and in OBS, you segue from one to the next whenever you want to go to different segments.

3. **Click on the "Live Scene" scene to see where your stream will happen.**

   If you have your webcam already plugged in, the template should recognize it straight away, as shown in Figure 6-5.

4. **Look into the *Sources* window a select the *Background* source. You will see the background image surround itself with a bounding box.**

   Sources are exactly what they sound like: sources of audio and video needed to make your stream happen. Instead of the console managing it, you and OBS are managing all sources independently of one another, and using OBS something like a mixer.

5. **Single click the + (plus sign) to add a source to this "Live Scene" scene. The Add Source window comes up. Select the *Video Capture Device* option, and then click the *Add Source* button.**

6. **In the Add New Source field, type "Console" for the name of the source. Click the *Add New Source* button.**

7. **This is your Properties window where you tell OBS where the signal source is coming from. From the Device drop menu, select your Capture Card. Click the *Done* button.**

   As shown in Figure 6-6, when OBS sees a signal, it will drop in the source directly into your scene's layout. We will adjust this in the next step.

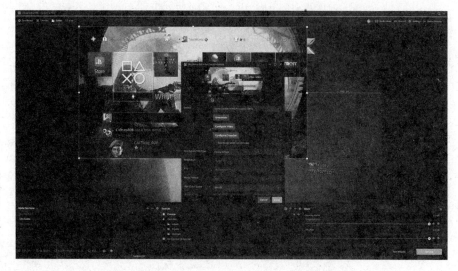

FIGURE 6-6:
Once you tell OBS where the signal is coming from, OBS will render the source in your template.

8. **Grab the bottom-right handle of the console video and click-and-drag the video to fill the entire screen.**

9. **In the Sources window, click-and-drag "Console" down the list of your sources until it is just above the "Background" source.**

10. **Single-click the "Background" scene and then click the – (minus sign) icon to remove it. Click *OK* when prompted.**

11. **Look at the Mixer section and click the gear icon off to the right corner of the window. Where you see the Console source, go to *Audio Monitoring* and select the *Monitor and Output* option from the drop-menu.**

Customizing your template

In bringing your game into the template, you also have an idea of how to customize your template to your own specifications. Let's personalize this template beyond just bringing in your console. Let's put your stream's title in here so people know exactly where they are.

1. **Find the header of your template in the Sources window and single-click the eyeball to the far right of it. This will hide the layer from view. Single-click the eyeball again to make the source visible.**

   These two icons are Source Lock and View/Hide options. When a source is locked, it cannot be edited (but it can still be removed). Single-clicking the View/Hide option will make a source visible or invisible. It can still be repositioned and edited, but it is either hidden from view or visible.

2. **Where you see the Stream Label widget, click on the *View/Hide* icon to hide it from view. Then lock it.**

3. **Where you see the *Text Element* (designated by an *A* icon), single-click and move that in place of the Stream Label, as shown in Figure 6-7.**

   Each template will be different, but in many of these templates, there will be *Stream Labels* in place, small widgets that offer up some simple automation between your dashboard and your template. (In the case of this template, the widget reports who gave the most recent donation to your stream.) *Text Elements* are just that: static text generated by OBS, most of the time used for headers, footers, and titles of some description.

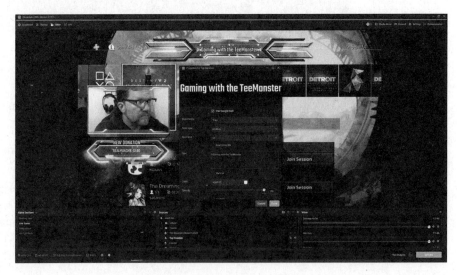

FIGURE 6-7: Templates in Streamlabs OBS are easy to customize and make your own.

4. Double-click the *Text Element* to get to its Properties window. In the Text field, type in a title for your stream. Hit the Tab button to see the changes, and click-and-drag the new title in your template to center it.

In the Properties window, you can change other attributes of the text, ranging from font to font size to color.

5. Click the *Done* button to accept the changes.

This is how you make the template your own. Perhaps you're beginning to see how your stream can evolve creatively with the help of Streamlabs OBS. This is a very common look you will find from stream to stream, a personalized look with animated elements adding a touch of flair to your Channel.

From here, you can tinker around with SLOBS to add more depth to your stream: extra cameras for in-studio co-hosts, a keyboard-mouse camera to show off your mad gaming skills . . . or your struggle to refine said skills, depending on what your stream wants. Or maybe adding in an external audio source to bring in some tunes of your own as a backdrop. The more you dive into Streamlabs OBS, the more possibilities are there for you. It's now a matter of what you want to accomplish and how you want to present yourself on stream.

But let's talk a little bit about audio. Oh, let's talk . . .

Video Is Easy; Audio . . . Is Hard

In setting up my dream stream machine, I discovered something unexpected: *Audio is a fickle mistress.*

With the PS4 console, everything is self-contained, including PSN Party Chat. Much like Xbox's own network, PSN's audio delivers a clear, clean signal, and everyone can easily join in on the fun, both in game and on stream. There are no real complications in set up. So long as you are using a USB headset and microphone, you're ready to go.

With the PS4-PC combination, however, things get complicated. *Really* complicated.

PSN Party Chat, once the PC becomes the streaming device, is no longer a self-contained option. In all the various combinations of devices, gadgets, and cables, either I would get audio from all sources but not be able to talk to Party Chat. Or I would get audio from Party Chat only, leaving both game and Twitch in the Cone of Silence. Maybe a little more research was in order, so I started asking other streamers about how they dealt with audio.

I discovered in my research that I was far from the only one grappling with this issue.

Regardless of the console and its network, audio is apparently far from "an easy fix" when working with a PC. While a PC does give you more creative options, audio can be tricky to manage.

I've come down to two solutions that could offer you the audio solutions you are looking for. Your mileage may vary if you are using different models of peripherals and different connections found between internal and external devices.

Using the Astro A50 MixAmp Pro as your Party Chat solution

For this solution, you will need this equipment:

>> an Astro A50 MixAmp Pro

>> a USB cable (included with the MixAmp)

>> an optical audio cable (included)

>> a male 1/8-inch jack to male 1/8-inch jack cable

>> a set of Astro 40 Pro headphones

— OR —

>> a set of headphones that can plug into an auxiliary jack

1. **Connect the USB cable between the console and MixAmp Pro.**

2. **Connect the optical audio cable between the console and the MixAmp Pro.**

3. **Plug the 1/8-inch jack into the "Stream" connection located between the "USB" and the "Optical" audio connections, as pictured in Figure 6-8.**

4. **Plug the other 1/8-inch jack into the PC's audio out connection.**

5. **Plug in your headset.**

6. **Go into your console settings and make sure the Audio Input and Output settings are set to the MixAmp Pro.**

7. **Go to your PC and make sure that your MixAmp is plugged into the internal audio card.**

FIGURE 6-8:
The Astro
A50 MixAmp Pro
acts as a bridge
between console
and PC, but
there is some
effort involved
in making it
work with your
headset.

From here, you can tinker around with audio settings for balance. Before going live, you will want to run a few audio tests and maybe even a live stream, just to be sure the signal is clean.

Using Discord as your Party Chat solution

The other solution is both the easiest and the most difficult solution to implement for your Party Chat. And you may hear streamers talk about it, because it is a multi-purpose app that you should have in your streaming studio. *Discord*, a Chat service offering audio options, launched in 2015 as an alternative for gamers to socialize in a network that was to platform specific. Discord has become what streamer, podcaster, and passionate gamer Danfinity (`http://twitch.tv/ danfinity`) describes as "Facebook for Streamers," and it serves as an audio.

First, you are going to need to download Discord. Once installed, you will set up an alert channel for our stream.

1. **Go to `http://discordapp.com` and install the app on to your laptop or desktop computer. Once installed, launch Discord.**

   Discord is accessible both as a web browser app and as a standalone app. You will want to install the standalone app. At first, Discord looks barren, but we will go through the process of setting up a server and channels dedicated to your Twitch stream.

2. **Look for the *Add Server* option (a large + sign in the center of a circle) in the left-side of your Discord window. Single-click *Add Server* and then click on the *Create a Server* option.**

3. **When creating your server, as pictured in Figure 6-9, an icon and a Server Name are needed. Enter in for your Server Name:**

   My Twitch Community

   For the icon, use either the icon used for your Twitch Channel or use a profile picture that can easily be associated with you.

   Both the Server Name and the Server Icon can all be changed after the server is established.

FIGURE 6-9:
Creating a Server,
a private line of
communication
for your Twitch
Community, is
how stream hosts
build and
maintain
communications
through Discord.

4. **Click the *Create* button and your server is live.**

   In Discord, servers are your own private areas of the Discord community. Within your server, *channels* are established where you can discuss with your community a variety of topics. We're going to explore Discord in chapter 7 and Chapter 13.

People who follow your Twitch Channel's Discord server can stop on by and look into what your group is talking about. They don't even have to be followers on your Twitch stream. All they need to do is have Discord on their computer, tablet, or smartphone, and be able to access your server, usually done through a URL you share.

Another option you have with Discord is voice chat. For this solution, you will need these items:

» Discord (https://discordapp.com/)

» a USB Cable

>> an optical audio cable

>> a set of USB headphones

1. **Connect the optical audio cable between the console and the PC.**

2. **Connect your USB headphones to your PC.**

3. **Launch Streamlabs and make sure you have a Source that recognizes your audio signal.**

4. **Launch the Discord app.**

5. **Go to *Voice Channels* at the bottom of the left-hand column of the Discord App. You can select the gear icon and rename the channel name "Game Chat," as shown in Figure 6-10.**

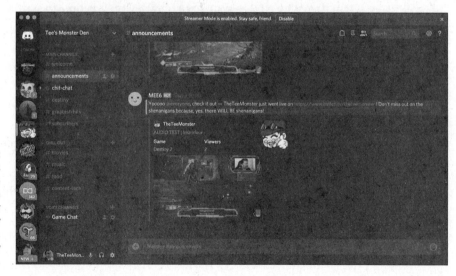

FIGURE 6-10: Discord offers you audio channels — open and private — for all your Party Chat, Fireteam, and Raid crew needs.

6. **Single click the *Create Instant Invite* icon to the left of the *Channel Settings* options and follow the steps to create a link you can use to send out to members of your Party Chat.**

7. **Once all your Party Chat gathers in Discord, launch your game and have Streamlabs all set and ready to go.**

While this option appears easier on the surface, Discord has a learning curve that some users may find difficult. Safeguards on browsers may also prevent audio connections. Again, I offer a more in-depth introduction to the popular Chat application in Chapter 13.

Before Returning to Orbit, Guardian . . .

I was asked several times *"You had a setup that was working, so why did you make his change?"* When it comes to streaming on a PC, things do get more complicated when compared to working on a console. There's a bit of resource management to get used to. Alongside producer, director, and on-screen talent, you now add I.T. Support to the many hats you wear. (Guess that would make me and *Twitch For Dummies* your own Help Desk. *"Hello, Help Desk, have you tried turning it on and turning it off again?"*)

PlayStation and Xbox make streaming easier than playing the video game itself, but let's not kid ourselves: There's only so far you can go with it creatively. The trade-off for the simple, quick way of console streaming is versatility. If you want to stream completely game-free, you can. If you want to stream with broadcast-quality graphics, you can. If you want more interaction with your Chat, you can get that, too. With a PC as your streaming device, it is time to start exploring.

> » What's "The Jar" and how does that work?

> » Oh, can I have a dynamic list of events letting people know who is hosting, subbing, donating, and all that?

> » Wait, I can make *custom* alerts on my stream? Seriously?

Yes, you can do all that, and with a little clever thinking and a touch of imagination, you can look pretty boss while doing it.

To quote ZGphoto when taking me into the Wrath of the Machine for the first time: *"Take a deep breath. This is only the beginning, my friend."*

Chapter **7**

Setting Schedules and Social Media

Whether you are sticking with console and a camera or working with the ultimate stream machine and gaming setup, you have arrived to the wonderful world of Twitch. It's an incredible community. For me, it's like stepping back in time to the early days of podcasting. There is a real, supportive network out there of like-minded creative types, either sharing their love and passion for a particular video game or exploring a topic of discussion or self-improvement, and they have invited the world to join them in this voyage of discovery.

Also, like podcasting, everyone appears to be approaching Twitch from various disciplines. Hop from one Channel to another, and you will see people all coming to their game or creative outlet of choice differently. There is nothing really wrong with any of these approaches to streaming on Twitch. Yes, Twitch has rules on what you can and cannot stream, but deciding how you stream is strictly up to you. As a Twitch Channel Host, you are essentially the producer, the director, and the star. You wear a lot of hats. This chapter explores all these various responsibilities that fall on you, and together we find a strategy and an approach that best fits you and your lifestyle.

Same Bat-Time, Same Bat-Channel: Setting Your Schedule

Think about your favorite television show. This is the show that, when it's running, you never miss the episode. You want to see it when it airs, not on-demand or when the season appears on Netflix or Hulu. You want to see the series in real time, when it drops.

Now, try to imagine how infuriating it would be if you found a show that you love only to discover it aired when it felt like it? Maybe it would play on Monday, but then it would pop up on Thursdays because that worked out best. Oh, and instead of airing at 8:00 p.m., it decided to air at 3:30 p.m. because *"Why not?"* You might not be all that inclined to catch the show if you never knew when said show was going to air. This is why we have schedules for cable, satellite, and all forms of media.

This is also why we have schedules for Twitch.

The schedule you set up for yourself should be a schedule that strikes a solid balance for you and your real-life demands, and it should be a schedule that you should be able to keep without burning yourself out. (*Burnout* we will be talking about later in Chapter 14.) Your schedule is not necessarily set in stone, but you should do what you can to make it.

From start to finish: A basic schedule

When you sit down and ask yourself the hard questions about your stream, one of the hardest is "Okay, when do I stream?" Look at your day, break it down to when you need to get things done, and then look at the best times when you want to unwind or relax because — in theory — your stream is your time to relax and have a little fun, all while sharing with the world your skills in game or whatever creative endeavor you are undertaking.

Using my previous morning schedule as a basis for an example, let's say you discover that you've been at your day job long enough to come into the office and settle in between 9:30 a.m. and 10 a.m. without anyone raising an eyebrow. You also know from where you live, provided you can either throw together a quick breakfast or pick up something at the day job, so you need an hour. 8:30 a.m. is now your cutoff time. So when do you log on, because it is looking like an *early* start time for you?

Across the streams I follow, I find the smallest streams are usually clocking in at three hours. If we are to use this as a guide, then your go time for streaming should be 5 a.m. So wake up at 4:30. Quick shower, shave, and teeth brushing.

Get dressed. Launch your stream at the top of the hour. There's no real science to why launching a stream at the top of the hour yields better results than starting at the quarter or half hour, but in my own experience, people just like streams starting at the top of the clock.

Your morning schedule for streaming would look something like this:

Monday — 5:00 a.m. – 8:30 a.m.

Tuesday — 5:00 a.m. – 8:30 a.m.

Wednesday — 5:00 a.m. – 11:00 a.m.

Thursday — 5:00 a.m. – 8:30 a.m.

Friday — 5:00 a.m. – 8:30 a.m.

Here is a proposed schedule for a morning stream. Notice that on Wednesdays, you tend to stream a little longer. That could be an "Extended Stream" day as you have designated that a "work from home" day and have managed, the night before, to get a few extra hours clocked in on projects due. Provided you are able to adjust your sleep schedule (and yes, I did), you have a schedule that can easily work for you and your stream in growth. Breaking down this former stream schedule even further, here's why this approach works so well for new streamers:

>> **Morning audience:** As I am based on the East Coast of the U.S., it is highly unlikely that I would get any sort of attention heading out West, but there are audiences that work the night shift and enjoy some Twitch distractions. Then you have people on your coast who are getting ready for the day, and I was their morning wake-up show. Finally, I had audiences overseas in the United Kingdom and Germany; and on some occasions, I heard from Australia and New Zealand.

>> **Limited competition:** An advantage to streaming early in the morning is that many of the headliner American streamers are offline. It doesn't mean you have Partnered Streamers out there with numbers worth reaching for, but the names seen often at the top of your Directory and others are still asleep. It's a good advantage to exploit.

>> **Less stress on the household:** Here was the biggest bonus for me, both as a husband and as a dad. At this time of day, everyone was asleep (provided I didn't get *too* wound up when I gamed). The time was mine to do with as I pleased, and as I was slightly burned out from working out on the elliptical, I could give early morning streams a go without feeling as if I was tuning out my family. Later in Chapter 14, we go into the ups and downs of streaming and real-life relationships, and how to strike a balance between the two. Reduced tension between significant others and life partners is a good thing to have in your Twitch routine.

WARNING

The temptation to wake up super-early and push yourself through a day can be strong, especially if you really find a love and a joy in streaming. However, your health does matter. It matters a lot. Maybe for a week you can function with four hours of sleep. Maybe for a month, the sleeping pattern of three hours and a solid nap after coming home from your day job is feasible. Eventually, time will catch up with you. Be reasonable in your routines, and make sure you're getting enough sleep.

Other schedule options

So how do you know when your schedule is a good fit? The best way to test out a schedule is to take a hard, critical look at how you feel after a week of streaming on this schedule. Once you get past a week, the next hump to clear will be a month. Within that time, you should find a routine within your schedule. If, however, your stream still feels off, you may need to reconsider your times to Twitch and see if another time of day is better suited for you.

>> **Afternoon streaming:** At high noon and in the hours following, you might find a sweet spot for streaming online and finding your audience. Many factors come into play for you. If you have the ability to stream in the after-noon and you are based further west, the audiences towards the east will be turning to you for early evening entertainment. Subsequently if you are an afternoon streamer based on the East Coast, there will be a morning audience watching you out west. It can be a difficult slot to manage, depending on your day job and the flexibility of your hours. Swing-shift jobs? Hardly a concern. If you are working a standard, 40-hour work week with no sort of deviation from the 9-to-5 clock, then streaming midday is not in the cards.

>> **Evening streaming:** You come home from work, grab dinner, maybe tend to a few odds and ends around the house, and then you stream until bedtime. Depending on agreements with significant others and life partners, this is manageable. However, the talent pool is a bit deeper and audiences have more variety to choose from. Also, when it comes to social engagements and relation-ship responsibilities, evening streams may prove more of a challenge than you may realize. What benefits an evening streamer best is two things. The first, communication. You should be making your intentions and your goals with Twitch crystal clear between you and your friends and family. Without that, you could be driving a wedge between you and people that matter. The second thing to work into your evening schedule: flexibility. There will be some nights that higher priorities crop up. Am I saying Twitch could not be a high priority in your life? Not at all. In the beginning, though, Twitch is a hobby with the potential of something more. Evening streaming is an option but can be harder to maintain.

>> **Overnight streaming:** Here's an alternative for the streamer who works on a flexible schedule and who can sleep during the day and stream for part of the wee small hours of the morning. Call it the "Red Eye" approach to streaming.

While you may reach the odd insomniac or possibly a few fellow night owls who work the third shift, the majority of your audience will be overseas. It doesn't mean you won't land subscribers or build a following. There will be a whole new set of challenges in front of you, many of them concerning the balance between real-life relationships and streaming.

Finding your own prime time may sound easy, but when streaming, you want to try to find a balance between your real life responsibilities, your stream, and simply taking care of yourself. Without that balance, you may find maintaining your commitment to your audience and your community something of a challenge.

Your own pocket of time: The length of your stream

You may look at that previous morning schedule and think, *"Those times seem a little . . . brief,"* and to some extent, they are conservative compared to other streamers. When setting up a schedule, you have to consider all of your other responsibilities when deciding on the amount of time you want to set aside for streaming.

Unlike podcasting where you allocate time for recording, editing, and scheduling, Twitch works in real time. You are creating content and posting it all in one shot, and your audience is more present when you're streaming. A trick with building your audience and your community is helping your potential audience find you, and the best way to do that is to stream.

A SCHEDULE? WHO NEEDS A SCHEDULE?

You can find many Twitch streamers who stream — quite honestly — whenever they feel like it. When they go live, social media and Twitch notifications serve as signal flares to their community: *I am live. Come join in the fun!* It's amazing how loyal these audiences are, waiting on the word from the channel host of when they go live. There is no real consistency between these streamers. Some of them are early adopters of Twitch. Others built a following based on long streams (discussed next in this chapter) and then scaled back their own stream to better suit a balanced lifestyle. Whatever the case, streamers do have an option to stream whenever they feel like it or when time allows them to schedule. The results are mixed, and your own mileage may vary if you decide to proceed sans schedule. While a schedule offers stability not only for your audience but for yourself, there is a sense of freedom in streaming on your time. Have fun and enjoy the stream as you are, in a sense, following the currents to wherever they take you.

But how long should your stream be?

>> **3–5 hours.** Streamers need to find you, but it helps to know your audience's viewing habits. Twitch audiences tend to float from streamer to streamer, usually after enjoying a stream for an hour or two. This means streamers need to stretch beyond a single hour or two to increase their chances to be found. Within the pocket of time suggested here, 3–5 hours offers you an opportunity to be found by not only potential streaming audiences but streamers themselves looking for someone new to raid or host. I recommend that streams should be no shorter than three hours, as the chances of audiences finding you (and getting to know you) within an hour or two is unlikely. Give yourself some time to let people get to know you.

>> **6–8 hours.** When streamers push their streams to pockets of time this substantial, there is an earnest push (adopting the term from video games, *grinding* through hours on Twitch) from streamers to either go part time or even full time with their stream. (I delve deeper into the business of Twitch and going full time with it in Chapter 12.) This slot has been regarded by many streamers as optimum time to find a groove in a stream and a great way for new audiences to find you. Casual Twitch viewers and streamers looking to end their own streams with a host or a raid have an even greater chance to find you, as you are on for a longer stretch. Committing to this kind of schedule, keep in mind, is a serious step into going full time with Twitch. With 6–8 hours on a regular basis, Twitch becomes something of a part-time job. Make sure to approach it as such.

>> **10–12 hours.** Investing this much time into Twitch is a commitment. You're now building a presence, and maintaining a presence, on the platform. With this much time streaming, hosts will usually state that there will be breaks (as, last time I checked, hosts are human and breaks are needed), but this stream is the kind of stream where different kinds of people are in and out, hosts and raids occur, and your ranks in a directory vary throughout the day. There is very little remaining in the day after a stream of this size, so plan out the day in order to take care of yourself. Pausing the stream for meals and taking a few moments AFK (away from the keyboard) are essential in keeping your feed a positive place to be.

TIP

Streams going beyond 10–12 hours (as discussed in the upcoming sidebar) are terrific for special occasions. Got a highly-anticipated game on your console and taking a day from work to enjoy it? Are you planning to host a charity stream for your favorite non-profit? If you have the time and the ability to host a longer-than-usual stream, but can't host long streams on a regular basis, find a holiday, a charity, or a special game release or project. Enjoy the occasional marathon stretch of gaming. It may even introduce you to new audiences.

THE LURE OF THE LONG STREAM

When you first step into Twitch, looking at the extended stream is tempting. Go in and go hard, right? And there are some streamers who go beyond the 12-hour streams. Some hardcore streamers even double down and attempt 24-hour streams.

Impressive. Also, something of a trap.

Analytics and statistics support the fact that long streams are the best way to be discovered. The effect longer streams have on your monthly average viewers should be kept in mind. In your own path to *Twitch Partnership* (discussed in more detail in Chapter 12), you need to strike an average of 75 viewers over the total number of hours you stream. Longer streams could potentially work *against* you as more hours added to your monthly hours on stream make it harder to keep the overall viewer average high. Also, longer streams tend to take a greater toll on the host as the energy needed to maintain the stream's pace, coupled with performance in game, fizzled out in the later hours. Another thing to seriously be aware of is how your overall quality of life is affected. Longer streams means you are sitting in front of a computer for stretches of time double that of desk jobs: It's a sedentary lifestyle that can take its toll on the human body. And it's also a hard habit to maintain when real world relationships, financial responsibilities, and other priorities become involved. Professor Broman, a successful streamer, wrote about this in 2017 at `http://bit.ly/twitch-balance` and his words still remain relevant today.

Long streams tend to also be a short-cut to *burnout*. This is when the stream no longer becomes a passion or a joy, but more of a chore. In a quick pursuit to partnership, streamers attempt to push their own limits only to tap out. Longer streams are a commitment, so make sure you are ready to undertake such a commitment.

Consistency and Communication

Now that you know when you want to stream and how long you are planning to stream, it is up to you to maintain your schedule and stick with it. While the longer the stream the better your chances are in being found online, you also need to build trust with your audiences that you are going to be online and what you are going to be streaming.

Communication with your audience starts on your Twitch dashboard.

Notifications on Twitch

Remember when you were setting up your Twitch account? If you recall, this is where you confirm the email where all our Twitch notifications are sent. Whenever you follow another streamer or someone follows you, the first notification arrives from Twitch, whether it is email or a mobile app alert. When these notifications are sent, your audience is told what you are streaming, what the title of your stream is, and even offers a quick note from you on what you have planned for your stream.

How does Twitch do that? Pretty easy, really.

1. Go to http://twitch.tv and log in. If you are already logged in, or once you have logged on, go to the top-right drop down menu of Twitch account and select the Dashboard.

2. Look for the Stream Information panel, located usually on the left-hand section of the Dashboard and pictured in Figure 7-1. In the Title window, enter in the following:

   [PS4] [Destiny 2] Gaming with TheTeeMonster | #TitanTuesday | Tank Life!

   The Title is the title of your stream as it will appear in the Twitch Directory. There are a lot of theories in what makes a title eye-catching, but the title can be broken down as such:

   [Platform] [Game] Title of Your Stream | Hashtag Describing Your Stream | Quick Summary of Your Stream

   Looking at other streamers, you'll see this format repeated with variations on a theme:

{PS4/PC} Flawless Trials w/ YOU HOMIE! // @OneActual on Twitter

Viewer EoW Prestige (PS4) | Destiny and Coffee

DBS | Then Raid fun with BDO, Zoe, Polar, Kepr and CG!

These Titles from OneActual, ZGPhoto, and Tiddly all serve a purpose in summarizing their streams. In the Directory, you can quickly and easily figure out what's in store for you here. Find a format that best suits you and make sure you change it before each stream.

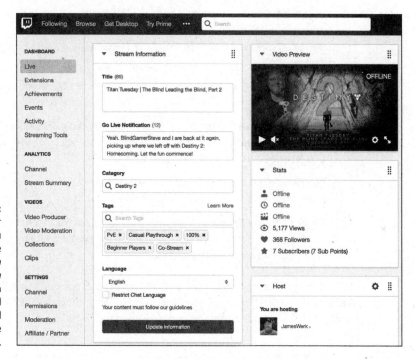

FIGURE 7-1:
In your Dashboard, you will find the *Stream Information* section, which helps you and your stream find its place in the Twitch Directory.

3. **Proceed to** *Go Live Notification,* **which is the message sent out with Twitch Notifications that you are going live. Send your followers and subscribers this message:**

    Good morning, everyone. Let's get things going with some Titan shenanigans. TANK LIFE!!!

    This message will only be seen by Twitch notifications, which show up in Twitch alerts and email notifications.

4. **Proceed to *Category* and search for the game you currently are planning to play.**

   If you are planning to do a creative, non-gaming stream, you can search for either one and then select it. Make sure if you change games mid-stream to change your game in order to be listed in the proper directory.

5. **Twitch offers a list of *tags* that help people find you and your stream. From the drop-menu provided, select five tags relevant to your game.**

   Tags are used to describe stream beyond the game or category. Viewers can use tags as filters within a directory, narrowing down specific detsils that views want in a stream. You are allowed up to five tags; but if you cannot find a tag that best fits you, go to `http://bit.ly/suggest-a-tag` and suggest a tag to Twitch.

6. **Proceed to *Language* and select your stream's preferred or dominant language.**

7. **After filling in all the fields, you will notice the link that take you to Community Guidelines. If you are not certain if your content falls into place with Twitch guidelines, click on that link.**

   You can also go directly to Community Guidelines at `https://help.twitch.tv/customer/portal/articles/983016`.

8. **Single click the *Update Information* button to accept all changes. If you have properly formatted and completed everything, the button with turn into a green button with a checkmark.**

When you go live, you will send out information to everyone stating that you will be going live with Twitch. In the next section, let's continue with the notifications and get the word out about your stream through social media.

Notifications on Facebook and Twitter

While Twitch works hard in getting the word out about your stream, you also have Facebook and Twitter you can lean on for support as well. There is a good possibility that authentication for these platforms has already been taken care of, and when you have connected your consoles to Facebook or Twitter, it is a process you only have to do once. By tapping into these social media platforms, you only boost your signal in reaching all those who are following or subscribing to you.

If you are streaming directly off your PS4 console:

1. **Turn on your PlayStation 4 and navigate with your controller to your Settings option. Press the *X* button to enter the menu.**

2. Under the Settings menu, select the *Account Management* option.

3. From the Account Management screen, select the *Link with Other Services* option.

   As pictured in Figure 7-2, the Link with Other Services option grants your PSN account access to various social media links.

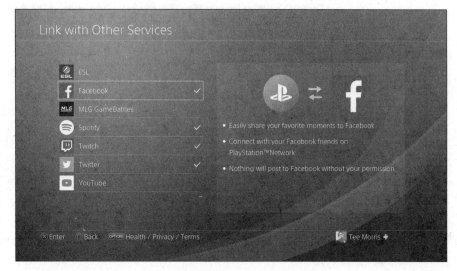

FIGURE 7-2:
The *Link with Other Services* option connects your PSN account to other social media accounts like Facebook, Twitter, Spotify, and YouTube.

4. Select the Facebook option and follow the login and authorization steps to connect your Facebook account with your PSN.

   Your PSN can only connect with personal account, not Page or Group accounts.

5. Follow the login and authorization steps to connect your Twitter account with your PSN.

6. Once you have authorized Twitter and Facebook, press the *Circle* button on your controller to return to the Main Menu. Find a game you want to stream and launch it.

7. Press the *Share* button on your controller, located to the top left off the directional pad. From the menu sliding from the left of your monitor, select the *Broadcast Gameplay* option.

8. Select Twitch and review your Broadcast Page options.

9. Scroll down to review the title of your stream.

   As mentioned back in Chapter 3, instead of using your controller and PS4 to edit your stream title, you can create and edit your title in your Twitch Dashboard. We have just done so in the earlier exercise, so you should see your title populating this field. You are good to go!

10. **Scroll down to Social Links to Facebook and Twitter. Select both platforms for you to notify followers in your networks that you are going live on PSN.**

11. **Under the Twitter and Facebook options is the Comment window. This is what will appear both as a post and as a tweet on your respective platforms. You can either leave the default message of "Check out my stream . . ." or create a custom message accompanying a link to your Twitch Channel by pressing the *X* button and composing a new message.**

    I recommend creating a more personal, customized message. Try a message similar to the following:

    Okay. It's been a heck of a week already, so let's punch stuff! #TitanTuesday #PS4 #Destiny2 #TankLife

    The breakdown of the message is **[Post/Tweet] #hashtags.** And when you begin broadcasting, your PlayStation generates a link back to your Twitch channel.

TIP

Go easy on hashtags. Whether it is here in your announcements or posting on Instagram as part of a social media promotional push, spamming with hashtags can be a real turn off and could set off a few SPAM flags. Five should be plenty. Any over ten is overkill.

12. **At the bottom of the screen, select the *Start Broadcasting* button. Your Facebook and Twitter are automatically updated.**

If you are streaming directly off your Xbox One X console:

1. **Turn on your Xbox One and navigate with your controller to your *Settings* option. Under the Settings menu, select the *Account* option.**

2. **From the Account screen, select the *Link Social Accounts* option and enter in your passkey, if applicable.**

    Similar to the PSN, the Link Social Accounts grants your Xbox account access to your social media platforms.

3. **Select the *Link to Twitter* option and follow the login and authorization steps to connect your Twitter account with your Xbox One.**

4. **Return to the main screen of the *Linked Social Accounts* option and select the *Link Facebook Account* option. Follow the login and authorization steps to connect your Facebook account with your Xbox.**

    You will be prompted to "Find Friends," which is Microsoft's way to help you broaden your Xbox Live network. Select the button to finish the process.

5. Once you have authorized Twitter and Facebook, return to the Main Menu. Find a game you want to stream and launch it.

6. Return to the Xbox home screen by pressing the *Xbox* button on the controller. From the Preferences, make sure the *Allow Broadcasts . . .* option is selected.

7. On launching the Twitch app, confirm your network settings and ensure that *Enable Microphone* is selected so your audience can hear you.

8. With audio levels set, go to the Broadcast Title window. If your title from the Twitch dashboard isn't there, edit the window to match your Twitch title.

9. Select *Start Broadcast* to begin your stream.

   Once the broadcast goes live, your Facebook and Twitter are updated.

Now you have two platforms covered. Your audiences are in the know of when you go live. We only have one more platform to tend to, and this one is a relatively new player in the social media arena but a familiar gathering space for streamers. I will go into more detail on this third platform in Chapter 13, but in the following section, I offer a quick introduction to a streamer's best friend in building communities.

Say "Hello" to Discord.

Notifications on Discord

As introduced in Chapter 6, *Discord*, is a Chat service offering text and audio options to its users. It also serves as another platform for your stream to notify subscribers and followers of when you go live.

1. Launch Discord either on to your laptop or desktop computer.

2. In the left-hand side of the Discord window, find the icon you created for your channel and single-click it. Here you will find in your server your text and voice *channels*. Under *Text Channels,* click on the *Add Channel* option (a large + sign located to the right of the Text Channels label) to create a new channel.

   As stated earlier, *channels* are dedicated topics that you want to share with your followers and subscribers. Returning to the "Facebook for Streamers" analogy, picture being able to make multiple sections of your Facebook dedicated to singular topics like Food, Sports, or Movies. Instead of sifting through your main feed for topics of interest, Discord offers you the ability to sort and organize your interests.

3. **In the Create Text Channel window, go on and label your new channel "Announcements" and make sure the Channel Type is *Text Channel*. Leave the *Private Channel* option turned off.**

   Again, I will explore Discord and channel options more in depth in Chapter 13.

4. **Single-click the *Create Channel* button.**

   You now have a channel created that is available to everyone. We have designated "#announcements" will be where you drop in automatic notifications for when you go online.

5. **With the Discord app still running, return to your browser and go to `http://mee6.xyz` and single-click the *Add to Discord* button.**

   MEE6 is a *bot*, but not the kind of bot that makes your online experience miserable. Bots add automation and extensions to your Discord and Twitch Channel, once permissions are granted.

6. **Once permissions are granted, you should be taken to a page prompting you to select a server. (If not, simply refresh the browser.) Select your Twitch Channel's server.**

7. **MEE6 takes you to a page of *plug-ins* designed to give your Discord a variety of extra functions. Look for the *Twitch* plug-in and single-click the *Enable* button.**

8. **In the Twitch plug-in Preferences page, single-click the *Add a Streamer* button.**

9. **In the *Add a Streamer* window, under the Channel Name field, search for your Twitch user name.**

   There is no need to type in the full URL for your Twitch Channel. Just the username you created will suffice.

10. **Proceed to the Announcement Channel drop-menu. From the Select a Channel . . . menu, choose the #*announcements* option**

11. **In the Announcement Message field, you can choose to leave the default message as is, or edit the message to make it more personal (see Figure 7-3). Edit this message to read as follows:**

    @everyone, {streamer} has just gone live on {link}! We'll see you there?

    The announcement message can be as personal as you like, but make sure the following elements are there:

    @everyone — this is the tag that makes sure everyone in the server is tagged properly and notified

    {streamer} — this is an element MEE6 needs in order to know where to put your streamer name when you go live.

{link} — this is an element MEE6 needs in order to know where to put your Twitch Channel's URL when you go live. Leave that space between {link} and punctuation. Otherwise the punctuation is made part of the URL and the URL will not work properly.

12. **Single-click the *Add* button.**

FIGURE 7-3:
Instead of creating a new message in Discord every time you go live, *MEE6* gives you the ability to send out automated notifications every time you go live.

Whenever you go live from this point forward, an automated message appears in your Discord, sending out to everyone in your server notification that a new stream is underway. Discord, the more you work with it, remains one of the most popular platforms for streamers to nurture the community around their stream, and gives you plenty of options in how you communicate with your audience. Discord can be as public or as private as you make it, and in Chapter 13, we will go deeper into its functionality and cover how you can leverage it to help grow your channel.

When Life Happens: Changes in the Schedule

Communication is key when it comes to streaming. With so many platforms able to help you boost your signal and get the word out on when your stream goes live, it's easy to think that all your bases are covered, and all you need to focus on is hitting that broadcast button and being awesome.

That's a safe assumption, but there's one obstacle in the way of your stream: Life.

Life, to pontificate in a somewhat Douglas Adams-esque style, tends to take a good look at you and your stream and says, *"Huh, this creative outlet of yours is running pretty damn smoothly. You must have read that book from Tee Morris. Good egg, that Tee Morris, but that's not why I'm pontificating at present. So, I think that I, Life, needs to mix things up a bit so . . ."* and suddenly you find yourself and your stream schedule thrown for a loop.

I'll use my own experience as an example. With a day job, I had been working effectively and efficiently at for a few years, I set up for myself a morning Twitch schedule:

> Monday — 5:00 a.m. – 8:30 a.m.
>
> Tuesday — 5:00 a.m. – 8:30 a.m.
>
> Wednesday — 5:00 a.m. – 11:00 a.m.
>
> Thursday — 5:00 a.m. – 8:30 a.m.
>
> Friday — 5:00 a.m. – 8:30 a.m.

For me, it was the perfect schedule, as I had stated earlier. There was no real encroachment on family time or even work time for that matter. People I usually watched during the day (iLulu, ZGPhoto, \Aura, Tiddly, and so on) were still asleep. I found my pocket of time to start building a stream and a community. In keeping this schedule, I achieved an *Affiliate* rank (explained in more detail in Chapter 12) within a three months. For over six months, I managed to build for myself a group of "Morning Monsters" that gamed with me and enjoyed a good laugh before going to work (in the United States) or heading to bed (in Australia).

Then, Life happened.

Changes at the day job compelled me to start circulating the resume. After a series of interviews, I landed a prominent position in Washington, D.C. I was thrilled. I was ecstatic.

And I was about to make some serious changes to my stream. After a lot of starts, stops, and hard exercises of time management . . .

> Saturday — starting at 6:00 a.m.
>
> Sunday — starting at 6:00 a.m.

Monday — starting at 8:00 p.m.

Tuesday — starting at 8:00 p.m.

How did my Monday–Friday find itself as a Saturday–Tuesday schedule? Before mornings and evenings set in place, I had to touch base with my wife and make sure that this didn't throw off anything in our relationship. (Yes, relationships are a thing.) Also, the various activities my daughter would be involved in after school — orchestra concerts, all day field trips, Krav Maga classes — would supersede any planned stream. Outside of the personal responsibilities at home, there was Twitch. New time block. New audience . . . with far more to choose from at 8:00 p.m. rather than 5:00 a.m.

So I should come as no surprise that my most popular days on Twitch are the morning streams when I "get the band back together."

TIP

There is a real joy and sense of satisfaction found in streaming, and turning it into a full-time activity is not easy. However, as much as I enjoy streaming, I would be the first to tell you not to let opportunities in life pass you by because it may inter- fere with your stream. Don't hold on to a job that makes you miserable because it allows you to stream. Don't miss your child's school event because you're stream- ing that night. Don't avoid taking a vacation overseas because you're worried about how it will affect your numbers. Live your life and enjoy it to the fullest. Nothing is worse than missed opportunities.

Resetting your schedule could be regarded as a setback. In a sense, maybe not completely, you are starting all over again. You are introducing yourself to a brand new audience, and depending on your schedule, the opportunities to be discovered by others could be slim as you are streaming in tighter blocks. Think of a schedule reset, though, as another opportunity for an audience to discover you at a time that works out better for them.

But here's where communication is key. You have Twitch, Facebook, Twitter, and Discord. And later in Chapter 13, we look at other social media channels that you can take advantage of to let your audience know exactly what is changing in your feed and how you plan to proceed. When keeping your audience in the know, it is completely up to you how much you share. Sometimes a simple message such as *"No stream tonight. Got to take care of things at home."* is more than sufficient. You have plenty of communications tools to take advantage of. Keep your community in the know.

TIP

One way of keeping your Twitch stream in the know is to take advantage of the *Video Player Banner*, mentioned all the way back in Chapter 1. Put your schedule up here so that people can easily catch at a glance when arriving to your Channel when you are on. You can also create various versions of the banner to give dates for when you will be offline, or when special events are happening on your stream. The graphic can then appear on your various social media platforms as pinned tweets and posts so that when others visit your social links, you let people know about any late-breaking or upcoming changes to your stream.

We know what we are streaming. We know when we are streaming. We also have ways of reaching out to our audience both on Twitch and elsewhere to let people know when we are live. As you should notice, your Twitch stream is starting to take shape. We have been focused a lot on how we stream from the consoles, but with the PC as our stream machine, we have many more options — some cosmetic, some functional, all pretty dang swish — to explore. Now, let's have some fun gaming your way. Let's go live, everybody.

Chapter **8**

Bells & Whistles: Nifty Add-Ons for Your Twitch Stream

With schedules set and your PC optimized, you are ready to give your stream a whole new look. I've said repeatedly that, yes, you really don't need a "stream machine" for Twitch. If you have a PlayStation or an Xbox, you're ready to go. Introducing a PC with Streamlabs OBS does grant you more creative choices which is always good, and you can manage Chat a bit easier and add more functionality to your stream.

So where do you go from here?

A stream is a solid stream when you have a template in place, a camera on you, and audio live for your team and your game. You still have more you can incorporate into your feed. The more time you clock on Twitch, the more you're going to need add-on's to help manage your stream, keeping you more focused on game and less on making sure your stream is progressing smoothly.

Stand By For Stream: Introduction and Intermission B-roll

As I cover in Chapter 6, Streamlabs gives you an all-in-one solution, complete with templates that you can customize for your stream. If, however, you wish to create a look truly original, truly your own, you can download the latest version of *Open Broadcaster Software,* or *OBS* (http://obsproject.com), an open source application that transforms your computer into a broadcast studio. OBS offers you a blank canvas for *overlays,* an image or looped video that offers your stream a signature look. You've been working with Streamlabs' templates. Now, we create these elements from scratch.

From television, film, and video production comes the term *B-roll.* This is extra footage compiled, edited, and used as something to set a mood. With Twitch Channels, B-roll is applied with templates to create snappy *video loops,* footage that seamlessly and continuously repeats to let people know that your stream is about to start. For Tiddly (http://twitch.tv/tiddly), her introduction video is an animated version of herself on a spacewalk, looking into a space station's Control Room, manned by cats. On Control's main viewscreen, the game she is planning to play is featured. For DrLupo (http://twitch.tv/drlupo), the looped video is a series of graphics featuring his logo and other information about his stream. Tessachka (http://twitch.tv/tessachka) opens her stream with images of her gaming, biking, and other off-stream activities while promoting what will be expected on her stream.

Other streamers keep their introduction B-roll simple. Aura (http://twitch.tv/3vil_Aura) features his stream logo with "Stream Incoming" as its caption. The Big Marvinski (http://twitch.tv/thebigmarvinski) runs a placard that reads "Starting Soon" with his name across the top. iLulu (http://twitch.tv/ilulu) has a similar banner, featuring her logo.

The idea of introduction B-roll is that, instead of starting cold once you hit the "Broadcast" button, you can ease yourself and your stream into the day's or night's activity. It's a nice way to slip into streaming, especially in you want to start on time but then the phone rings, your coffee needs topping off, or you suddenly need to visit the Little Guardian's room before you go live.

For this exercise, we will create a static introduction image. Then we will incorporate it into OBS to make it work.

1. Open a photo editor that you are comfortable using. Go to File ⇨ New to create a new document. Make sure the dimensions of your new image is 1920 x 1080 pixels, which is the dimensions for high definition (HD) television.

   For this exercise, I am using Adobe Photoshop.

2. Create for yourself a fun "Welcome" image like the one pictured in Figure 8-1.

   Your image should be output as a JPEG or as a PNG.

FIGURE 8-1:
A Welcome Screen can either be video or a still image. The image can be as flashy or as simple as you want it to be.

3. Launch OBS on your PC and in the Scenes window, click the *Add Scene* option (the + sign) to create a new scene called *Game*.

4. Return to the Scenes window, click the *Add Scene* option (the + sign) to create a new scene called *Introduction*.

5. Make sure the Introduction scene is at the top of your Scenes window by selecting it and using the *Move Up* option (the ^ icon) and clicking it above the scene for *Game*.

6. With Introduction still selected, go to the Sources window and click the *Add Source* option (the + icon) to create a new source labeled *WelcomeBanner*.

7. Single-click the *Browse* button and find the Introduction image you just created.

8. Select it and click the *Open* button to make it the Source of the Introduction Scene.

Now with OBS, you can easily segue from a simple introduction screen to the game or project you are about to stream. From here, you can expand on how your stream looks by creating other B-roll such as:

>> **Intermission or "Be Right Back" screens:** If you are staying hydrated while you game or waking up in the morning with a cup of joe, eventually Nature will call. Or when you are talking with your stream, UPS, FedEx, or Amazon will knock at your door. Then you have those moments when the phone rings. All of these spotlight a need for an *Intermission* screen as the sight of an empty chair and your game on a menu loop does not quite scream "engagement" with those new to your Channel. The Intermission screen lets people know that you are taking a quick break and your stream will be resuming in a few minutes.

>> **End screens:** Some streams just end, much like classic Jackie Chan movies. Slam on the breaks, shut the lights off, and high tail it offline. An *End* screen can be something as simple as *"Thanks for watching!"* or can remind viewers old and new about your schedule along with any potential changes coming. (See Chapter 7 on communication with your Chat.) Look at it as the closing credits of a film and the End screen as your own personal "Fade to Black" for the day's stream.

>> **Video loops:** The difference between static screens and video loops is that one is created in photo editors like Photoshop while video loops are edited in programs like Adobe's After Effects. If you want your B-roll to be more dynamic, more eye-catching, then look at creating video loops that kick up the production level of your stream up a notch.

This is just one of many little touches you can do with OBS; and unlike Streamlabs where the templates are available to everyone using Streamlabs, what you create and incorporate into OBS here is unique to your stream. There is nothing that says you need B-roll to be part of your stream, but in doing so, audiences will sit up and take notice. You should take these production flourishes one step at a time, gradually building up your stream to create the best look for your Channel.

There has been a lot of work on your part to make this stream happen. It feels like you have been single-handedly (with a little help from this book) building from the ground up a video production of epic scale. Again and again, I have stressed that no matter how simple your stream or how complex you make the production, you make the call on how far and how fancy your stream is in the end. There is a lot to manage in a stream, though, and consequently the more you add to your stream, the more you have to manage.

This is why it is okay to ask for help.

LETTING OTHERS DO THE HEAVY LIFTING

When searching for additional help and resources online (and yes, I encourage you to do that), you'll hear about many online vendors, all ranging in price, offering *video templates* for you to download and implement. What exactly are these packages? Production houses like IVIPID (http://ivipid.com), Digital Juice (http://digitaljuice.com), and Scene Maker (https://nerdordie.com/product/scene-maker-free/) all offer up prefabricated video templates that you can use for a variety of applications on your stream. Some of these online vendors offer you online editors that allow you to customize your animations and video loops with your name and images. Other vendors will simply hand you all the elements of an animation, leaving it to you to control all the elements. For the latter, an understanding of video editors such as Apple's Final Cut, Adobe Premiere, or Adobe After Effects is necessary. If, however, you have it in your budget to hire someone, find streamers with slick video segues and ask them where they had those done. It is more than feasible to find a talented video production artist who can come through with a look and a feel for your stream.

Second-in-Command: Channel Moderators

You have taken a look at working with bots (on the most rudimentary of levels) and have turned on and off a variety of options that will help you keep trolls, SPAM, and out-of-control behavior at bay. There is, though, a need for people — real people — to become involved. These are people who are responsible. These are people we know. These are people we trust.

In Twitch, these unsung heroes of many, many Channels are known as *moderators*.

When you can't enforce the rules of a stream as you are tied up in a game, working on a particular tricky pattern on a cosplay-in-progress, or following a train of thought, moderators are the individuals in Chat who pick up the sword (pun intended) and defend your Chat. When wielding the moderator badge, seen in Figure 8-2, the individual has a responsibility to enforce the rules of your Chat and your Community. These guardians fill the shoes of Security, Public Relations, and Marketing Representative, all in one.

How does one become a Moderator? A lot of it comes from spending time in other Channels. So is the case with Realmunchie (http://twitch.tv/realmunchle), a UK gamer that taught himself the in's and out's of Twitch and made himself part of many communities. "I mod in other Channels, and that is a severe learning curve in the Twitch process," Munchie says. "As a mod you are taking on the responsibility of someone else's Chat and you're participating while, at the same time, offering a degree of lenience. You have to put yourself into someone else's shoes. Someone comes in, start saying nasty things about you — not how you are playing necessarily, but *you* personally — then you're out the door." For Munch, his job is to keep a watch out for the streamer first, then the stream itself second. "When people visiting a stream are critical of how you play, you give that polite warning of '*I see you.*' and then it's a game of where the exchange goes. And that's a lot of trust. You can really do a lot of things as a mod to someone's stream, and that trust should be taken seriously."

FIGURE 8-2:
The green badge featuring a white sword designates a *moderator* in Chat. Moderators (also known as *mods*) enforce the rules of the host when the host cannot.

So what should you look for in a moderator?

>> **A regular visitor to your stream:** Moderators should not be those folks who occasionally pop in and out of your stream, say a quick greeting, accomplish in-game what you need to get done, and then leave. You are looking for regulars who come into Chat, greet people coming in and out of your Chat, and are active participants in your stream even if they aren't present in the activity you are doing. They are the Norm and Cliff of your Twitch Channel (and if you don't know who Norm and Cliff are, we cannot be friends), and they show up because they enjoy your company that much.

>> **An active participant:** Some people tend to *lurk* which is when people come into your stream, drop a quick greeting, and then disappear into the wood- work. Then you have some who come in and take part in the conversation. They pay attention to what people are saying, respond to it, and encourage interaction with others in your Chat. This sort of participation not only fosters engagement in your Chat but also tells you that this individual is paying attention to the Chat. That is a real attribute of a potential moderator as they need to watch what, in some situations, you cannot.

>> **Someone who understands (and respects) your rules:** As I mention in Chapter 3, your Channel comes with a set of rules. Sometimes, these rules are detailed and clear as crystal while others are painted with a more broad of a brush. Regulars to your Chat know how you run things, and they are the first to stand up and say, *"Tai ho, bro!"* (Kiwi-speak for *"Hold up there, Sparky!"*) when people come in and start spamming their own links, throw insults at you, or just come in and try to hijack the Chat for themselves. If you are busy in game, these individuals in your Chat may ask the person to respect the stream.

>> **Someone you trust:** It doesn't get any simpler than this. When you hand someone the mantle for being a moderator, you are saying with a quick granting of permissions that you trust this person to make judgment calls when you can't. They know you. They know the kind of community you are building. They know what you do and do not tolerate. This person is a confidant. This person is an ally.

Trust is a major reason why ModSherpa (`http://twitch.tv/modsherpa`) is often offered the responsibility of moderation. "When you offer the mod sword to someone, you are telling them in so many terms that you trust them with your stream and your community, and that should not be taken lightly." ModSherpa takes the title of "moderator" very much to heart, but he warns of streams that tend to make everyone moderators. "You see this a lot in smaller streams where everyone has the sword by their name. It's seen as an attempt to promote engagement in a stream, but giving everyone that level of influence over your stream benefits no one. Not you. Not your stream. Being a moderator is a serious responsibility. It should be taken as such."

When you find people like the ones listed here in your Chat, you may have a potential moderator on your hands. If you find that, yes, you have a moderator in the midst, reach out to that person privately and ask them seriously if they would be okay with becoming a moderator. Sometimes, individuals may turn down the opportunity because they may not feel ready or may not want the responsibility in being a moderator. That is perfectly acceptable, too, as you really don't want a reluctant moderator in your Chat. You need someone who won't be drunk with power but is also ready to drop the ban hammer, if needed. Always ask before granting that person Moderator status, though. It's good etiquette.

Nightbot: Your Friendly Neighborhood Virtual Assistant

If you have a team of mods (a team defined here as maybe around 2 to 5 mods in Chat) that are keeping an eye on your stream, it's easier to focus on the main creative task at hand. You can stream stress-free knowing that if you really get into your stream, you are not going to have any problems with less than respectful visitors. When you are starting off, though, getting people in your stream is difficult enough, let along finding regulars that will want to mod your channel. Instead of driving yourself nuts by wearing yet another hat in your stream and moderating your Chat, you can reach out to *Nightbot*, a free, online service that is here to help you focus on your stream while it helps you in the background manage your Channel.

Nightbot (`https://beta.nightbot.tv`) is a virtual assistant, set up by you, and managed by you and mods (once you assign mods, that is) to help police your stream. The setup may feel a little awkward, at first, but once you get Nightbot up and running, some details of your Chat needing your attention will be tended to while you remain on the in-game task or creative project in front of you.

Say it again and again: Custom commands

One way Nightbot helps out streamers everywhere is how you can create your own custom *commands*, something we have dabbled with in previous chapters. These commands are messages that you frequently post in your Chat. Instead of having to type out the same message again and again, or copy and paste the same message from an open text document, you can create a custom command.

1. **Go to** `http://beta.nightbot.tv` **and authenticate your Twitch Channel with Nightbot. Once you have authenticated Nightbot, go to the menu on the left-hand side of your browser window and click the *Commands* option. From here, select the *Custom* option.**

2. **Single-click the blue *Add Command* button to create your first command for your stream.**

   For your first command, we will create a *Sub Hype* command, which is used when people subscribe to your channel. It's a spamming of *emotes* (Twitch's version of *emojis*) to show gratitude.

3. **In the Add Command window, starting with the *Command* option, type** `!subhype` **into the field.**

   Many commands in Twitch begin with an exclamation point immediately followed by a keyword. No spaces. No numbers. Keep keywords for commands simple.

4. **Within the Message window, compose the following (shown in Figure 8-3):**

   <3 <3 PogChamp PogChamp FutureMan FutureMan KAPOW KAPOW FutureMan FutureMan PogChamp PogChamp <3 <3

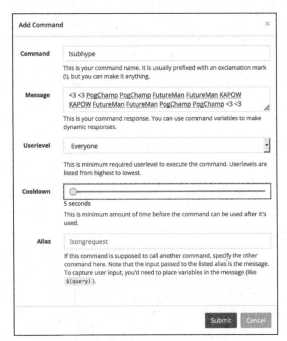

FIGURE 8-3:
Nightbot's *Custom Command* feature allows you to create frequent messages by dropping in a quick keyword into your Chat.

REMEMBER

Twitch offers a bank of emotes for everyone in the Chat window. There is an icon for *Bits* to the left (the triangular icon) and Emotes to the right (the smiley face). Click on the Emotes icon to see what icons you have available.

As you make your way through Twitch, you may see different emotes not available in the public well. Once you reach Affiliate level, you are given slots for three emotes unique to your channel that only your subscribers can use. Emotes is one way of enticing people to subscribe to your channel. For more on Subscriptions and generating revenue on Twitch, check out Chapter 12.

5. **In the Userlevel drop menu, make sure *Everyone* is selected.**

   If you want to create commands available to everyone in Chat, available to subscribers only, or available only to you, you set permissions for commands here.

6. **The *Cooldown* option is where you set a clock for when the command can be used again. Set this option to *5 seconds* by moving the slider all the way to the left.**

7. **The final option, the *Alias* option, is used when embedding this command into another command. You can either call it the same name as the command or leave it blank.**

8. **Click the blue *Submit* button to add this command to your list of custom commands.**

With this custom command, you can now type into your Chat window !subhype and drop a quick thank you message to the person now subscribed to you. As the command is open to everyone in Chat, you can then say to your Chat *"Can I get some sub-hype in Chat?"* which will cue those watching to also drop into the Chat window your command or encourage them to drop in their own emote parade.

Commands can really be for anything in your Chat that you feel is needed often. Instead of having to type the same message over and over again, you can make your moderation and your moderator's job a little easier with some quick short-cuts. Some suggested commands you may want to think about incorporating may include:

» **Greeting/Icebreaker:** A command to bring up a message like *"Good evening, Twitch Monsters! Make sure you say 'Hi' and @TheTeeMonster will give you a shout on stream!"* is a nice way to invite lurkers, newcomers, and regulars to your stream to start talking. Come up with a nice way to welcome people to your stream, and try to give the command some sort of action item.

» **Lurk:** Sometimes, Life calls. You will leave the stream on in the background, but your attention is elsewhere. A !lurk message lets both host and Chat know you are within earshot but not necessarily watching.

» **GamerTag:** You will get asked often, *"What is your GamerTag?"* in Chat. So make it a command.

» **Shout-outs:** If you're talking about a streamer you were recently watching, or maybe you met them at a meetup, or perhaps they are dropping by your stream, dropping a shout-out is a good thing to do. The command itself is a bit more complicated:

```
Please take a moment to check out some $(twitch game
$(touser)) action with $(touser). Give them a follow at
twitch.tv/$(touser) and check out their amazing content!
```

The extra elements in this command not only offer custom URLs to the streamer mentioned but also look at the last activity that streamer broadcast. This command, labeled !so in your command collections, allows you to type !so theteemonster into Chat. The command generates the message *"Please take a moment to check out some Destiny 2 action with theteemonster. Give them a follow at twitch.tv/theteemonster and check out their amazing content!"* complete with links back to the streamer's page.

There are a lot of other commands you can create, and as you get into a rhythm with your stream, you will build on your commands catalog and incorporate everything from captured clips to sound cues to inside jokes with your Chat.

Nightbot offers a lot of features to streamers, from a *Giveaways* function that allows you to do drawing for any contests you host on your Channel to a *Song Request* option if you want to open up your background music. Instead of going through all the various options that Nightbot brings to the table as a virtual assistant, let's focus in the upcoming sections on two features: one that will help you keep your Twitch Channel a nicer, safer place, and one that will help you get more out of your Chat.

Locking it down: Spam protection

In *The Dark Knight*, when Bruce Wayne asked Alfred about the kind of mind the Joker possessed, the sage butler replied with *"Some men just want to watch the world burn, Master Bruce."*

There are people like that on Twitch. We call them *trolls*.

Trolls happen to the biggest and smallest of streams. It is an "honor" I share with DrLupo, Professor Broman, iLulu, and others. Trolls are everywhere, and they are out to make you and your stream. Why? If the above statement from Alfred Pennyworth isn't good enough of an answer, then consider this: These are the most miserable of people in the world, and they feed on making others feel just as bad as they do. Trolls may also have an agenda, be it self-promotion or the promotion of others, and as it is *your* stream, you should have a say in who's promoting what. You would think that people would practice common sense online, but that's not necessarily the case. Sad, but true, as Metallica would say.

Nightbot knows how Trolls and Spam can really throw off a positive atmosphere, so it offers you some protection against unsavory or unwanted messages in Chat. With a series of clicks, you can take measures to assure that safe measures are in place.

1. **Return to Nightbot, go to the menu on the left-hand side of your browser window, and click the *Spam Protection* option.**

2. **The first filter — *Blacklist Word/Phrases* — puts users in a "timeout" (suspends them from posting) if they post something you find offensive. Click the *Enable* button.**

   Some of these filters rely on extra data from you which we will take care of in this exercise.

3. Single-click the *Options* button to access the preferences for this filter.

4. In the Blacklist window, list any offensive words or phrases that you would prefer not to have appear in your Chat.

   You might blush a bit at some of the things you type in this window, but remember, it's for the Chat's betterment. Be offensive. Get nasty. Go dark.

5. For the *Timeout Length* option, make the offense — usually the first one on your Chat — timeout for 30 seconds.

   If after 30 seconds, the offender continues, you have another option coming up to help you out.

TIP

If you find success in Twitch and experience busy Chat sessions during your streams, you may need the Silent option, located underneath the Exempt Userlevel option. The Silent option completely blocks the offender.

6. Under the Exempt Userlevel drop menu, make sure you set your *Moderators* to be exempt, to assure they are never timed out, even if they slip up.

7. You also have an opportunity to send a *Custom Message* to the offender and Chat. If you want to have some fun, paste this link in the Custom Message window:

   `http://bit.ly/GOT-SHAME`

   The URL goes to a GIF from *Game of Thrones*. And yes, it is more than appropriate.

8. Click the blue *Submit* button to accept these Preferences to your Blacklist filter.

9. Go the *Links* option and click the *Enable* button.

   If you are hesitant to allow random people to your Chat posting URLs that you have no idea take people, you can prohibit the ability to post external links with this option.

10. Single-click the *Options* button to access the preferences for this filter.

11. In the Whitelist window (as shown in Figure 8-4), list any URLs that you would do not mind appearing in your Chat.

12. For the *Timeout Length* option, make the offense timeout for 10 seconds.

13. Under the Exempt Userlevel drop menu, allow *Subscribers* to be exempt, making the ability to post URLs an incentive for subscribers.

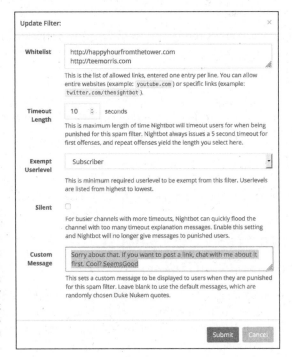

Update Filter:		×
Whitelist	http://happyhourfromthetower.com http://teemorris.com	

This is the list of allowed links, entered one entry per line. You can allow entire websites (example: `youtube.com`) or specific links (example: `twitter.com/thenightbot`).

Timeout Length `10` ‡ seconds

This is maximum length of time Nightbot will timeout users for when being punished for this spam filter. Nightbot always issues a 5 second timeout for first offenses, and repeat offenses yield the length you select here.

Exempt Userlevel Subscriber ▾

This is minimum required userlevel to be exempt from this filter. Userlevels are listed from highest to lowest.

Silent ☐

For busier channels with more timeouts, Nightbot can quickly flood the channel with too many timeout explanation messages. Enable this setting and Nightbot will no longer give messages to punished users.

Custom Message Sorry about that. If you want to post a link, chat with me about it first. Cool? SeemsGood

This sets a custom message to be displayed to users when they are punished for this spam filter. Leave blank to use the default messages, which are randomly chosen Duke Nukem quotes.

Submit Cancel

FIGURE 8-4: Nightbot's *Links* feature, located in the Spam Protection section, gives you the ability to prevent unwanted links showing up in your Chat.

TIP

The idea of posting URLs as an additional incentive to subscribe to your Twitch Channel may work in the early stages of your stream, but you might wind up revoking this perk if you get those subscribers that don't know when to quit spamming URLs. Be ready to revoke this privilege at any time because, remember, this is your stream, and posting links to parts unknown should remain under a decorum of control.

14. **You also have an opportunity to send a *Custom Message* to the offender and Chat. Go on and type in this message into the Custom Message window:**

Sorry about that. If you want to post a link, chat with me about it first. Cool? SeemsGood

Feel free to change the above message to whatever you want your message to read.

15. **Click the blue *Submit* button to accept these preferences to your Blacklist filter.**

You might notice I skipped *Excess Caps* and *Excess Emotes* here. In the case of these two options, activating them will prevent your Chat to cheer you on with "HYPE!!!" followed by a deluge of emotes, be they your own emotes, emotes from other streamers, or emotes from the Public Well. Creating a Blacklist for your stream along with locking down URLs will go a long way in protecting your Community from trolls.

Not completely, mind you, but preventive measures are in place. This makes your Moderators' jobs a little easier, too; and yes, they will also have a say in how Nightbot operates.

We have one more option to explore in Nightbot. This one will help you to hype up your own channel with important messages that you want your Chat to know while you are busy gaming or getting creative on your Channel.

Self-promotion on Twitch: Working with timers

Promoting your own stuff, even when it is your own channel, just feels . . . weird. You really don't want to be *that streamer* where you are constantly shilling your Channel. Have you subbed? You can click here! Want to drop a tip to the host? You can click here! Have you listened to the host's podcast? YOU CAN CLICK HERE!!! Even though this is your Channel, you really do not want to be labeled the eternal huckster. You want people to enjoy your Channel and have fun . . .

. . . but here is the truth: No one is going to toot your promotional horn better than you. It's up to you to let people know about your YouTube channel, where previous streams are archived. It's up to you to let people know where they can find your Channel's swag. It's up to you to let your Chat know where to find you online.

Here's where Nightbot can take some of that pressure off of you, and do a little bit of shilling on your behalf.

1. **Return to Nightbot, go to the menu on the left-hand side of your browser window, and click the *Timers* option.**

   Timers are commands that you can create and then set on two kinds of triggers, one designated by time and the other designated by chat messages. This way, if your Chat is lively, the command will execute. If, however, Chat executes the command first, the timer supersedes the Chat trigger.

2. **Click the blue *+Add* button, and in the Add Timer window, type "Social Media" in the Name field. (See Figure 8-5.)**

3. **In the Message window, type the following:**

   Want to find me online? You got `http://yourwebsite.com` - `http://www.facebook.com/YourPage` - `http://www.twitter.com/YourTwitter` - `http://www.instagram.com/YourInstagram`

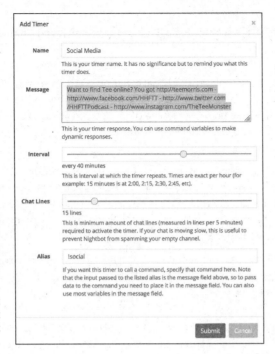

FIGURE 8-5:
Timers are
commands —
usually of a
promotional
nature —
that repeat
throughout
your stream at
various intervals.

Feel free to edit and add into this step your own social links, but you should see what we are doing here. These are all the locations where people can find you online.

4. **Set the *Interval* slider to "every 40 minutes" so that your message will fire off at this desired interval.**

5. **Set the *Chat Lines* slider to "15 lines" in order to have your message trigger every 15 lines of Chat, provided your Chat has that sort of activity within five-minute intervals.**

Nightbot uses these five-minute intervals in order to avoid your Timer from spamming an empty Chat. If there is a slow Chat in your stream, the Timer defaults to the Interval setting.

6. **Click the blue *Submit* button to accept the new Timer.**

Timers, when created, are automatically enabled. They can be disabled at any time, if you need to give the Timer a break.

If Timers strike you as commands of a more promotional nature that repeat on a designated schedule, you would be correct. No, not all Timers need to sell or promote, but they should be messages you want to get out to your Chat. The difference here from Commands is Timers take a priority, so much that they head out automatically. Some suggested Timers for your Twitch Channel could include the following:

>> **Tip Jar:** People visiting your Channel can drop you a *tip*, a cash gift as motivation or as gratitude for a good tip. Tip services have their own third-party services, and these tip services have URLs. You can go on and set up a reoccurring link to your Chat stream, just to remind them of where they can drop you a quick gratuity.

>> **Subscribe:** You have heard us mention *subscriptions* throughout the book, and while you can go on and ask your viewers to subscribe in order to show a support and an investment into the Channel, you can also have Nightbot remind your Chat when you can't that following and subscribing to your Channel is a good thing.

>> **Podcast:** Many streamers are into podcasting, and if you are one of these streamers — or if you become one of these streamers — then you will want people to know where they can find your podcast.

The more things to you have to promote — Stream Swag, special events, a YouTube channel for previous streams — the more Timers you will create. Make sure to space them out so you are not dropping promotions one on top of another, but don't be shy about letting people know about what you do beyond streaming. This is one reason Nightbot offer us Timers. If we feel a little weird always promoting, Nightbot will take that hit for us.

And we do love Nightbot for that.

With these add-on's, your stream is not only locked down and protected to some degree from spammers; but you have a few automated commands that will help you keep your Community in the know. You are also stretching your creative talents by working with OBS, creating your own flow and your own unique look. You also have prerequisites set up for assigning moderators to your stream. These mods will keep an eye on your Community, keeping it troll-free while still keeping the banter lively and fun. You should be seeing your stream becoming well-rounded, and you're focusing more on the game and less on managing Chat. This means you're having fun with the game.

And if you are having fun, your Chat is having fun. Something we all aim for.

Chapter **9**

Setting the Stage

You're working with mods and virtual assistants to make your stream not only safer but incredibly efficient. You have placards that let your Community know when you are about to stream or when you've stepped away for a moment. You're also streaming off a PC with OBS or Streamlabs, and you're even pleasantly surprised, if not a little proud, in how far you have come in building yourself a channel. You've accomplished a lot, so well done!

Now that you have been streaming for some time — that time being designated by you — you may want or need to give things a different look, or perhaps a new setting that will make your stream more personal, more — you know — *you*. Upgrades no matter what they are should improve the quality of your stream, be it a visible improvement or behind-the-scenes.

Love What You've Done with the Place: Overlays

Back in Chapter 8, I talked about B-roll and how to create placards for the show. Along the same lines as Introduction B-roll, *overlays* are a way to create a signature look for your channel. Some streamers keep their Channels "bling-free," preferring to let the game take center stage while their own inset video is simple and basic. Other streamers go with planned out themes for their overlays, even having their accompanying *alerts* (notifications that someone has followed, someone has subscribed, something where your Chat has interacted with your stream) match the theme of their overlay.

To create an overlay, though, you will need to create an image within an image editor that works with layers and also create transparent images. The preferred format for overlays is the *Portable Network Graphic (PNG)* format, as it does create transparent backgrounds without the degradation of *Graphics Interchange Format (GIF)*.

Creating an overlay

For this exercise, much like we did in Chapter 8, we will create a static image in an editor like Photoshop (which I am doing), but we will be creating a multi-layered image that will work as an overlay. Then we will incorporate it into OBS to make it work.

1. **Open a photo editor that you are comfortable in using. Go to File ⇨ New to create a new document. Make sure the dimensions of your new image is 1920 x 1080 pixels, which is the dimensions for high definition (HD) television, and — if possible — make the image transparent.**

2. **Create a new layer. Make it black or white. It should be a solid color that should serve as your canvas.**

TIP

Instead of a solid color for your canvas, use a screenshot from your preferred video game. This will help you design an overlay theme better suited for the gamer you tend to frequent.

3. **In a new, separate layer, create a banner across the top that has your name or your Channel's name across the top (see Figure 9-1).**

4. **In a new, separate layer, create a border that you can frame the top section of your overlay with. Repeat this step in order to create images for the bottom of your overlay as well.**

5. **Once your overlay design is completed, remove the "canvas" layer so that your overlay has a transparent background. Export or "Save As" a PNG file. Call the image "overlay.png" and save it in the same location as your "Welcome" image from Chapter 8.**

Make sure, when saving the PNG file, you preserve the image's transparency.

6. **Go back to OBS on your PC and in the Scenes window, click the *Game* option to review the *Sources* currently in play here.**

If you need a refresher on OBS, head back to Chapter 8.

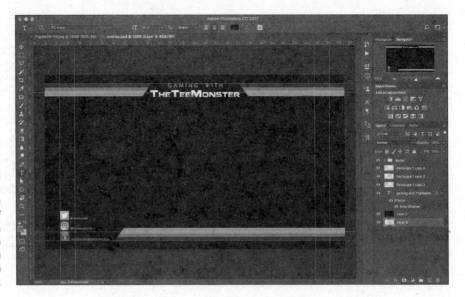

FIGURE 9-1:
In creating an overlay, you take advantage of layers and a variety of design elements you create in Photoshop.

7. Go to the Sources window and click Add ⇨ Image option.

8. Single-click the *Browse* button and find the overlay image you created just now.

9. Select it and click the *Open* button to add it as another source of the Game Scene.

10. Once back in OBS, single-click the *Preview Screen* button.

11. Resize or reposition any objects by single-clicking the *Edit Scene* button. You can also move elements as layers (similar to working in Photoshop, InDesign, or Powerpoint) by right-clicking on the sources in the Sources window and changing their order.

12. Once the video preview looks good, single-click the *Edit Scene* button to save your work. Figure 9-2 shows the finished product in action.

Your overlay is now in place and you have a distinct look for your Twitch Channel. While you game, work on a particularly creative process, or simply enjoy some one-on-many IRL time with your Chat, you are working on the branding of your Channel with that snazzy overlay you have in place.

REMEMBER

Fiverr (http://fiverr.com) is a terrific resource for Twitch streamers to shop for artists and video editors who are looking to offer their talents and services to create a sharp look for your stream. When making a budget for your upgrades, factor in some quotes from Fiverr or from other artists in your Chat or IRL network who would like to work with you on this Channel of yours.

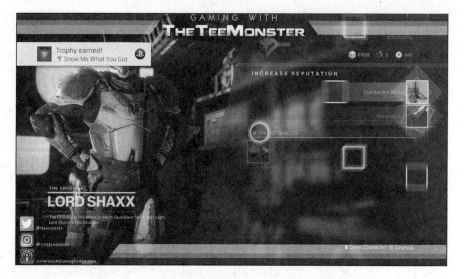

FIGURE 9-2:
Once your
overlay is in
place, your
game-of-choice,
your stream,
now has a
signature look.

I bet the look you've created for yourself is looking good, I have no doubt. I mean, it is *your* look after all. No one else has what you got. This is a look for your digital stage, and with the curtain up, your digital stage is now set for you and your stream.

But where exactly are you streaming from? What does your *actual* set look like, and what exactly does it say about you? Look around you just before your next stream. Maybe you're ready for an upgrade.

Quiet on the Set: One Final Look at Your Twitch Studio

What remains in this last look at your Twitch Channel is the location of your stream. Before you say, "*In front of my monitor . . .*" check your snark at the door and read on. There are all sorts of different places you can stream from, but it's good to know from where you stream intimately so as to avoid any sort of distractions for yourself and your stream. While you may have put a lot of thought into how your stream appears and how it handles everything from potential SPAM to unruly visitors to your Chat, you should know your environment as well.

Couchcasting

Before the acquiring of a gaming chair, before the careful eye for detail of in-studio audio gear, there is a starting place for many a streamer: the couch. As shown in Figure 9-3, my own Twitch stream knew humble beginnings as a *couchcast*. This is where you fire up the console, make yourself as comfortable as possible, and stream. For my own person, I was couchcasting from a sectional in a finished basement before a large, mounted television. This is as simple a setting as you can get.

FIGURE 9-3: When Tee started his stream, he kept it simple with a *couchcast*. No fancy gaming chair, no special lighting, no green screen. Just him, a console, and a PS4 camera.

What do we need to know about this sort of setting?

>> **What's on the walls:** You are giving the world a sneak peek into your home. This means that whatever you have on the walls becomes something of public knowledge. Why does this matter? It won't matter if you don't mind that level of sharing. Some people put thought into it and line their walls with private collections (Funko Pops tend to be a trend with streamers.) while others just go with confidence on their décor. Your wall adornments can make for good conversation starters, but if what hangs there leans more towards the sensational or controversial, you may find that affecting your numbers, or saying too much about your personal life.

>> **Lighting:** If you decide to work with a camera, you will want people to see you, so lighting will be a priority. With a couchcast, your lighting choices will be limited. In my case, I took advantage of the Phillips Hue Lighting System, creating a variety of *recipes* (color themes you create on the Hue app) to fit my mood or game. I made the most of my Hue, and managed to bring in a little atmosphere to my stream.

>> **Field-of-view:** Continuing with the topic of what you have hanging on the walls, what is the visible *field-of-view* for your camera? This is the area captured by your camera and following the resolution you set in the Preferences, either *square* (usually a ratio of 4:4) or *widescreen* (usually 16:9). This matters when you are streaming from a high traffic area. My wife, for example, may need to get to the utility room (behind me), but she would prefer not to be on camera. Good news: My camera's field-of-view is narrow enough that the access point for the utility room is cropped out. No need to worry about being seen there. Also, with a narrow field-of-view, I simply have to make sure when couchcasting that no one sits directly behind me in order to remain off-cameras.

Couchcasting is a common starting point for many streams as it is casual. Still, the couchcast should be inviting, and to be as such, you want to be aware of where you are and what is around you before you start streaming. You also want to know what is visible and what is off-camera, both for your benefit and anyone else in the home.

Deskcasting

If couchcasting is the most common beginning for a stream, then *deskcasting* is the most common of destinations for streamers. Here, your computer desk, gaming console, and monitors are all set up, and you keep track of your game, your Chat, and your OBS settings from this corner of your home or apartment. This space is your Control Center, and you manage every aspect of your stream from here. It can be a tight space, too, if you apply a privacy filter.

When deskcasting, what should you be aware of?

>> **Lighting:** Especially with the incorporation of a privacy filter, lighting is essential. You must light yourself enough that the green backdrop behind you appears solid and seamless, making you "pop" off it. Lighting will make the masking process for your hardware and software easy and effortless. Amazon offers plenty of lighting packages like the Zomei 18-inch LED Ring Lighting Kit with Tripod Stand and Phone Adapter, priced at just over $100 USD. Kits and prices vary based on brightness and accessories, but you will need to figure out where these lights will reside. On or around your desk? How easily will you be able to get in and out of your deskcasting set? With the sophistication of a privacy filter, you will need to take these details into consideration.

>> **Field-of-view:** Doing away with the privacy filter, streamers also contend with field-of-view for their cameras. Regardless of whether your resolution is square or widescreen, you should take a close look at what your cameras

capture and how much you want to share with your Twitch Community. ZGphoto, as shown in Figure 9-4, retired his green screen, opting out for a more open feel with his camera picking up all background. So long as you are aware of possible traffic moving behind you, be it a household pet or a significant other, make sure to know there might be behind-the-scenes distractions to contend with now that your studio is including a busy background.

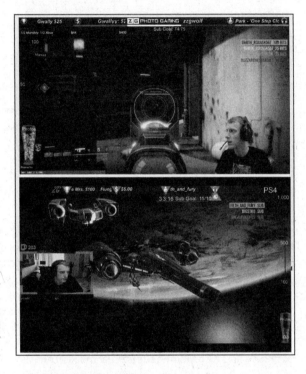

FIGURE 9-4: ZGphoto streamed for years using a privacy filter (top) but presently opts out for the more open background (bottom) for his feed.

From the set

The construction of a full set is a massive undertaking, but if you have the space, the resources, and the budget — all of which you have when you are Bungie (http://www.bungie.net), creators of the award-winning video games *Halo* and *Destiny* — then a set, complete with lighting, sound, and multiple cameras (if you are really feeling ambitious), is right for you to stream from. And for Bungie, a set like the one pictured in Figure 9-5 is exactly what they use.

Even in this controlled environment, you want to be aware of . . .

>> **Sound:** Depending on the set you create yourself, you want to check your audio. The audio test will not only be for balanced levels but also for any odd echoes that might crop up. A sparse, minimalist set may lend itself to sound bounce every which way, making your stream sound very hollow. Thick carpet, furniture, and set fixtures will dampen potential echo spots, but they may call on you to boost your microphone levels in order to pick up your subjects. Set design will always have an impact on your audio, so make sure to run sound checks before stream.

>> **Lighting:** In this situation, you will want to make sure your set is adequately lit. Without proper lighting, shadows can distract from the subject matter at hand. Make sure that those on camera are not casting any odd shadows, or that the set around and behind them is not changing the aesthetic you intend.

>> **Set integrity:** The last thing you want to worry about with a set is that it falls apart during your stream. Before any stream, it wouldn't be a bad idea to walk the set, checking to see if any of the set pieces are in danger of an unexpected collapse. There should be no question or hesitation about this: If the set piece is wobbly, go on and replace it. If your instincts tell you that part of your set is unstable, either secure it or remove it entirely. It's best to be overcautious when it comes to your set.

>> **Camera angles:** In the case of Bungie's stream (`http://twitch.tv/bungie`), there are three cameras at work: one primary camera that covers the host and special guests, a second camera for the host exclusively, and the third on the guests in studio. Routed through a control board or even something like OBS, action cuts from camera to camera. Before streaming, though, directors and operators check camera angles just to make sure there are no unaccounted sightlines revealing backstage or off-camera personnel. Viewers should be focused on the guests in studio, not anyone moving in the background. Cameras should also be capturing a balanced image of guests and host, as opposed to off-centered or at odd angles. You're streaming, not shooting a David Fincher film. Stick to the Rule of Thirds (look it up online if you don't know what that is), and shoot your stream's cast in focus and balanced.

Take a look at where you are streaming, and see if where you have your stream set is a good atmosphere for you. Maybe you have reached a point where change is needed, so think about your set. Think about what you want to say and how much you want to share, then make it happen.

Now what happens when you take on the words of Shakespeare to describe your stream: All the world's a stage? Your Twitch stream is wherever you are, provided your Internet connection is strong. Your environment is your set. How do you manage a setting that is constantly changing?

FIGURE 9-5:
When Bungie streams their latest game reveals, DeeJ hosts the stream straight from a Destiny-inspired set, giving them complete control over their stream setting.

Twitch on the Go: Streaming from the Twitch App

One last place from where streamers can hop on stream and connect with their Chat is only a quick tap on your smartphone away. The Twitch mobile app (`http://mobile.twitch.tv`), available on the App Store, Google Play, and Amazon, puts streaming into the palm of your hand. Provided your connection is solid and you are ready to go live within the moment — your stream promising to be the most raw of raw streams — then jump into the Twitch mobile app and enjoy the stream.

1. **After you have installed the Twitch app on to your smartphone, tap it to launch and then log in.**

2. **When you have logged into Twitch, tap in to top-left corner your Account Icon to go to your Channel. Tap the *Go Live* button in order to set up your stream.**

   The Account icon located at the top-left of your smartphone accesses your Twitch Channel Page. It shows you available Past Streams, Clips, and whatever stream you are presently hosting. From here, you can set up your Channel for a new or future stream.

   At the time of this writing, the Twitch app for smart devices (like the iPad) can set up titles for streaming, but you cannot stream from these devices.

3. **Tap on the View Dashboard window and type in the Title field the following:**

   Just Chatting | What I Am Up to Today. . .

   Feel free to edit and add into this step your own title attributes, but as you are going to go live on the phone, you should plan it out as if it is a stream on our console or PC.

4. **Type into the Go Live notification the following:**

   Working on Twitch For Dummies so trying out the app to see how to write about it.

   Feel free to edit and add into this step your own announcement. As you can see, the same steps for setting up the Channel is the same as you would be on your desktop or laptop.

5. **Search in the Game/Category field "Just" and then select "Just Chatting" from the listed options, as shown in Figure 9-6.**

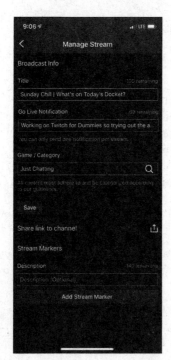

FIGURE 9-6:
Setting up a stream on your phone is very much like setting up a stream on your desktop or laptop.

6. **Tap *Save* and then tap the arrow in the upper-left corner of your screen. Then tap the down arrow also in the upper-left to return to your Account Overview.**

7. **Tap *Go Live* and then tap the *Start Stream* button. Rotate your phone into the landscape position when you are ready to stream.**

   Following a three-second countdown, your stream will begin.

8. **Once you're streaming, start talking. Watch Chat. Respond. Flip the camera forward if you're showing off something, and remember to look at the phone camera (not the actual phone surface) when streaming.**

Streaming from the app is a real challenge as you have to remain aware of . . .

>> **Distance from the camera:** Sure, you could grab a selfie stick and star streaming, and the selfie stick will give you plenty of space between you and the camera. Reading Chat? Unless you have exceptional vision, you might miss a few comments coming into your Chat, so fair warning on that. Keeping the phone close will keep Chat in sight, but just be aware that may mean you will have a tight shot of yourself.

>> **Speaking into the camera:** Remember when you are filming on your phone, you should not be looking at the actual screen of your phone, but more towards the earpiece of your phone. That is where your smartphone's "face camera" resides, and this is where you should keep your eyes focused on. That way, you don't look as if your attention is slightly off screen

>> **Who or what is behind you:** As you can see, in Figure 9-7, you may catch a glimpse of my wife, Pip Ballantine. While it may seem that was an unintentional cameo she is making in my stream, it is not. I knew where she was and how to frame it so that she was there . . . making the snarky references she is known for when I stream and she joins in from the peanut gallery. The camera in your phone does have a wide and deep field-of-view, so remain aware of what happening both in front of as well as behind you. Make sure people around you know you are streaming and that they may be caught on camera.

Each setting for your stream comes with its own unique challenges. Your job as host and as producer is to manage and mitigate those challenges. The set should be a space you are confident in. This is where your stream will happen on a regular basis, so your set should be not only a place from where you enjoy streaming from but also a place where your Community will feel right at home visiting. Consider your streaming space and make it work for you.

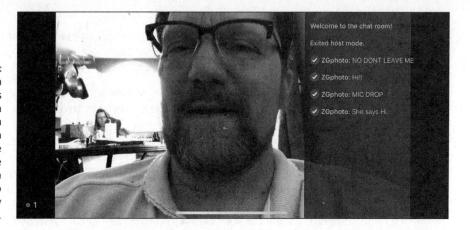

FIGURE 9-7:
Streaming from
the Twitch app is
no different than
streaming off a
console or a
PC with the
exception of the
camera being a
little closer to
you — literally
arm's length.

From the humble beginnings on PS4 or Xbox to here, we have been steadily and gradually building on this Channel of yours. Even with upgrade on upgrade, you can always work on refining your channel and making it an eye-catching corner of the Twitchverse. Finding a look for yourself is always difficult, but once you know *"This is me . . ."* the next step for you is to build on that look and make your Channel your own. So what does your Channel say about you? What do you want it to say? And what can you do to improve your Channel's branding and messaging?

Always look for the next improvement, and see whether or not your Channel heads in the direction you want. Remember: your stream, your look, your rules.

3

Getting Busy with the Business of Twitch

Create and sharpen a structure for the show, including pointers for hosting interviews.

Create highlight reels of previous streams.

Turn your stream into an income revenue.

Chapter **10**

Let's GOOOOO, Chat: Welcome to the Show!

Overture, curtains, lights,
This is it, the night of nights!
No more rehearsing and nursing a part.
We know every part by heart!

Overture, curtains, lights
This is it, you'll hit the heights!
And oh what heights we'll hit
On with the show this is it.

A nd if you are old enough to remember that anthem from Saturday morning cartoons, bless you.

Chapter 10 may seem pretty deep into a book to talk about the introduction of your stream, and I've already spent time looking at how to kick off a stream way back in Chapter 4. I also spent some time breaking down our stream and giving it some tough love in Chapter 5.

So why am I returning to the basics five chapters later?

When you start streaming, rarely do you give any though about your opening other than *"Woah, it's 7:55, and I'm live in five minutes. . . ."* When the red light flips on in your Twitch app and you see your count flash up on your PS4, you know the camera is on and you need to turn on the charm. Starting cold on a stream can be not only jarring for your stream, but for you as well

Have you thought for a moment how you want to introduce yourself?

That's what we're taking a moment to look at: How are you communicating with your stream? I'm going to break down when we make those connections and then ride that current into how we connect with guests in your studio and stream. If you are creating a Twitch stream that centers around interviews, how do you make those interviews happen?

Let's begin by taking a look inward.

Who, What, Where: Your Show Intro

Twitch has an organic feel when you watch it, and it's that natural, improvisational nature that makes Twitch so much fun, both for the host as well as the audience. I mention in a previous sidebar how many of my stream harken back to my days with the improv troop, ComedySportz. However, much like how Penn & Teller reveal the best secrets from the professional magician's industry, the truth about improv is that we rehearse. We are working off the tops of our heads, yes, but we are also working from a well of tricks and ideas that we practice and keep in our back pocket to kick things off.

So when I go live on Twitch, do I always know what my first words are going to be? For some viewers, I'm about to make a first impression. What do I want that first impression to be? Something spontaneous? What about creating a more familiar greeting that makes Chat, and those returning to it, feel like old friends?

It's up to you, but think about how strong a first impression and a cool intro can make. Consider four words that became the signature introduction for a science fiction dynasty:

> Space. The final frontier.

Yeah, I still remember the first time heard that when I was a kid, and this intro was so unforgettable as a first impression that they went back to it for the next generation. When you go live, you are establishing yourself as a personality (and a stream) that people will enjoy and anxiously wait for you to go live again. You want the first impression to be a positive one, so let's work on it.

Kicking off a stream is always hard, so if you have a few notes or topics to talk about, you can ease your audience into your game or featured project. So remember to talk candidly and stay on point.

Each streamer is different. Some would probably just dismiss all this deep thought of mine and jump on in with a quick "Good morning/afternoon/evening, Chat . . ." and then talk a bit about what the plans are for the stream. Others have more of a routine, one familiar to those that return to the stream. When it comes to an introduction, there are some elements that should always be present:

>> The stream's name, if it has one.

>> The name(s) of the stream's host(s).

>> A quick introduction of who you are and what you're planning to play.

>> Any possible changes to your schedule for the day.

Sit down and brainstorm a few ideas on how to introduce your particular stream. For example, my own stream tends to kick off like this . . .

>> "Good evening, Chat! You're gaming with TheTeeMonster. How are you this Monday? Hope it was a good start to the day. For those of you new to stream, I'm the TeeMonster. You can call me Tee or TeeMonster. I am a science fiction and fantasy author, I'm a podcaster, and I play *Destiny* . . ."

>> "Hey, Chat, how are you tonight? I'm the TheTeeMonster. You can call me Tee or TeeMonster. And I — am — ready — to —c v game. Had a bit of a crappy day. Things at the office? I could have brought a better game to my boss. There's always tomorrow . . ."

>> "What is up, Chat? You're enjoying Saturday Morning Cartoons with TheTeeMonster. Pajamas and bowls of cereal are encouraged. For those of you new to stream, I'm the TeeMonster. You can call me Tee or TeeMonster. I am a science fiction and fantasy author, I'm a podcaster, and this morning we are playing *Destiny*. But today? Yeah, I need to end the stream early because . . ."

As you see in these examples, you can mix and match the elements to drop into an intro. Come up with what feels right for you and your stream, and if you mention another project you are involved with (like a podcast) or a special event you may be attending, have a Nightbot command with a relevant URL ready to drop. Your stream's greeting is just another way of bringing your audience into your game or creative project, making them feel like a part of it.

At the top of every hour, it's a good idea to repeat your introduction. In the time you've been stream, you may have picked up a few new names in your Chat. Repeating your message of who you are, much in the same way a radio station or a television station runs a station identification, is a nice way to let those new to your stream get a snapshot of your stream.

Gitting Gud at Multitasking: Responding to Chat

When I first watched OneActual on Chat, followed by ZGphoto, followed by 3vil_Aura, followed by many others, I kept asking the same thing: *How are they talking to Chat and still playing the game without fail?*

I know my own limits in multitasking and Twitch, I feel, go continuously challenged. However, on stream, multitasking and Twitch work together. Does Twitch push my own comfort zone with multitasking out further? Maybe. A little? The idea that I can go into a six-man raid lair against Argos, all while tracking a conversation in Chat about where Chris Evans was better suited as an actor — as Johnny Storm in *The Fantastic Four* or as Steve Rogers in the *Captain America* films (and before you ask, I'm firmly a #TeamCap guy) — is ridiculous. If you add to this mix my wife coming downstairs and asking if I have medicated one of our cats, I pretty much collapse like a cheap lawn chair.

Still, I am finding a method to the madness.

Checking with Chat in real time

I've been playing video games since . . . well, a long time. True, I stepped away from games for a long time as I didn't have the time, or think that I had the time. In making baby steps back into this delightful world of space opera, superhero standoffs, and battle royales of all kinds, I have noticed there is something that games of today offer that games of yesterday share in common: *the grind.*

The grind in video gaming, from Wikipedia, is defined as repetitive tasks that level up characters and offer advantages in upcoming levels. Grinding is usually for "experience points," and some gamers live for the grind as the payout is worth it. A good example of a grind is *Destiny 2's* quests like "Cayde's Will" which earns the Guardian the powerful "Ace of Spades" hand cannon. To earn this weapon, you need to perform certain tasks like "Eliminate 250 hostiles in strikes with hand cannons" (see Figure 10-1). Once you reach the end of the challenges in Cayde's Will, this powerful hand cannon becomes yours. Some players turn their nose up at the grind, claiming that the rewards are not worth the work; or complain they lack the amount of time needed for some grinds, and call for developers to create a bypass through in-game transactions.

FIGURE 10-1:
Grinding offers streamers opportune moments to interact with Chat. Here, Tee is talking with his Chat while pushing through a *Destiny 2* strike he is more-than-familiar with.

But the grind is a streamer's gift. The grind is truly the best time to check your Chat window, reach out, and talk to those hanging out. With a repetitive, somewhat grindy game where you can still get things done while on auto pilot, it's easier to glance at Chat and see who's talking and what they're talking about. Interacting with Chat, I have found, makes the grind go by a little faster. Granted, you might suffer moments during a grind where you may forget about Chat; and you may have to scroll back to see who said what. This is when moderators are good to have watching your back, just in case you do get lost in the game.

Your Chat does understand though, especially when you are busy in-game, that you aren't able to get to Chat straight away. Also, when you have hundreds of people in your Chat, it gets a little difficult to catch everyone's greetings, questions, or comments, and usually any tension rising up from missed comments is disarmed when the host says, *"Sorry if I missed your comment in Chat. This game can get a little crazy."* When you can, catch up with your Chat and touch base with folks there. I've found most of Chat does understand that games, even the grindy ones, can get pretty intense.

Checking with Chat at specific segments

If you have ever played the video game *Fortnite*, shown in Figure 10-2, you know that things can get incredible tense. Especially if you find yourself in the remaining ten of the initial 99 that kicked off the game.

Fortnite is much like those tense moments in *Detroit: Become Human* or *Tomb Raider* where you have to make a decision, aim, and then open fire . . . only the *entire* game is like that. I've watched many amazing streamers get down to the final five. Then down to the final three. Then down to the final two. And like clockwork, someone in Chat will pop up and say . . .

> *"Oh hai, strimmer!!! How u doin'?"*

Within a few seconds, as the host is building, shooting, building, shooting, and reloading (and all as they are jumping from spot to spot, as you do in *Fortnite*), the Chat visitor posts again . . .

> *"Yo, strimmer!!! Y U no say hai?!"*

This is when a moderator may step in and politely say, *"As you can see, our host is somewhat busy right now . . ."* which they are. It can be a little frustrating as you want to connect with those cheering you on, but at the moment when thing reach a fever pitch, it may be impossible for you to talk to Chat.

FIGURE 10-2:
Battle Royale games like *Fortnite* do not lend themselves to Chat interaction. When streaming games like this, find moments when you can reach out and say "Hi!"

Intense as player versus player (PVP) games are by design, or when games demand your full attention, there are moments where you can and will catch up with your audience. For *Fortnite*, the game does offer moments to catch your breath and reach out to Chat, catch up with comments, and also give out thank yous for new follows and subscriptions. Finding pockets of time and opportunity where you can talk to Chat in between the more attention-intensive moments of a game can work for you and for your audience. This way, a happy medium is struck, so Chat feels acknowledged and you can land that "Winner Winner Chicken Dinner" title at the end of a particular tense standoff.

Taking a Bow: Ending Your Stream

At the time you've set — hard stop or something a little more fluid — the end is upon you. What's a nice way to wrap things up and close your stream? Do you just say, *"Thanks, everyone, see you next time . . ."* or just a basic *"Bye,"* and then it's over? Some streamers do that, and the quick and simple signoff works for them. Whatever you decide, closing your stream can be as basic or elaborate as you want to make it. Putting together your closing comments is no different from putting together an intro: same approach, only you're doing it at the end. So review the earlier suggestions for intros and consider what seems a likely direction for a solid close.

Here are a few ideas:

>> "Thanks, everyone, for watching. It's been a blast today, and I'm thrilled you spent some time to hang out with me. I'll be back tomorrow night, same time, and I'll be continuing my journey through *Detroit: Become Human.* I will see you then! Goodnight!"

>> "Alright, Chat, it's time I wrapped up. So we're going to go raid Danfinity, so copy this line of text and spam Dan's Chat with it when you get there. Thank you, everyone, for the love and support. Big shout-out to my moderators and to all of you who followed, subbed, and raided. All this helps support the channel, and that means a lot to me. I will see you all tomorrow night, 8 p.m. ET, and we will be back with more *Destiny*. Take care of yourselves."

>> "Right then, I am calling it a stream. Thank you all so much for the tips, the bits, the subs, the follows, the hosts, and the Auto-Hosts. Remember, it is your support that helps this channel grow, and I appreciate each and every one of you for being here. Remember, tomorrow — no stream. I'll be out of town this weekend, but I will be back Monday night for *Fortnite.* Thanks again for being there. You all have a nice weekend. Until next time, be good to each other. Peace."

Just as your Introduction works as the first impression of your stream, alongside your own presentation on stream and the shenanigans you are getting up to while live, your closing statements are a nice nod of appreciation and sincere thanks for the support shown by your Chat. When you kick off a stream with a high burst of energy, it's just as good to end on an equally positive, energetic note.

With an approach to your introduction and a positive ending to your stream, you now have to fill the middle with content. Depending on your personality, you may be the sort of host that enjoys back-and-forth banter. You may invite conversation completely unrelated to the game you are playing, or the creative project you are working on. It can be the host and the Chat. It can be the host and their own Party Chat. Whatever the makeup of the group, talk is key. Conversation invites participation from Chat and also invites those new to your Chat into the Community you are building.

Conversation also leads to another kind of content found everywhere across Twitch: *interviews*. The more you talk to friends, the more you talk to people, the more comfortable you become in asking questions. When you host a good interview, it can be a great time for the host, the interview subject, and the Chat.

Creating Content for Two (or More): Hosting Interviews

There's something about sitting down with a guest, be it in studio or from a remote location, that grants you a hint of courage. Suddenly, you're not afraid of anything. Oh yeah, you're "running with the big dogs" now, and like Anderson Cooper, Paula Zhan, or even BCC's own Stephen Sackur, you're asking the questions to find out what makes your guest tick.

What sets you apart from those big dogs, though, is skill. The late, great Anthony Bourdain of *No Reservations* and *Parts Unknown* made interviewing look easy. You're just sitting down, enjoying food, and talking to people. That's all there is to it, right?

Make no mistake: Interviews are not easy. For anybody.

I speak from authority, not just from my own foundation of interviewing writers, actors, musicians, and creative individuals, but from my own experience interviewing streamers for this book. On speaking with many of these talented content creators, I was told often *"These are great questions. A lot of thought went into these."* It makes me wonder what kind of questions these streamers were asked in the past.

But asking the right kind of questions is only part of the interview process.

Interview requests

The courage to submit an interview request comes simply from your interest in the interview subject. Instead of throwing together a query in an e-mail app, settle in behind a word processor and compose an to ask your favorite author, actor, sports celebrity, gamer, streamer, podcaster, or whomever you want for an interview. You may need to submit the request multiple times, and sometimes you may have to work through numerous people simply to get a "no" as your final reply, if you get a reply at all. That happens. It doesn't mean that individual is mean, a rude person, or otherwise. They just don't do interviews. For every "no," you will find others who will enthusiastically say "yes."

Here are some things you should keep in mind when working on the interview request:

>> **Market yourself.** Your interview request needs to sell your services to the prospective guest. If you've got previous bylines in social media or experience with journalism, be sure to mention that. Do you have solid numbers in Twitch? Mention that. Have you done interviews before? If so, drop a few names. Let people know who you are and why you are interested in talking to them.

>> **What can I do for you?** The perspective guest (or agent) is going ask *"What's in it for me (or my client)?"* Does he or she have a new book coming out? Perhaps he or she is about to launch a special product? Are your guests into game development? Find an angle and work with it.

>> **Be flexible.** Remember, you're asking for *their* time. There may be restrictions in your schedule and theirs. Sometimes you can get an interview within 24 hours or you have to schedule it weeks or months in advance. You may also have to rearrange your plans, just like the interview subjects who are taking time out of their day to chat with you.

REMEMBER

Don't assume the person reading your interview request is going to know you, your stream, or even what Twitch is. (Or be ready for the question, *"Isn't Twitch that thing where people watch other people play video games?"* delivered in a somewhat sardonic tone.) You may have to explain your platform using alternative terms or a short explanation.

THE INTERVIEW REQUEST E-MAIL

One of the easiest ways to do interview requests is via e-mail. It's time to put on your marketing hat on top of your public relations hat and consider how you want to represent your show when sending queries. First, putting words like "Interview Request" or "Query for Interview" in the subject tells the reader what you want before they even open the message. Use a warm greeting like "Hello" followed by the person's name is always a good start. You may send the initial query to the potential guest first but end up working through an agent, media representative, or handler.

Explain why you want to speak with that person. Do they have any upcoming books, movies, or appearances they are interested in promoting? This would be a good time to mention how much time you are asking for, and be considerate and reasonable with your guest's time. If you say thirty minutes, stick with thirty minutes. If you find during the interview you may go long, ask permission.

Now is when you can get on with describing your show, but don't drone on — a couple sentences and perhaps some other notable names whom you have interviewed ought to be all you need. Then close with a respectful yet positive salutation, such as "I look forward to hearing back from you." Remember, most people are very busy and may not respond back right away, so you might need to follow up periodically. No more than three.

And if the interest is there, be flexible. You may face more challenges in schedules, but it will be worth the effort.

Asking really great questions

Chances are good that if you're new to interviews, you've never had an interpersonal, casual chat with someone you don't know very well that could get a bit thought-provoking or downright controversial, depending on your stream's subject matter. This could be a somewhat nerve-wrecking experience, but there's a science to it. Here are just a few tips to take to heart so you can hold a good, engaging interview:

>> **Know who you're talking to and what to talk about.** When guests appear on your show, it's a good idea to know at the very least the subject matter on which you will be talking about. Let's say, for example, you are having an author appear on your show. If the author has written over a dozen books, be they fiction or nonfiction, trying to find the time to read all of your guest's books would seem an impossibility. So do some homework. If the author

guest has written a popular series, go online and research the series. Visit `Wikipedia.org` and see if the series has a summary there. If you can only find limited information, find websites relevant to the topic of the series. If the series is steampunk, dig up information about the Victorian era. If the series follows a snarky, sentient robot, look up Artificial Intelligence. This has two effects: (1) You sound like you have a clue what the writer is writing about, and (2) it allows you to ask better questions. These same rules apply for nonfiction authors and really for guests of any particular background.

TIP

It's also a good idea to perform a search on your guest. You don't have to be a super fan, but you should be familiar with the guest, their past, and their experience in order to know what direction to take the interview.

» **Have your questions follow a logical progression.** Say you're interviewing another streamer who specializes in horror video games. A good progression for your interview would be something like this:

- What made you decide that horror games would be your steam's subject matter?

- What makes a really good horror game?

- What games inspire you in this genre?

- What is the scariest game ever made?

You'll notice these questions are all based around horror video games, beginning and ending with the streamer's choice. The progression of this interview starts specific on the current work and then broadens to a wider perspective. Most interviews should follow a progression like this, or they can start on a very broad viewpoint and slowly become more specific to the guest's expertise. Interviews on Twitch are driven by conversation. You can still have fun with an interview, as shown in Figure 10-3 with Ashnichrist hosting Smirky on her podcast, and also be professional.

» **Ask open-ended questions.** To understand open-ended questions, it's simpler to explain closed-ended questions. Close-ended questions are the kind that give you one-word answers — for example, "How long have you been streaming?" Don't count on your interviewee giving a dynamic answer to a question like that. Close-ended questions make the process harder than it needs to be. Instead, rephrase your question like "So why did you start streaming? What was the appeal of Twitch?"

TIP

Always offer to your potential guest the option of seeing the questions before the interview. This establishes a sense of trust between you and the potential guest, as well as gives the potential guest an opportunity to prepare for the interview.

THE **STREAM COACH** PODCAST

Ashnichrist - Stream Coach and Content Creator

Smirky - Twitch Partner and Toontown Creator

FIGURE 10-3:
Ashnichrist
hosting Smirky
on her podcast.

>> **Prepare twice the number of questions that you think you'll need.**
Some interviews will grind to a halt for no other reason than the interviewer
believed that the guest would talk his head off on the first question, and they
run out of questions to ask.

TIP

Have a pad and a pen on hand, ready to go. In the middle of your interview,
an answer may inspire a brand new question you would want to ask your
guest about. Jot it down so you won't forget it. Then ask this new question
either as a follow-up, or in place of another question you have up and coming.

>> **Never worry about asking a stupid question.** When asking questions that
may sound obvious or frequently asked, remember: Chances are good that
your audience has never heard them *answered* before. Okay, maybe a writer
has been asked time and again, "Where do your ideas come from?" or a
politician has heard, "So, when did you first start in politics?" often. When you
have a guest present, there's no such thing as a stupid question. What's really
dumb is not to ask a question that you think isn't worth the guest's time. He or
she may be champing at the bit in hopes you *will* ask it.

Avoiding really bad questions

Before you start brainstorming questions based on my preceding tips, stop and
think about interviews you've listened to . . . and think about where things
suddenly took a wrong turn. Usually the interviewer finds themselves with a

guest they know nothing about and they are expected to interview them on the fly, or the host ambushes the guest with questions that dig into something that's out of the guest's scope or none of the interviewer's business.

Within minutes, you can go from being a promotional opportunity to one of *those* interviews. Here are a few blunders best avoided when hosting interviews on your stream:

» **Ask inappropriate questions.** Your stream is not *60 Minutes, HardTalk,* or even *Jerry Springer.* If you want to fire off hard-hitting-tell-all-mudslinging questions, think about who your audience is, who you're talking to, and whether the question is within the ability of the guest to answer honestly and openly. If not, an awkward moment may be the least of your worries. Inappropriate questions can also be those irrelevant, wacky, off-the-wall, and far-too-personal questions for your guests. "Who was the rudest person you have ever worked with on a game?" or "Why did this DLC drop the ball so hard? Did you know the storyline alone was a red-hot mess?" could put a developer's career into jeopardy if answered earnestly. Maybe these "wild card" questions work for shock jocks, but when you have an opportunity to interview people you respect in your field, do you really *want* to ask them something like, "Boxers, briefs, or none of the above?" Think about what you're going to ask before you actually do.

» **Continue to pursue answers to inappropriate questions.** If a question has been deemed inappropriate by a guest, don't continue to ask it. Move on to the next question and continue forward into the interview. Streams are by no means an arena for browbeating guests into submission till they break down in tears and cough up the ugly, sordid details of their lives.

Of course, if you're after irreverent material for your show and push that envelope as far as you can, your guests may not want to play along — especially if they don't get the joke. If that's the case, expect your guests to get up and walk away. Even in the most idyllic situations, guests can (and do) reserve the right to do that.

» **Turn the interview into the Me show.** Please remember that the spotlight belongs to your *guest.* Yes, it is your stream, but when a guest is introduced into the mix, you're surrendering control of the show to him or her. That isn't necessarily a bad thing. Let guests enjoy the spotlight; your audience will appreciate them for being there, which adds a new dimension to your feed. One way to avoid the "me factor" is to think of yourself as a liaison for the listener. Ask yourself, "As a listener, what questions would I ask or information would I be looking for from the guest?"

>> **Respect your guests. Period.** Following an interview with a streamer for *Twitch For Dummies*, I was asked to omit one of the questions that I asked. Personally, I found the answer to be a positive, informative one, but this was not my judgment call to make. This was the judgment call from the streamer in question. To establish trust, honor the request of the interview subject. Why? You want to avoid blacklists as interview subjects talk to their friends. You want them to speak positively of you and your stream. Show them respect, and those guests worth your time will do the same.

One final note on preparing for interviews: We've heard some guests say, "I'm doing these interviewers a favor by going on their show." And we've been told by other show hosts, "We're doing you a great favor with this chance to showcase your work on our show."

Both of these opinions are not just arrogant, but they're just flat-out wrong.

The reality is that host and guest are working together to create a synergy. The interviewer has a chance to earn a wider audience and display mastery of journalistic techniques. The guest has a chance to get into the public eye, stay in the public eye, and talk about the next big thing he or she has coming in sight of said public eye. Working together, guest and host create a seamless promotional machine for one another.

Prepping Your Green Room for Guests

A guest could be your dad, your mother-in-law, your best friend, or the man on the street. It could also be the friend of a friend who can get you on the phone with your favorite author, actor, or athlete. When you're interviewing, you have a second party to worry about.

Removing the "technical difficulties" element usually means either taking the show to the guests or bringing the guests to the show. This kind of interview not only is the most fun to do, but also gives you direct contact with the subject so you can observe body language, facial expressions, and reactions to questions and answers.

Welcoming in-studio guests

When you have guests visit your facilities — and because you're podcasting, this is probably your house — make them feel at home. Offer them something to drink. Offer to take them on a tour of your humble abode. Introduce them to your family.

The point is to be polite. You don't have to cook dinner for them, but offering a hint of hospitality, be it a glass of water (or a beer, if you've ever worked closely with me), is a nice touch.

If you're having in-studio interviews, it's also a good idea to get your home and yourself ready to receive guests. Sure, on Saturdays, Tee streams in his pajamas, but because he's flying solo and it's Saturday Morning Cartoons on his stream, he's allowed. If authors Alex White or Piper J Drake are coming over to his house for an interview, don't think for a minute he'd be greeting them in his Avenger jammies and Dogfish Head Brewery slippers.

Okay, maybe he *would* greet them wearing the Dogfish slippers, but he would be bathed and dressed and have his teeth brushed and hair combed. The key word here is *guest.* Treat them as such. Be cool, be pleasant, be nice. And if you're a guest on someone else's stream, the same rules apply. Don't prop your feet up on the furniture, don't demand hospitality, and don't be a jerk during the interview.

The in-studio visit is an audition for both guest and host. If the guest is abrasive, abusive, and just plain rude, chances are good that the guest will never be invited back, no matter how well the previous interview goes. If a host asks unapproved questions, continues to pry into personal matters that have nothing to do with the interview, or seems determined to take over the interview spotlight as if trying to impress the guest, said guest may never return, even if extended an invitation.

Meeting guests on their own turf

Be cool, be pleasant, be nice. These same rules apply when you take your podcast on the road. You may find yourself at a person's home, place of business, or some other neutral place. With Twitch running off your phone, you're now practicing — for the lack of a better term — guerilla journalism. It can be prearranged, or you could be at a special event like GuardianCon, ambushing unsuspecting people with questions that may not strike you as hard and probing but could be to people who don't expect them. Make certain to show respect to your guests, wherever you are when the interview takes place.

A good approach for getting good interviews is to ask permission of your guests, be they passers-by or experts at their place of business, to interview them. If the guest you want to interview has a handler or liaison, it's good protocol to follow the suggestions and advice of the guest's staff, as outlined earlier in this chapter.

If you start out with a warm, welcoming smile and explain what you're doing and why, most people open up and are happy to talk.

REMEMBER

Before going mobile, test your equipment. You're now out of the controlled environment of your home studio; you have to deal with surrounding ambient noise and how well your interview is recording in the midst of uncontrolled background variables. Set up your equipment, if you can. Power up your laptop and portable gear and perform a test stream through Twitch. When you have your setup running, you're ready to get your interviews.

And although this may sound a bit pessimistic, be ready for things to go wrong. Guests might not show up for interviews. New high-tech toys, if not given a proper pre-interview shakedown, may not come through. Prepare to have plenty of topics to discuss on your own, and then your live stream can continue following a quick disclaimer.

Chapter **11**

The In-Between Streams

This has been an amazing journey so far, hasn't it? And no doubt, along the way, you've been experiencing streams you wish didn't have to end and other streams you wish you hadn't started. Twitch is like that. Some streams, you are the windshield of a high-performance sportscar. Other streams, you are the unsuspecting bug cruising along the highway, enjoying the air currents until you find yourself in front of a high-performance sportscar.

Regardless of the kind of stream you most recently hosted, you can't shake that itch to stream again. When you feel that pull to get back online, that's when you know the stream has got a hold of you. (Maybe that's one reason why they call this platform Twitch? You're fidgeting all day, watching the clock, just waiting to get back to the game and your Chat.) It feels like a long pull in-between streams, and during that stretch, your mind may be racing to figure out what you can do to keep your stream active, especially when you visit other streamers and note their success. What are they doing to nurture and cultivate their Community?

Meanwhile, at Penguin's Secret Lair: Your Channel between Streams

It is always a lesson to watch other streamers, take an active part in their Communities, and see how their Channel operates. One of the first things I noticed when jumping from stream to stream was that the Channel's Video Player Banner (which I cover way back in Chapter 1) is present when the host is offline. However, the banner tends to come out only when there's no programming happening on the stream. When I say programming, I don't mean content that you are creating. I'm talking more about content being created by other streamers.

Remember when I walked you through the process of a *raid* back in Chapter 4? When you lead a Twitch raid to another streamer, you are essentially doing two things. The first and foremost, you are taking your assembled Chat and leading them to another streamer that you think your stream will appreciate. The other thing you are doing, though, is *hosting* that Channel, as seen in Figure 11-1. When you host another streamer, their programming is now featured on your Channel.

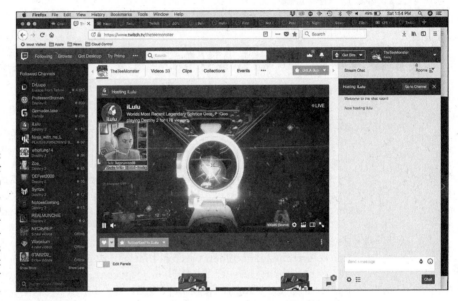

FIGURE 11-1: When you *host* another stream on your Channel, you are sending a message to your Chat and your stream that this is a streamer that warrants your attention.

If you want to host another streamer's Channel, it's not that hard:

1. **At the end of your stream, let your Chat know that you are going to host another stream.**

2. **In the Chat window, type in the following command:**

    ```
    /host td0013
    ```

    You can host a streamer without a raid. It's up to you if you want to either make a big splash with your Chat or simply "change stations" and treat your Chat to someone new or maybe to an old friend of the stream. Hosting is one of many commands that you can review on Twitch at https://help.twitch.tv/customer/portal/articles/659095-chat-moderation-commands.

3. Single-click the *Chat* button or press the Enter key, and your Channel will be hosting the streamer you designated.

It's pretty easy to invite other streamers on to your channel, and as it's so easy, you might not think it's a big deal, right?

Actually, hosting other streamers and getting hosted yourself is a pretty big deal.

Why host other streamers?

When you are trying to build a name for yourself, it may seem a little counter-intuitive hosting other streamers. Why invite "the competition" over to your stream so that your audience can check out their mad skills at *Destiny, Fortnite, Overwatch,* or some other game du jour? There are a lot of benefits behind intro-ducing your Chat to other streamers, and they should be considered whenever you decide to raid or host.

Hosting and raiding promotes goodwill

When you are bringing a new stream into your own Channel, whether new to your Community or new to you, you are saying *"I am trusting you with my Chat."* to the hosted Channel. That is quite a responsibility, not to mention a sense of faith from the hosting streamer that the incoming programming is relevant to his or her Channel. In turn, the hosted streamers open their doors to viewers, welcoming them to their Community. It's a reciprocating agreement between Channels and should help both grow.

REMEMBER

While hosting other Channels does promote goodwill on Twitch, this does not mean you should head to the Twitch directory, find the Top Streamers, start host-ing them, and then wait for people to find you. Just because you host one of the biggest names in streams does not obligate him or her to return the favor, send their Chat to you anytime in the near future, or even acknowledge your host or raid. (Depending on their Channel and activity, they may not.) That's not how goodwill works, and this may be an exercise in futility if you pursue it.

The hosted channel is a favorite of yours

Before you were streaming yourself, you went to this Channel often. The host was always kind and welcoming. The level of skill featured at this streamer's corner of Twitch was nothing less than inspiring. The Community around this stream was never anything other than positive, inviting, and fun. You want to introduce your own Chat to this streamer. Maybe your own growing Community will find the same enjoyment that you found and still continue to find there when you visit.

It's a good idea to know about a Channel before you send over a raid or a host. Sometimes, you can get lucky and meet some really nice people that way. However, if you don't know the streamer and roll the bones to see where you and your Chat land, you might find yourself in a dark, sinister corner of Twitch that may not reflect all that back on you.

You might just make a streamer's day

When you visit `http://bit.ly/TeesFirstRaid`, you will watch a video of me blissfully coming off a somewhat disappointing Crucible match . . . only to have that loss supplanted by me saying "I'm being raided!" I then watched (and, of course, hyperventilated) as I watched my numbers go from 6 viewers to 25 viewers . . . then to 35 . . . then to 135. This was my first-ever raid from the overnight streaming machine that is JSniperton (`http://twitch.tv/jsniperton`), who not only dropped in a huge amount of people into my Chat, but also introduced my stream to a new group of people and catapulted my Channel into the Top Five of Twitch's *Destiny* 2 Directory that morning. It was unexpected. It was a wild ride with so many new names in Chat. It also made me a new friend and contact in Twitch.

And yes, I was walking on air for the rest of the day on account of that.

Selecting other streamers

As mentioned in a tip earlier in this chapter, it's always good to know where you are sending your stream. You could cover your eyes, throw a dart at a board, and see where it lands . . . but as Twitch is on your computer, it really doesn't make sense to anybody — especially those watching as you are still streaming, you nimrod — that you suddenly decide to start playing darts. Come on, butterfly Boy, focus. Where exactly are you going to find a host for your Chat?

Your Follow List

Look to the left of your browser window and see who is live, as shown in Figure 11-2. Is TD0013 live, making props and costume gear? Or is Alkali Layke multitasking between a costume build and rounds of Heartstone? Take a look at who's online when your stream is about to conclude, and then let your Chat know who you are about to introduce them to and why. It's always good form for you to talk a bit about the streamer you are about to introduce to your Community.

Before launching a raid or a host, make sure to confirm that the streamer is live and not in a rerun.

Followed Channels

DrLupo
Escape From Tarkov ● 4,359

ProfessorBroman
Destiny 2 ● 803

GernaderJake
Fortnite ● 284

iLulu
Destiny 2 ● 164

Ninja_with_no_L
PLAYERUNKNOWN'S B... ● 92

whoflung14
Destiny 2 ● 84

Zoe_
Destiny 2 ● 65

OEFvet2006
Destiny 2 ● 35

Syntzx
Destiny 2 ● 17

REALMUNCHIE
Destiny 2 ● 13

FIGURE 11-2:
Take a look at who is streaming from your own Followed Channels List, and see who would make a good fit for your Chat.

The Game Directory

When I was raided by JSniperton, my first reaction was *"How did this guy know about me?"* as I knew about him through other streamers I had seen before. Then I found out about how some will go to their Game Directory and see who is at the bottom of the list. After looking at the person's profile (again, the importance of a complete profile) for a few moments, just to see what kind of streamer they are, seasoned streamers will raid that unsuspecting streamer to give their numbers a boost. You can tell a lot about a streamer from how they handle monster raids. It's a wonderful gesture and always welcome.

WARNING

Random hosts and raids from streamers you don't know are done out of goodwill . . . in most situations. However, this is the Internet, which means some people — men and women alike — can be jerks. A trend that seems to linger in Twitch is known as the *malicious raid,* where broadcasters — some of them, partners — will send their community somewhere else to harass someone. When a raid happens, watch your Chat.

Auto-Hosting

As you continue to stream and as you continue to explore the various streams that are out there, you get a feel for the streams that you think best represent you, your own stream's philosophy, and games that you really like to play. You might also note that some of these streams are hosting at all hours gamers, creatives, and engaging personalities from all over the world. It would be nice to be able to do that for your stream, now wouldn't it? Why don't you, then? The *Auto-Host* is a function in the Twitch Dashboard that allows you to go on and host someone on your stream with you having to initiate the host command.

1. **Go to your Twitch Dashboard and go to Settings ⇨ Channel in the Dashboard menu, located on the left-hand side of your browser window.**

2. **Scroll down to the *Auto Hosting* option and then single-click the *Host List* option.**

   The *Host List* is a collection of streams that, when they are online, will automatically appear on your own Channel. This way, when you are unable to stream or are in-between shows, your Channel will feature programming of some description.

3. **If you are wanting to begin or add to a list of auto-streams for your Channel, click in the *Search* bar across the top of the stream. Twitch will look at your Follow List and offer options for you to add these streamers, as shown in Figure 11-3.**

FIGURE 11-3:
Auto-Hosting
allows you to
provide Twitch
content on your
stream without
you having to
authorize it. Add
a streamer, set
the priority, and
let Twitch do the
work for you.

4. **In the stream you wish to add, click on the corresponding *Add* button to the left of the desired stream.**

5. **If you wish for one stream to have preference over another stream in being hosted, click-and-hold your mouse over one stream and then drag the stream higher into your list.**

6. **If you want to remove a streamer from your Auto Host list, move your mouse over the streamer in question. The stream will highlight, and to the right, you will see a trash can icon. Single-click the trash can to remove the stream from your Auto Host list.**

Hosting other channels also turns your Channel into something of an active network. Through your host, be they ones you yourself have initiated or others where you let Auto-Host do its thing, you are providing programming. People surfing through Twitch, provided they would prefer not to interact but simply watch streamers, will finds on your Channel a collection of streamers that you think are talents to watch. Enjoy tonight's playbill, and give out a few follows. Remember, following a Twitch streamer is free.

Twitch on Demand: Past Broadcasts

Let's say you are a fan of DrLupo, Ninja, or SheSnaps . . . but your day job has you stuck in meetings, attending a special after-work function, or dealing with a sudden crisis in the office. Not to worry, you can always catch a rerun, right? Oh wait, you missed the rerun, too?

That's okay, too. Why not watch Twitch on *your* time?

Past broadcasts on Twitch

We have already looked into the *rerun* (back in Chapter 4), but I'm talking more about Twitch on your time. When you visit a Channel, there will be a tab at the top marked *Videos,* taking you to a section of your Channel as shown in Figure 11-4. This is where you should find the most recent broadcasts of Twitch streams, along with *Highlights* (also covered in Chapter 4) you've created. Your Video Directory organizes your previous broadcasts and Highlight Reels by the most recent and can conveniently bring you up-to-speed on what is happening on your favorite Channel. When you roll your cursor over a *video-on-demand* (or *VOD*), you should get a quick animation preview of what to expect in the segment. Single-clicking it brings you into a viewing mode almost indistinguishable from an actual live stream. The main difference is that you will not see the usual "LIVE" icon anywhere. And while you see Chat, you can't really interact with people there as this is a replay of a previous broadcast. Beyond that, it is no different than watching a rerun with the exception that instead of the host replaying it, you are.

Let's speculate though that your week is busier still, and there was an episode of a stream you really wanted to catch as you heard it was definitely worth seeing to be believed. *"Eh, I'll watch it over the weekend."* The weekend comes and goes and you put off seeing the previous stream for another few days. What you might not realize is that your window of opportunity to catch that video is growing smaller and smaller. Twitch, by default, grants access to your previous streams for only two weeks. Once the two week period has expired, the video is deleted from the server. So while Twitch is a convenient platform for streaming and video-on-demand, it does have its limitations.

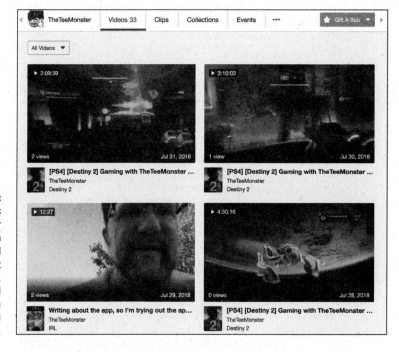

FIGURE 11-4:
The *Videos* section of your Channel is a Twitch-managed archive of Past Broadcasts, Highlights, and other events you have hosted or created.

TIP

For Twitch Prime users and Partners, VODs are available for 60 days. For regular broadcasters, Twitch Prime users, and Partners, highlights are available indefinitely.

In the spirit of binge watching, there is a way to access your previous broadcasts after their expiration dates. It may seem unlikely to you that anyone would want to watch archived shows of you playing *Borderlands*, *Magic: The Gathering*, or *League of Legends*, but it might surprise you how tenacious new audiences and Twitch fans can be. They want to see those early days of your stream, see where you started, and note how far you have come in streaming. So where can you send people to view this video time capsule? Read on.

Past broadcasts on YouTube

This may sound like an unexpected sort of tip in a book dedicated to Twitch seeing as *YouTube* (http://www.youtube.com) has a similar platform to Twitch — *YouTube Gaming* (http://gaming.youtube.com) — now available. Before becoming competitors, Twitch and YouTube worked together to effectively archive all this content Twitch streamers had created around their favorite video game. Unedited, raw, and completely intact from the beginning of the stream to the end, YouTube offered a more permanent home to hours of information and entertainment that streamers provided (see Figure 11-5).

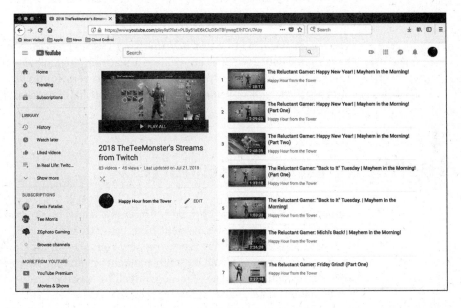

FIGURE 11-5:
YouTube offers a more permanent place for all your previous Twitch broadcasts.

To make YouTube a "forever home" for your past broadcasts (provided none of the Terms of Service for either Twitch or YouTube change), you will need to set up a YouTube account, a channel, and a playlist. These finer details are all presented to you in *YouTube Channels For Dummies* by Rob Ciampa, Theresa Moore, John Carucci, Stan Muller, and Adam Wescott. Once you have your YouTube channel set up, you can begin the process of archiving your previous Twitch broadcasts on to your YouTube playlists.

The day after finishing up a stream, you can begin the process of exporting your broadcasts from your Twitch Channel.

1. **Following your stream, go to the Twitch Dashboard and go to Videos ⇨ Video Producer in the Dashboard menu.**

2. **Find your most recent broadcast and select from the Options icon (the three vertical dots to the far right of the broadcast) the *Export* option.**

   The Export option should remind you of when we were creating highlights earlier in Chapter 4. Similar to that process, we will be exporting an entire stream to a YouTube playlist.

3. From the *Export to YouTube* options, you can add in a *Description, Tags,* and the choice to make your video *Public* or *Private.* Edit these options accordingly.

4. Select *Start Export* to begin the export process.

You will be notified by email if your YouTube video is successfully exported. Once done, your stream finds a permanent place on YouTube.

REMEMBER

The reason you need to wait a day after your stream goes back to the contract you have signed with Twitch as an Affiliate or Partner. Twitch owns the rights to your content for 24 hours. This means you cannot post your content to YouTube directly after a stream ends or you run the risk of your affiliate/partnership becoming null and void.

Highlight Videos: Revisited

Remember our overview of *highlight reels* in Chapter 4? To review quickly, the *highlight* is a quick clip of a moment from your stream. A *highlight reel* is a collection of clips edited together reviewing how your stream unfolded, your proudest moments in game, and your funniest moments in stream. Alongside frequency of reel posting and what to look for in a compelling highlight reel, perhaps the greatest demand is *time.* Digital video applications like iMovie and Premiere have dramatically simplified the process of editing video. Commercials aren't quite honest, though, when depicting video editing as a push-button technology.

Depending on the power of your computer's processors and the length of your video, digital video production can take anywhere from a few minutes to an hour to a full eight-to-nine-hour work day.

I'm the first to admit there is an allure to video editing. It is *intense!* And here's a true confession: I love it! You just have to give yourself *time.* Time to edit. Time to review. Time to render.

Before you start posting highlight reels, go on and make that first highlight reel for yourself. Keep it under ten minutes. Then edit a second highlight video, and make it fifteen minutes. Go for three, if you can. Make it whatever a running time you want. Once you have those reels edited and ready to go, you have an idea of how long you want your reels to run and what kind of posting schedule you want for your highlight reels.

iGame, Therefore iTwitch: Creating Highlight Reels with iMovie

New Mac devices have *iMovie* (www.apple.com/imovie) installed, but iMovie can easily be downloaded from Apple's App Store. This unassuming application grants you the ability to edit video by dragging and dropping clips where you want them on your project's timeline.

Import video with iMovie

When you go to the Video Producer and select from the options menu *Download*, your broadcast will be downloaded as an mp4 file, a versatile video format that keeps a good amount of resolution (clarity) while being manageable in data size. You need to get the video into your copy of iMovie. Importing video into iMovie is a quick and easy process.

1. Launch iMovie.

2. From the intro window, select *Create New* by clicking the giant plus sign and selecting the *Movie* option.

3. Single click the *Import Media* option and from the Import window, navigate to where your footage resides.

   When downloading your previous broadcasts, Twitch will default to the *Downloads* folder unless you designate a different location on your Mac.

WARNING

   You might look at your Finder and actually see a media clip present, but iMovie will not. Check to see if a copy is present on your drive or if the clip is available through iCloud, Apple's cloud storage service. Unless it is on an internal or external drive, iMovie will not see it.

4. Select the clips you wish to import and single-click the *Import Selected* option.

   Your clips are imported into the *My Media* pane, as shown in Figure 11-6.

5. When your import is concluded, iMovie closes the import window automatically and returns to the main editing window.

This is part of the process known in the video editing industry as *logging.* Before you start humming Monty Python's "Lumberjack Song" and dress in flannel, let me quickly explain what "logging" is in this respect. Logging video is where you go through all your footage, organize your media clips as needed, and finally settle on what you want to use and what you don't. This is where time comes into play as the game footage in this respect is your stream. Hours on hours of gameplay now waits for you to sift through so you can find the "best moments" from the stream.

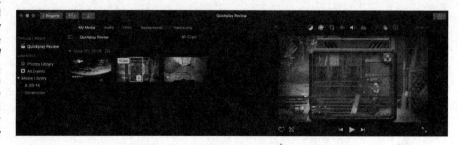

FIGURE 11-6:
Once you find
your gameplay
footage, the
Import Selected
(or *Import All*,
depending on
how your files are
set up) option
brings all your
video into the *My
Media* pane.

This could take a while.

TIP

It's not a bad idea when you do have a memorable moment in your stream to make a note of the time. If it happened around 35 minutes into your stream, then you will know when logging that you can mind the moment somewhere in the 35-minute mark in your media. This will serve as a handy timesaver for you.

Once you have your media imported into iMovie, we can now start on assembling a highlight reel.

Creating your highlight reel with iMovie

Let's work on creating that first Greatest Hits video of yours.

1. **Single-click a full clip in the My Media pane.**

   When clips are selected in the My Media pane, a gold frame with two handles will appear on the clip. These handles are your *In Point* (left) and *Out Point* (right) handles.

2. **Click and drag the *In Point* handle to a rough estimate of where you want your first clip to start. Then drag the *Out Point* handle to where you want your opening clip end.**

   If you click-and-drag the clip from the My Media pane without adjusting the In and Out points, you import into your Timeline the entire file. By adjusting points, you can easily farm multiple clips from one file.

3. **Click and drag the clip from the My Media Pane into the Timeline along the bottom of the iMovie interface.**

   The *Timeline* in your iMovie interface is where you assemble and edit your clips. Simply drag and drop clips in the order you want them to appear.

4. **Repeat Steps 2–3 for the remaining clips in your My Media pane until you have a collection of clips in the order you want, as shown in Figure 11-7.**

What you have now is commonly referred to as a *rough cut*. This is your reel without transitions, set volume level, or any detailed editing. It gives you an idea of what the video will look like when it's done.

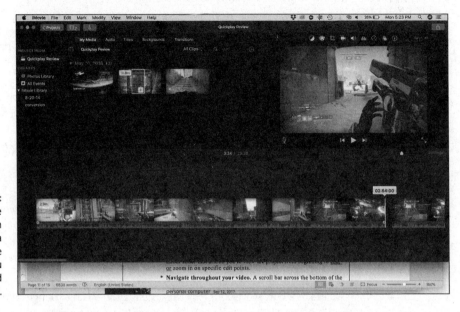

FIGURE 11-7: After you move your clips from the My Media Pane to the Timeline, you have completed your rough cut.

5. **Move your cursor to the end of your first clip in the Timeline. You should see the Adjust In/Out Point tool (←|→) appear. Click-and-drag the clip forward or back to adjust its Out point.**

   When you drag In and Out points of clips, you can see a preview of the new Out point in the Preview window.

6. **Move your cursor to the beginning of the next clip in the Timeline. When the Adjust In/Out Point tool appears, click-and-drag the clip forward or back to adjust the In point.**

7. **Repeat Steps 5–6 to change the running time of your clips throughout the Timeline.**

8. **Return to the beginning of the Timeline once you have adjusted all the clips, and then click at the beginning of the first clip. Press the space bar to begin a playthrough of your rough cut.**

   If you need to adjust your clips after the review, repeat Steps 5–6 to refine your work.

9. **Repeat this entire exercise if you wish to add clips to your Highlight Reel.**

REMEMBER

The best practice when it comes to defining In and Out points in video is to log when the best moments before you begin the editing process. Without logging, you could be searching through clips and refining In and Out points in clips well into the night and even the next morning.

The amount of editing your highlight reel needs depends on the amount of footage you have to choose from and how detailed you this "Best Of" production to be. When you have a rough cut, here are some editing tricks to try:

- **Zoom in and out.** Above and to the right of the Timeline window is a Zoom slider that allows you to view the project from beginning to end, or zoom in on specific edit points.
- **Navigate throughout your video.** A scroll bar across the bottom of the Timeline will allow you to move from the beginning to the end of your rough cut.
- **Scrub through video.** Rolling your cursor over individual clips, you can *scrub* through the video. *Scrubbing* is the process of viewing playback at a user-designated speed. You scan through segments, find what you're looking for, and make edits. With the left and right arrows, you can also advance through a clip frame by frame.
- **Make a cut.** Move your *Playhead* (the grey line with a triangle at the top, seen in Figure 11-8) in the Timeline to where you want to make an edit. Choose Modify⇨Split Clip (or press ⌘+B).

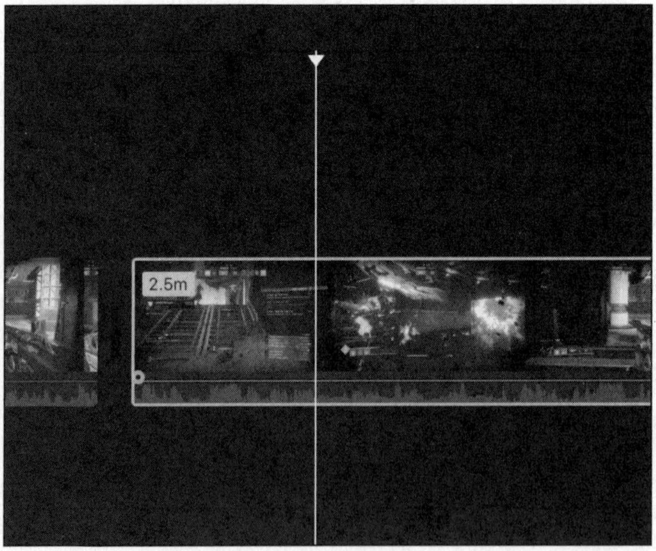

FIGURE 11-8: Where you click on a clip in your Timeline, the Playhead will jump to that point and start playback from there.

>> **Delete a segment.** Click the segment you want to remove and press the Delete key to remove the unwanted video.

>> **Drop in a transition.** If you want to go from clip to clip in a more creative fashion, take a look at the *Transitions* pane at the far-right of the various options next to My Media. A transition is a cool way to get from one clip to the next (a crossfade, wipe, or some interesting bridge), unlike a *cutaway* or *jump cut* where one video source switches to another. Click and drag the desired transition between two clips to apply it.

>> **Place a title at the beginning of your video.** Click Titles (on the same row as My Media and Transitions) to bring up the Titles pane. Choose a title and drag it to the timeline just above the first clip. Once you place your title on the clip, double click the new bar above the first clip to edit the text in the Preview window. The Titles pane is the feature of iMovie where you can place animated or static text at the beginning, middle, or end of your movie, giving your reel a polished Hollywood touch.

TIP

Something to think about with your highlight reel is how you want it to begin and how you want it to end, commonly referred to as an *intro* and an *outro*. After you create your first highlight reel and you get comfortable with the editing process, you can go back and create an intro and outro, and then simply import them in as clips of their own. Go to `http://bit.ly/HHFTT-video01` for a video featuring a set Intro and Outro and then think about how you would like your reels to begin and end.

Exporting Your Highlight Reel from iMovie

When you have fine-tuned your video how you want it, follow these steps to export your highlight reel:

1. **Choose File ⇨ Share and select *File*.**

A dialog box like the one in Figure 11-9 opens, giving you the option to set the video title, description, metatags (optional), format, resolution, quality, and compression options. The dialog box also lets you know playback time and approximate file size based on the selected settings.

2. **After reviewing the dialog box, click the *Next. . .* button.**

3. **Select a place where you want to keep your highlight reels, and then single-click the *Save* button.**

And there you have it. Your first highlight reel as made in iMovie.

FIGURE 11-9:
The Export ⇨ File window offers you a final review of how your video will be exported.

TIP

iMovie is not only designed to be easy; it's designed for you to have fun with video. Remember to go exploring with its various features such as *Slow Motion* (an icon of a turtle) or the *Voiceover* feature, which allows you to watch the footage and record a narrator's track as you watch the playback. You can also take your finished highlight reel and create a Hollywood-style *trailer*, a preview of what's coming soon, using iMovie's built-in templates.

While this exercise touches on the basics of video editing and things look super-easy, time plays into this highlight reel of yours as you are the last word on how long your reels are, how many clips are involved, and how polished your highlight reel will look in the end. If you want to find out more about editing with iMovie, there are many books on the market that will take you deeper into the power of this application. If you decide to take the next step up, Final Cut Pro X (`www.apple.com/final-cut-pro`), consider looking into Tom Wolsky's *From iMovie to Final Cut Pro X: Making the Creative Leap.*

Elementary, Dear Watson: Video Editing with Adobe Premiere

The PC market offers many video editing packages, some of them free and others coming with a price tag. For streamers on this platform, I focus on the Adobe products that have not only been tried and tested but are considered trusted and reliable by editors of all backgrounds. Premiere Elements (`www.adobe.com/products/premiere-elements.html`) is Adobe's professional grade video editing suite made available and affordable to consumers. There will be a slight learning curve in finding the workflow that suits you, but the user interface is accessible to newcomers to video editing. It does have a price tag around $100 USD, but that should fit within most streamers' budget. If, however, you are looking for something with more options, also available is Elements' big brother, Adobe Premiere Pro (www.adobe.com/products/premiere.html) for the more advanced producer.

Importing video with Premiere Elements

As depicted earlier in this chapter for iMovie, we are starting off this tour of Premiere with the prerequisite that you have downloaded a stream, or several others, that you will be editing down to a single highlight reel. This could be a daily edit, taking the most recent stream and whittling it down to a few minutes, or a weekly recap of what people are missing when they don't tune in live. Whatever the case, the footage is on your hard drive in its raw, unedited form.

1. **Launch Premiere Elements.**

2. **Under the Add Media drop-down menu, as shown in Figure 11-10, select *Files and Folders* if your video is on your PC's hard drive. If it is coming from an external drive, you should be able to access it using the *Videos from Cameras & Devices* option.**

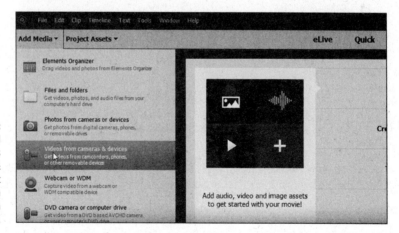

FIGURE 11-10: Use the Add Media ⇨ Videos from Cameras & Devices to import your clips when kept on an external drive.

3. **In the Video Importer window that appears, check clips you wish to import, or rather, uncheck the ones you don't wish to import since all clips are checked by default.**

Don't forget to check out the other options available on the Import window such as naming your clips, deleting them after import (to reclaim space on your drive), and where video clips are being stored.

TIP

By default, Premiere Elements will add all your videos to the timeline. If you'd rather have them save as *Project Assets* that you can pick and choose later, uncheck the *Add To Timeline* option.

4. **Click *Get Media* to import the selected clips.**

5. **Once your clips are imported, use the *Project Assets* drop-down to copy the clips you want to the Timeline, as shown in Figure 11-11.**

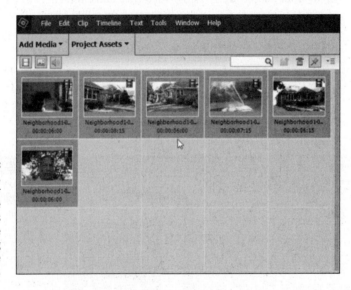

FIGURE 11-11:
Once imported, you'll find your clips in the Project Assets collection where you can drag them to the timeline.

You may notice that, if you are jumping from iMovie to Premiere, the steps are somewhat similar. That's because the basics of video editing from platform to platform, from application to application, are identical. You have media clips that you import into the application. *Check.* You click and drag them into a Timeline. *Check.* You adjust In and Out points in the clips. *Check.* What we do to achieve the end results are similar, only the smallest of details differing between iMovie and Premiere.

Creating your highlight reel with Premiere Elements

We've got our clips imported. Now let's start editing in Premiere. You'll find that while iMovie is more basic than Premiere, the concepts are very close to the same.

1. Click and drag the desired clip into the Timeline.

2. Click and drag the Playhead to where you want your clip to start (and you should see the new *In Point* in the Preview window above the Timeline . . . just like in iMovie). Then single-click the scissors icon appearing on the red line attached to the Playhead.

   The red line is called the *CTI* or *Current Time Indicator*. You can use this to trim up a clip and split one clip into multiple clips.

3. Click and drag the Playhead to where you want your clip to end, and then single-click the scissors icon to create an *Out Point*.

4. Click the clips you do not want, and hit the Backspace/Delete key to remove them from the Timeline.

5. Click-and-drag your remaining clips to put them in the order you wish.

6. Repeat Steps 2–5 for any remaining clips in your Timeline until you have a rough cut, as shown in Figure 11-12.

FIGURE 11-12: After you move your clips in the Timeline to the order you wish, your rough cut is ready for review.

7. **Go to the Action Bar in the Menu and select** *Transitions*.

8. **Click-and-drag a transition from the Transitions window, and place it in-between any two clips in the Timeline.**

   Again, just like iMovie, you have applied a transition.

9. **Repeat this entire exercise if you wish to add clips, transition, and additional elements to your highlight reel.**

Take a look at that list of suggested editing tricks for iMovie. Many of those suggestions also apply for Premiere Elements. For the most part, you can apply the same tricks and techniques in both applications.

And just like with iMovie, after some tweaking and fine-tuning, we are ready to export our highlight reel.

Exporting your highlight reel from Premiere Elements

How does your video look? All good? Then let's export your highlight reel:

1. **Choose Publish & Share ⇨ Computer.**

2. **Choose the format you want for your file.**

3. **After reviewing the dialog box which includes a preset of the format, the name of your highlight reel, and where you are saving it on your computer, click the** *Save* **button.**

Pretty simple, isn't it?

WARNING

Although programs like iMovie and Premiere have simplified video editing dramatically, as mentioned before, this isn't a quick-and-easy process. When the video is done, it must be processed, and that can take anywhere from a few minutes to a few hours, depending on the length of your episode, the dimension of your video, and the compression format. Give yourself that time to edit and time to process the video you're creating. Before announcing your video podcast, try to find out how those first few episodes will progress in production and finally what the processing time will be for a single episode. You may find that a missed mistake can cost you hours. Always preview and then preview again before processing. You may also pick up a few cool tips from John Carucci's *Digital SLR Video and Filmmaking For Dummies.*

SERIOUSLY? A SELFIE STICK?

The much-maligned selfie stick has been either a source of ridicule or, for those really lost in their own narcissism, a source of horrifying (if not comical) death. But when it comes to taking advantage of the Twitch mobile app — provided your Internet connection is incredibly solid — a selfie stick saves your arm from a lot of cramping and offers your video a bit of stability. With the right angle and the right leverage, your selfie stick actually works as a collapsible steady cam and can allow you better options in capturing more people in the moment and even more activity in your shot. Just remember to be aware — well aware — of your surroundings. Getting the best shot for your stream will not matter one bit if you fall off a cliff or get hit by a train and are recovering in a hospital — regardless of how awesome that would be for your stream.

And yes, Tee was being very careful with a vintage steam train slowly advancing behind him.

Photo credit: Babs Daniels, taken at Steampunk unLimited 2015.

Chapter **12**

From Hobby to Side Hustle . . . to Full-Time Job?

Perhaps you have skipped the previous eleven chapters to go on and jump into this chapter. After all, that is why you are here: to make money.

Yeah, okay, I'm going to have to ask you to slow your roll there, Sparky, go back to the beginning of the book and start reading.

No, seriously. Honor system. You go back to Chapter 1 and then, once you've gone through all the other stuff, I'll be here to talk about making bank. I'll wait. . . .

Hey there. Welcome back.

As this is the honor system we're working on, you know from previous chapters just how much work there is in hosting a stream. Sure, you watch Ninja, DrLupo, or xMinks (http://twitch.tv/xminks) and they make it look easy. This is because they have been at this for a good stretch of time and have found their groove. You, on the other hand, as you are reading this, are still learning what kind of platform

Twitch is and what its potential could be. You should also know, at this point, that Twitch is not a turn-key business. You just don't stream and — boom — instant success, unless of course you are a celebrity of some stature or notoriety. If you are starting at this cold, you have a long, hard road ahead. If this really we're as easy as the aforementioned streamers, so many others would not quit after a month.

The lure of easy money is hard to ignore, but what you might think is "easy" is anything but when it comes to Twitch. You have to be there, on camera, when you say you will be there; otherwise, your audience will check the directory for some-one else. Also, when it comes to making money on Twitch, a lot of things change. Numbers suddenly become a priority. The demands on you to perform become higher. There is an unspoken contact drawn up between you and your audience. Simply put: If you want their investment, you have to offer something worth investing into.

And from the start, Twitch is expecting you to fulfill a few requirements:

>> **Start your first stream.** I know: Thanks, Captain Obvious, but this is the baptism by fire. You set up Twitch, jump into the stream, and see where it takes you.

>> **Explore your dashboard.** Thing is, if you've started this book from the beginning (Ahem!), this would already be in your rear-view mirror.

>> **Update your stream title.** You might be surprised how many new streamers don't do this. As this book is out to make sure you don't develop any bad habits, you should have this down along with your Dashboard.

>> **Update your Stream Category.** Again, establish good habits by making sure you update this when necessary.

Revenue on Twitch doesn't happen straight away, and Twitch is determined to make sure the first few steps are quality steps. It is important that you really know the platform and understand how it all works. Complete the achievements I just listed, and Twitch becomes an online location for opportunity.

Be patient, though. Between you and the highly-coveted tier of Partnership remain a few steps for you to take.

Entry Level Pro: The Affiliate Streamer

We all start somewhere. It seems just only yesterday — and depending on your schedule, it might have been just only yesterday — you were streaming off your gaming console from the couch. We have made quite a few upgrades between then and now, and we are always looking to improve our stream, its quality, and our performance on camera.

Through it all, though, we have been making progress towards becoming an *Affiliate*. You can track your progress, shown completed in Figure 12-1, by going to your Channel's Dashboard and selecting the *Achievements* option. What exactly is an Affiliate, you ask? What's happens when you become one? How do things change with you and your stream? Is there an initiation I need to prepare for? Will there be a plaque of any kind presented?

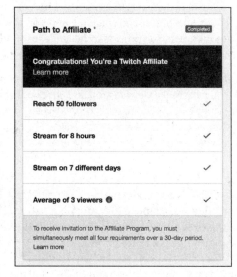

FIGURE 12-1:
The touchstones needed to reach the rank of *Twitch Affiliate*, listed in your Dashboard under *Achievements*.

Becoming an Affiliate does not involve any sort of trophy, no ceremony is centered around it, and your stream will not appear any different than normal. That is not to say you shouldn't be proud of what you have accomplished. In becoming a Twitch Affiliate, you have met the following requirements:

>> **Reach 50 followers.** Starting off, this requirement may feel like a real uphill battle, but once you go live with Twitch, let your social networks know. Facebook. Twitter. Tumblr. Wherever you are, throw out there that you now have a Twitch Channel. This milestone is your first, and remember, following people on Twitch is totally free of charge. It also helps your channel grow.

Notice how I didn't say *"Go onto other Twitch Channels that you follow and let people know"* because that is the fastest way of getting blacklisted. Twitch is a Community, sure, but it is a Community about participation. Streamers should get to know you, should recognize you and your contributions to the Channel. If Mods recognize you, they will give you the shout-out, but not if you drop in a

WARNING

quick plug for yourself and then disappear. Do not self-promote in others' streams unless you are given a green light to do so. I will cover more etiquette tips in Chapter 14.

>> **Stream for eight hours.** This is the average amount of time over 30 days that you spend streaming, and it is easy to think, *"Oh sure, piece of cake!"* Thing is, Life can happen. That four-day schedule could easily be scaled back to two days if family commitments come up, but make sure you find a pace and a schedule you can keep. And if you've done it already, then well done!

>> **Stream on seven different days.** Again, based on a 30-day period, your average days spent streaming happens across seven different calendar days. Depending on how much time you spend steaming and how driven you are to make this goal, this requirement can provide a challenge for some. For others, it is one of the first challenges met.

>> **Average of three viewers.** Alongside followers, this can be a pretty tough requirement to fill. You can't make viewers stop and check out your stream, which can be a real struggle as you hope audiences will give you a chance. Twitch knows this isn't easy, and that's why Hosts, Raids, Premieres, and Reruns all count towards your average, putting this Achievement will within reach.

REMEMBER

Numbers can drive you crazy. Numbers can also have an effect on the mood of your stream. It may be difficult to "ignore the numbers," so practice this Golden Rule of Streaming: Whether it is 1, 100, or 1000, stream as if the world is watching because they are, and can drop by your stream at any time.

So maybe you are saying, *"Cool story, bro, but seriously — what does it mean?"* There are a few extra perks in becoming an Affiliate Streamer, and these perks unlock a whole new world of opportunity for you. One of these perks is a small perk, that goes without saying, but *"It's the little things that count"* really does come into play when we talk about Twitch.

Expressing yourself: Emotes

Probably the biggest (and yes, coolest) thing to have happen to you when becoming an Affiliate is that you unlock three positions for *emotes*. I touched on emotes back in Chapter 8 when I was talking about timed commands from Nightbot, and you may have already seen and — if you have subscribed to another's channel — used a variety of different emotes, both from the public bank and those exclusive to the streamer you are visiting. Emotes are tiny caricatures that express something unique to your channel, and when you become an Affiliate, you are given the means to offer Channel *subscribers* (or *subs*) emotes only available on your Channel.

So what exactly makes a good emote? Really good emotes say something about you and about your Channel. For TheBonj (`http://twitch.tv/thebonj`), his emotes are dragon-themed as he is based out of Wales, the birthplace of Western dragon lore. The emotes for Aura (`http://twitch.tv/aura`) are loving nods to Layla, his rescue pit bull. And mine? As shown in Figure 12-2, my emotes from the talented Bellla (`http://twitter.com/_zulubravo_`) are steampunk-themed, as I am an author of steampunk. These tiny images of hype and mischief are ambassadors to your Channel and should be something that your subs enjoy using both in your Chat and in the Chat of others.

FIGURE 12-2: Emotes, like the ones featured here from the artist Bellla, provide a nice perk for subscribers and can also help promote your Channel elsewhere.

After taking a look at the emotes of those you subscribe to, you may be faced with an even harder notion to consider: What emotes do you want? You start off with three slots, one for each Sub Level; so here are a few ideas for what to have on hand for emotes.

>> **"GG" or Good Game.** Some Twitch Channels have fun with the gamer's salute *"GGs!"* which stands for "Good Game!" and is sometimes called on by Stream Hosts after accomplishments are made. Some "GG" emotes are as simple as a block-font with a sniper's crosshair across it. Others can be a rendering of the Stream Host with "GG" underneath them. For my own emote, Bellla made the Gs interlocking gears, staying with the steampunk theme.

>> **Greeting.** Munchie's emote is a caricature of himself waving at you. DrLupo has a wide-eyed wave with *"Hey!"* across the bottom. iLulu's greeting is an anime-style Huntress throwing a peace sign. ZGphoto offers a multitude of greetings ranging from fist bumps to a simple *"HI FRIEND"* text greeting. When you drop into a Chat, these are great icebreakers.

>> **Encouragement.** Emotes are a great way to encourage people in your Chat, whether it is to show affection in rough times or just a way to show support

while gaming, encouragement emotes run a wide gambit. A muppet-like happy face (Tiddly), a sideways smile (DrLupo), or toasting you with a beer (ZGphoto), encouragement emotes are fun to spam when people need a smile. My own, a chibi-style rendering of me giving a thumb's up, can also double for . . .

» **Hype.** Danfinity's got one. James Werk's got one. Bungie has one. So does cosplayer and Hearthstone player Alkali_Layke (`http://twitch.tv/alkali_layke`). When you hear your host call out for *"Hype in Chat!"* it is good to have a Hype emote at the ready. Usually the word *"HYPE!"* is visible, but it doesn't have to be. However, actually seeing the word repeated over and over again serves as a digital equivalent to stomping your feet in high school bleachers. When you're coming up with emotes for your channel, you might have to think about a Hype emote.

TIP

When coming up with emotes, try to come up with ideas and images that scale. If there is too much detail in your emote, it will be impossible to figure out what it is when used in Chat.

Expressing your loyalty: Sub badges

Referred to as *loyalty badges* by Twitch, *sub badges* are icons that you create (similar to Emotes) that appear next to the names of people who subscribe to your feed. They can be color coded to signify how long someone has been subscribed to your feed. For example, in my feed, all new subscribers start out with a white teacup as their beginning level. After three months of subscribing, the teacup automatically goes from white to purple. On remaining subscribed to your stream for 6-months, sub badges change again to a silver gear. After one year, the gear turns gold.

With both emotes and sub badges ready for uploading, pay a visit to your Dashboard.

1. **Once the Twitch Dashboard loads into your browser, go to Dashboard ⇨ Settings ⇨ Affiliate / Partner in the Dashboard menu.**

2. **Select the *Emotes* option and then look at *Upload Emoticons* near the bottom of the screen.**

   In this section, you will upload your emotes for the three various tiers of subscription. You will need to have your emotes saved as PNG files with transparent backgrounds and available in the following sizes:

   - 28 x 28 pixels

   - 56 x 56 pixels

   - 112 x 112 pixels

3. **Where you see the Unique Code field, you will be requested to come up with a quick and easy prefix code for your emotes, not exceeding 6 characters in length.**

    My own prefix code for my emoticons is *thetee* as my online screen name is TheTeeMonster.

4. **With the prefix created and approved, upload the three sizes for the Tier 1 emotes. In the Unique Code field, shown in Figure 12-3, come up with a code for your emote. Keep it simple and short.**

    The unique code for my Tier 2 emoticon is *OK*, so if I type *theteeOK* in Chat, my "steampunk thumbs up" emote appears.

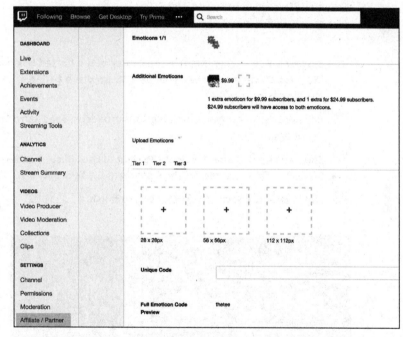

FIGURE 12-3:
For each tier, once Affiliate status is reached, you are allowed one emote to offer your subscribers. With more subscribers, additional slots for emotes are unlocked.

5. **Single-click the + (plus sign) in the center of the dotted box over "28 x 28px" and navigate to your 28 x 28 sized emote. Click *Open* to upload it.**

6. **Repeat Step 5 for the remaining emotes.**

7. **Single-click the *Tier 2* link to the right of the "Tier 1" header and repeat Steps 26. Do the same for *Tier 3* if you decide to activate a Tier 3 option for subscribers.**

8. Single-click the *Submit Changes* button to finish, and then single-click the *Emote Settings* header at the top of the browser to return to the Affiliates / Partner main menu.

9. Select the *Loyalty Badges* option and then look at the Base option under *Manage Badges* section of the screen.

The setup and process of uploading your sub badges are similar to your emotes with some differences. You have four various tiers of subscription loyalty this time. You still need to have emotes saved as PNG files with transparent backgrounds, but now they must be available in the following sizes:

- 18 x 18 pixels
- 32 x 32 pixels
- 72 x 72 pixels

10. Single-click the + (plus sign) in the center of the dotted box over "18 x 18px" and navigate to your 18 x 18 sized sub badge. Click *Open* to upload it.

11. Repeat Step 10 for the remaining "Base" badges. See Figure 12-4 for some examples.

12. Single-click the *3-Month* link to the right of the "Base" header, and repeat Steps 9–11. Do the same for the *6-Month* and *1 Year* options.

13. Single-click the *Save Changes* button to finish.

FIGURE 12-4:
Loyalty badges or *sub badges* designates how long someone in Chat has remained with a Channel. In SheSnaps' Channel, subscription length is measured by bacon and pizza.

Don't be afraid to brainstorm on what would like to use for emotes and badges. Maybe you want a *side-eye* emote as you give that often on stream. Do you blow your stack on stream when the game goes poorly for you? Why not a *rage* emote?

If you are into sports, why not use different kinds of sports balls as badges? Again, hop around the streams you follow and look at the emotes offered. You can then get an idea for what others are using and maybe find some inspirations of your own. To unlock more slots for emotes and badges, you will need to be a partner and earn subscriber points. The *Subscriber Emoticon Tiers* can be found at `https://help.twitch.tv/customer/portal/articles/2348985` and will probably motivate you to push for more subscribers to your Channel.

Now what about those subscribers? What makes them so special?

Showing support: Subscribers

Now that you have become an Affiliate, you are eligible to take on *subscribers*. These are people who not only follow you but also want to support your stream from a monetary point of view and are signing up to pay you a monthly fee. You have three levels of subscription you can offer your stream:

» $4.99/month

» $9.99/month

» $24.99/month

The three levels will all come with an emote, if you decide. If you decide to start off humbly and drop in only one emote for your starting $4.99 and that's it, you can do that. It's up to you to decide how you offer incentives, but consider that if you have a really smart emote, reserve that one for the higher levels. Strategy is key. Give incentive for people to subscribe, but make sure the higher levels offer something tantalizing.

REMEMBER

When you subscribe to a Twitch channel, you can make the re-upping process easy for yourself by setting the subscription to automatic renewal. At least, you can do that for *regular* subscriptions. Subscriptions made through *Twitch Prime* (part of your Amazon Prime account, if you have one) must be renewed manually.

Speaking of tantalizing, let's talk about the money earned. The more people you have subscribing to your channel, the closer you get to your payouts with Twitch, which happen either on a monthly basis within 45 days after the end of each calendar month, or when you finally crack $200 USD. 50% goes to Twitch; the other half goes to you. So the more subs you get, the more money you can earn with Twitch. Rather nice set-up when you think about it.

Other perks subscribers can earn on your Channel can include exclusive channels on your Discord where you can keep the conversation going, ad-free streams if hosts designate that it is a sub-only perk (reserved for Partners), and other privileges. More importantly, subs can help you generate revenue in order to purchase upgrades for your studio.

WARNING

There is a feature you will find under your Affiliate/Partner Settings called *Subscriber Only Chat* that limits your Chat window to subscribers and mods only. This is a great mode for your Channel if you are at the level of someone hosting thousands or hundreds of thousands of people in your Chat, and if you are playing a game that you would like to keep spoiler free or (unfortunately) if you are getting harassed. Some new streamers, though, believe if they make their Chat a subscription perk, it might generate revenue. It's a bold idea, but not a good idea. People want to interact with you before subbing to you, and making the Chat for your new stream a sub-only perk is presumptuous.

A penny for your thoughts: Bits

Subscriptions are not your sole stream of revenue on Twitch. There are also *bits*, which is Twitch currency that Chat can offer up to Affiliates (and Partners) during a stream. Bits roughly translate to a penny per bit, so if someone sends you 100 bits, you've just been tipped a dollar. Bits can be purchased through Twitch in a couple places. You can find them at the Bits menu that pops up on single-clicking the triangular icon found at the left of the Emotes icon. Or you can purchase bits at any time by single-clicking the *Get Bits* menu, shown in Figure 12-5, located at the top of your browser.

FIGURE 12-5:
You can purchase bits individually or in packages and then drop your favorite Twitch streamer some extra cash, one penny at a time.

But why would you give bits? Can't you give actual *tips* instead? Yes . . . and I will talk about tips in just a moment. Bits are a little different as, if you play around with virtual assistants and their various add-ons, they become another way to interact with the stream. Bits can trigger animations where emotes explode on the screen, or they can fill up virtual tip jars or glasses (seen on-screen), usually resulting in some sort of fun payout for Chat. Bits remain a popular option for Twitch streamers as Chat becomes, once again, part of the show.

Just the tip

While you are collecting revenue from subscriptions and from bits, it is good to know that subs and bitties all go through Twitch first. They need to take their percentage, of course, and therefore subs and bits tend to be seen by the streamer long after they have been gifted. *Tips,* on the other hand, are more direct ways of giving to a streamer. Tips are usually set up through a virtual assistant like Nightbot or Streamlabs and connected with a PayPal account. You send off a tip, and much like with a sub or bits, the Host gets an alert. Unlike subs and bits, tips go directly to the streamer and only PayPal takes a percentage. This is the most direct way to *financially* support a streamer, and many streamers earn a healthy revenue solely on tips. I stress "financially" as tips are not necessarily a way to make your stream grow. That happens with follows and subscriptions. Tips are simply a way for your Chat audience to express gratitude.

WARNING

This is where I say point blank, *"I am not an accountant,"* but when collecting this revenue, note that you are collecting money without any deductions for taxes. This means that, at the time of turning in your yearly income report to Uncle Sam, you are responsible for payment of both federal and state income taxes. If you find your Twitch Channel is performing well above and beyond your expectations, it might be a good idea to talk to an accountant about how to cover your taxes without getting slapped hard with penalties.

When I said at the beginning of this chapter that opportunities would open up, I was not kidding. Becoming an Affiliate Streamer is a big deal, and what success you achieve from here is really up to you. This is a first big step in an even larger realm of Twitch that, depending on who you talk to, is either an ultimate goal or an all-in-one-blessing-and-curse. Your next goal, at least as outlined by Twitch, is *Partnership.* Reaching Partnership is not easy, and hanging on to it can be even harder.

Achievement Unlocked: Partnership

The more you find out about being a Twitch Affiliate, the more you also find out about *Partnership*, something you've seen mentioned throughtout this chapter and this book. Already, you notice how new slots for emotes and badges remain locked, reserved for when you become a Twitch Partner. For streamers who have done their research before jumping into the platform, or maybe on seeing how things are a little different for Twitch Partners, partnership becomes a goal similar to landing a promotion at the day job, winning the fantasy football season, or landing two "Winner, Winner, Chicken Dinner" wins in *Player Unknown Battlegrounds*. Sure, Affiliate was a big deal. But now we're talking about Partnership.

How do things change?

Why become a Twitch Partner?

Peter Parker lives by the mantra *"with great power comes great responsibility,"* which makes his choice of mentors — Tony Stark — a little bit of a contradiction, but I digress. Becoming a Twitch Partner means you have achieved an even higher level of standing, based on dedication, hard work, and excellence in building your Community.

You have all the same perks as an Affiliate. You can have sub badges and emotes, you can accept bits, tips, and subscriptions. You get all the stuff you earned on reaching Affiliate, but with a few more bonuses:

>> **Advertising revenue.** Partners can, in order to generate income for their Channel, can run commercials running 30 seconds in length or up to 3 minutes in length. (More on this later in the chapter.)

>> **Ad control.** Partners have the ability to also decide if subscribers are excluded from ads. So, while new visitors and Followers watch an ad for an upcoming film or PSN's latest upcoming release, subscribers are treated to extra content from the host.

>> **User-controlled video quality.** Sometimes, Twitch Channels freeze. In some cases, the problem is coming from the source. Often times, it's the computer the viewers are on. The Internet is somewhat dodgy (Come on, McDonald's, step up your game!), or your computer's built-in video card cannot handle the incoming stream. Partners offer viewers the ability to scale back the video quality from the outgoing resolution to a lower one, making the job easier on your computer to bring you their Channel.

>> **More emotes and sub badges.** As we mentioned earlier, new slots are unlocked when Partnership is achieved. The more subscriptions you land, the more slots are unlocked for you to offer your Channel subs. Again, brainstorm on ideas for emotes. If success comes to you, you'll want to be ready.

>> **Longer archive time for past broadcasts.** By default, Twitch archives your past streams for 14 days before removing them from their server. Partners can keep their previous streams online for 60 days, giving you more time to download and archive them elsewhere.

>> **Larger payout.** Twitch Partners split revenues with Twitch at 70-30 as opposed to 50-50 with Affiliates. This is only after hitting and holding 500 sub points for two months, with less than 50% gifted. Partners at base get 50-50 on tier 1 subscribers, 60-40 on tier 2 and 70-30 on tier 3.

And then, of course, there is the coveted Partnership Badge, shown in Figure 12-6. There is a lot to celebrate when you reach this level. When you do, your Community along with other Twitch streamers celebrate with you.

FIGURE 12-6:
Tiddly (`http://twitch.tv/tiddly`) celebrated with her Channel at the sight of the Partnership Badge by her name. It had been a lot of hard work that paid off for her.

With the Achievements needed to become a Twitch Affiliate, you could easily be lulled into a sense of comfort that Partnership is a status easily reached. In the early years of Twitch, streamers did wonder how fair the system was, as there seemed to be no real consistency as to who got partnered and why?

Then, with a surge of popularity between 2015 and 2016, Twitch decided to refine the path to Partnership for new streamers. Being a Partner is a big deal, and now it's clear what you need to accomplish in order to be eligible for it.

The checklist for a Twitch Partner

Some streamers are still gobsmacked that they brandish the Partner badge. In 2017, Twitch announced at TwitchCon a revised, standard process for getting started on the platform, for achieving Twitch Affiliate, and finally for becoming eligible for Partnership.

Over a 30-day period, a Twitch streamer must meet the following requirements:

>> **Stream for 25 hours.** This is a notable jump from the modest 8 hours, but I did say hard work earlier, didn't I? Now, over a month's time, a streamer is expected to stream for 25 hours within a month. If you love it, this is easy.

>> **Stream for 12 different days.** Again, if you love it, streaming 12 different days over a 30-day period should be easy. Granted, schedules can get complicated, especially if you are busy on the weekends or you find yourself on vacation, but 12 days — once you find a groove — is easy.

>> **Average of 75 viewers over current hours streamed.** Here comes the achievement that could prove a challenge. 75 viewers on average, over hours streamed. Before thinking that a few well-timed Raids from influential streamers could get this accomplishment licked, think twice. Unlike the Affiliates achievement, where Hosts, Raids, Premieres, and Reruns all count towards your average viewership, these quick boosts are excluded from your 30-day average. This means facing a grind towards 75 viewers and maintaining it.

TIP

At the time of writing this, my average is roughly 4–5 viewers over 50 hours streamed in a 30-day period. Yes, I'm at barely 10% of this Achievement — the final Achievement — and I celebrated my one-year anniversary on Twitch in September. So what can I do? Honestly, the best thing to do is to keep going. What you should *not* do is quit, unless Twitch is no longer fun. You shouldn't be on Twitch simply to reach Partnership. It is a goal, but it shouldn't be the only reason you stream.

You may notice I am using a slightly different turn of phrase here: becoming *eligible* for Partnership. When I talk about reaching Affiliate, there is no question in becoming an Affiliate. You meet the requirements, you complete the onboarding process (which is a nicer way to refer to the paperwork you need to do), and then you can begin earning revenue. When you meet the requirements for Partnership, you must submit an application to Twitch and undergo a review process. There are no guarantees that Twitch will accept your application on the first attempt. Some Twitch streamers have met and maintained Partnership requirements only to be passed over for the promotion. The final decision for Partnership rests with Twitch, and these steps are simply achievements that make you eligible for it.

Show me the money: Revenue opportunities

Whether you've an Affiliate or Partnered Streamer, you may take a step back and wonder *"What's next?"* when it comes to additional streams of income. Twitch lends itself to promotion and awareness based on the nature of video. For years, marketing experts — particularly in the social media field — have encouraged businesses to invest more into video. Video can be dynamic, engaging, and eye-catching, depending on the production behind it, and analytics tend to back these claims. So yes, Twitch is not only a terrific platform for you to promote your passion or raise awareness for a cause, but Twitch is also a potential platform for advertisers.

This Twitch Stream is sponsored by . . .

When you are starting off, or even as an Affilate, you may have advertisements of all kinds appear at the beginning of your stream or when people tune into your Channel. These commercials are not for your benefit but for Twitch's. Once you are accepted as a Partner, though, you control whether or not you want to run ads at the beginning or end of your stream. Additionally, if you feel the need for a break from the stream, you can run ads while you are AFK (away from keyboard). You can also designate how long you want the ads to be and how long your overall commercial break lasts. The more ads that Partners run, the more revenue they generate for their Channel. This is why you'll hear Twitch streamers say, *"Remember these ads benefit the Channel, so please don't skip these ads."*

So, Chat, let me tell you about this amazing product from . . .

If you have solid gaming skills (iLulu), a unique angle on your stream (Aura), or an incredibly vibrant community (SheSnaps), you may be able to land product sponsorship for your stream. Each of the examples here did just that. iLulu (http://twitch.tv/ilulu) has sponsorship from Kontrol Freek (http://www.kontrolfreek.com) for those gamers who want a little more grip in their controllers. If you are a pet human for a for a four-legged friend of the canine variety, Aura (http://twitch.tv/aura) offers from BullyMake (http://bullymake.com) a wide variety of toys and treats for doggos of all kinds. And then there is SheSnaps (http://twitch.tv/SheSnaps) who can offer you a variety of gamer accessories from Steel Series (http://steelseries.com) to ScufGaming (http://scufgaming.com) to DXRacer (http://www.dxracer.com), just a few of the fine vendors who sponsor her stream.

POWERGPU'S HELP DESK: HAVE YOU TRIED TURNING IT OFF THEN TURNING IT BACK ON AGAIN?

Jese Martinez (http://twitch.tv/powergpu) is the name you hear often on Twitch when it comes to solving problem and creating solutions for streaming. Under his moniker of PowerGPU, Jese discovered an unexpected revenue stream for himself on Twitch. "When I was getting into streaming, I wanted to know how streaming actually worked. I'm one of these people that doesn't want to make a recommendation until I've done it myself. So I was on Twitter, watching people put out calls for help concerning this technical issue or that technical issue, and Twitch creators were getting advice of all kinds, all these different *'Have you tried . . .'* tweets, which just led to the content creator being frustrated. That was when I realized there was no one out there who was really dedicated to troubleshooting and resolving technical issues for streamers. I started helping content creators on stream, going for six-to-seven hours, tackling challenge on challenge, all free of charge. When I helped Myth (www.twitch.tv/tsm_myth), that was when things blew up. I took a risk, stopped streaming video games, and focused on troubleshooting, on computer building, and on support." PowerGPU now offers his services at affordable rates. "I've always been an entrepreneur, but I want to make sure that streamer can afford what I have to offer."

So if you can't find the solutions here or on my Sunday Specials where I open up my Chat for your questions, reach out to PowerGPU. Take it from the guy writing this book: He *knows* his Twitch.

Sponsorship can happen for Partners and Affiliates, but landing sponsors happens in a variety of ways. It can happen with a simple email request. Other times, it may mean putting together a full proposal with analytics, project plans, and strategies for community engagement and growth. On the most basic level, your email or proposal should cover these topics:

- » **The number of viewers** on average you reach.
- » **The demographic** of your audience.
- » **What is your stream about** and how does that appeal to the vendor's products?

Find a vendor that you think is in line with not only your audience, but your own beliefs, interests, and passions. Go on and make your pitch, and see if you strike out or knock it out of the park. You won't know if you have an opportunity unless you go on and give it a try.

Show me your SWAG!

You have a logo from your show. You have commissioned artwork that people quickly associate with your Channel. You have an account with Design by Hümans (www.designbyhumans.com). Guess what? You are only a few clicks away from show merchandise.

Tee shirts. Coffee mugs. Hoodies. Prints. Stickers. Depending on where you go to produce your promotional items, it's up to you where you want your brand to appear. So long as the quality of products produced are good (remember, this is a reflection of you and your stream), then go on and try out where you want your artwork to appear. You will probably not get rich from your merchandise, but when you see a fan wearing your logo on a tee shirt or a hoodie like the one pictured in Figure 12-7, it will make you smile.

FIGURE 12-7: Designed by TD0013 for Tee's stream and companion podcast, *Happy Hour from the Tower*, tee shirts sporting your brand are a great way to promote your show.

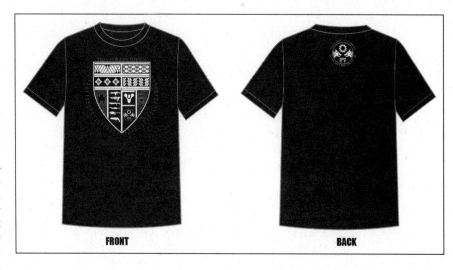

FRONT   BACK

Don't Quit Your Day Job Just Yet

Full-time streamers are something of a wonder. They are making a living — supporting families, making house payments, and continuing to upgrade their streaming rigs, for example — while playing video games, offering self-help advice, creating costumes, and pursuing other creative endeavors, all while the camera is live. It's inspiring, and when success comes your way, the idea of *"Yeah, I can go full time with this"* is very tempting.

Well, okay, let's take a step back and really consider this:

>> **Revenue from streaming does not come with deductions.** As mentioned earlier, federal and state taxes are not taken into account. Responsibility falls on the streamer to set aside those funds for taxes, and when the check arrives and bills are waiting to get paid, it's hard to remember that. It's also easy to play the *"I can set aside the next Twitch check for taxes"* card, but when the next Twitch check arrives, there will be new bills waiting to be taken care of. It's imperative to make sure deductions are set aside in order to avoid hefty penalties at tax time.

>> **Twitch numbers are not consistent.** One month, your numbers are up. Another month, your numbers are down. Gifted subscriptions from other streamers will not always renew their subscriptions. And Twitch Prime streamers may not renew. And for some loyal subs, the next month may mean putting their subscription to your channel on hold. (It bears repeating that Adulting can be really hard sometimes.) You can't count on your numbers to remain stable from month to month, and variations can affect on your Twitch take-home pay.

>> **Lack of security.** As volatile as the job market can be, this factor could be easily dismissed, but think about how fickle audiences can be. At the time of this writing, the building-battle-royale game *Fortnite* dominates the charts. The numbers and the attention the unassuming game has garnered is nothing to ignore, but how long will this last? And even if you are able to adapt your Channel to the next big game, will your audience stay with you? Similar to games, viewers come and go. Sure, you'll find loyal fans in your numbers and even make friends along the way, but will those loyal fans and friends be enough to keep you streaming full-time? Welcome to a full-time career in the Arts.

Make no mistake about what you are considering when making the jump to full time. You are entering an avenue of the entertainment industry. The same risks you are taking are not really all that different from musicians, actors, or artists of any medium planning to launch a full-time career. There is the "High Risk–High Reward" aspect to all this, sure, but there is also that elusive, lightning-in-a-bottle factor to keep in mind: luck.

DrLupo (`http://twitch.tv/drlupo`) does not mince words when it comes to his success. "I got lucky," he told me in an interview. "It was another day in *PUBG*, a well-placed grenade, and I killed Ninja. I joked, *'Wouldn't it be great if we squaded up together?'* Then Ninja contacted me. Then we ran Squads together, then we became friends, and then all this happened. You want to know what got me here? *Luck.*" While many (me included) would say that Lupo had a lot going for him — incredible gaming skills, innovative strategies, and insatiable curiosity over the limits of a game or gaming console — the Twitch superstar did have impeccable timing for emerging on the platform. Look at the circumstances: his joining of Twitch when he did; his stream of hacking a PS4, an Xbox, and one controller connecting both going viral; the arrival of *Fortnite*; his partnership with Ninja. To say that luck wasn't playing a little bit into DrLupo's success would be naïve.

Also, Lupo backs that. Luck and timing were on his side. I'm not saying that this sort of success can't happen to you as well, but a good month or two on Twitch is not a sign for you to pack it all in and go for a full-time career. Planning, preparation, and — especially if a family is involved — communication should happen before making that jump.

4

Beyond the Console

Use social media and community management to publicize your stream.

Get to know some rules and etiquette about Twitch.

Use Twitch for creative endeavors other than gaming.

Chapter **13**

Building Your Twitch Community

N ow that I have covered all aspects of the stream, from getting started to turning it into a side-hustle, we can look a little closer at that element of Twitch that can be easily taken for granted but should be appreciated every day: your audience.

When you hear Twitch streamers say *"I appreciate you . . ."* at the end of their streams, that is not some throw-away sentiment. (At least, not with the likes of streamers I have seen and been fortunate to meet.) Those three simple words are coming from the heart as there are hundreds of thousands of Twitch streamers currently online, all sharing with the world a favorite video game, a creative passion, or a stream of consciousness that might hopefully provide their audiences with some insight. When viewers show up and hang out with you, they have either stumbled upon you in a random search, following up on a recommendation, or may have met you at an event and want to see what you are all about.

Simply put, your audience is there because they *choose* to be there.

With people coming and going from your stream and regulars making small talk or undertaking a more active role in your stream, you as the host need to figure out how to let people know you are out there, streaming your heart out. How you interact with Chat sets the stage for your Community, but your cultivation of this growing audience of yours can't happen in Twitch alone. You have to look at other places where people can find out about your Channel.

Check Me Out Now: Publicizing Your Stream

With so much variety to choose from, how are people going to find you out there in the stream? With the likes of streamers such as Namaslays (http://twitch.tv/ namaslays), JSniperton (http://twitch.tv/jsniperton), JewelsVerne (http:// twitch.tv/jewelsverne), and Clyde (http://twitch.tv/gsxrclyde), how can you boost your signal without being overly hype-tastic?

Tooting your own horn when it comes to letting people know about you and your Channel is hard. It's not just all the extra work (which is easy to mitigate, provided you are smart about it), but it is also trying to walk a fine line between being just being you (or your persona) on Twitch and being a salesman constantly pushing your stream. *"Lemme tell ya, this baby can go for hours without a bio-break!"* Um . . . yeah-nah.

WARNING

I said this in Chapter 12 . . . and I'm going to say it here again: Going onto other Twitch Channels and telling others to follow you, or even saying *"Follow for Follow, my fellow Twitch streamer?"* is the fastest way of getting ignored, or even worse, banned. For more valuable etiquette tips in the Twitch Community, take a look at Chapter 14.

The good news is there are plenty of resources out there for you to tap into to help you publicize your Channel, help your Community grow, and still allow you to be yourself without de-evolving into that constant huckster who loves to talk over dinner about the importance of generosity but then disappears into the bathroom when the check arrives.

Don't be afraid. Let's hype.

Podcasting

Once again, we blur the lines between streaming and podcasting only to erase the divider altogether. *Podcasting*, I have found, is a massive outreach venue for streamers. If you have heard the term before but have never given it a go or only know podcasting from a consumer's perspective, podcasting is the delivery of media (audio, video, PDF, and so on) via RSS to computers and mobile devices alike.

Through apps like Apple's Podcasts app, Overcast, Stitcher, Google Play, and many others, media is either streamed or downloaded to your playback device of choice.

Now you may be shaking your head, thinking *"Are you kidding? Streaming is hard enough, and now you want me to learn how to* podcast?! *Faggedaboudit!"* But I got some good news: By streaming, you have already done the heavy lifting.

You might be surprised how easy it is to podcast now that you are streaming. For myself, I was already podcasting when I discovered streaming. I performed a quick upgrade to my recording studio (which involved downloading and installing OBS, and then investing into a few more webcams), and then *Happy Hour from the Tower* (`http://happyhourfromthetower.com`) offered a live component where Chat could easily interact with us (see Figure 13-1).

FIGURE 13-1:
The gaming podcast, Happy Hour from the Tower, now offers up a live component, thanks to Tee setting up his recording studio for streaming.

So how do we turn all this into a podcast? Here's one way to do it:

1. **Go to your Twitch account's drop menu and select the *Video Producer* option. Find your most recent stream and, as shown in Figure 13-1, select from the Options drop-down menu the *Download* option.**

2. **Using your video editor program of choice, open your recent stream and export the audio.**

   Apple's iMovie and Adobe Premiere Elements both can easily output the audio from an imported clip, usually a setting under an *Export* menu.

Other video editors offer this ability but go about it different ways. Check your application's documentation to find out how to export audio only.

3. **Launch iTunes and choose File ⇨ Add File to Library from the Menu bar.**

   Or you can press ⌘+O (Mac) or Ctrl+O (Windows). We are using iTunes as it is a free download and one of the most common of media players found online.

4. **Browse for the audio file you just created from your stream, then click Open.**

   Your file is now in the iTunes Library.

5. **Find the audio file in the iTunes Library and click to select it.**

6. **Choose File ⇨ Convert ⇨ Create MP3 Version.**

And there you have it. You have created a podcast episode. That's all there is to it.

Well, kinda.

There is a lot more to podcasting than just creating an MP3 file. There's finding a host server, ID3 tagging, and listing yourself in directories. But all that is quick-and-easy compared to the really hard part: content creation. That you have already done. If you decide podcasting is something you want to pursue, go on and pick up the latest edition of *Podcasting For Dummies* from John Wiley & Sons, written by Chuck Tomasi and some dude who has been podcasting for a long, *long* time. . . .

Twitter

While you would think that Facebook would be the social media platform where you would find your favorite Twitch streamers, *Twitter* (http://www.twitter.com) is a preferred method of notification, communication, and integration with streamers everywhere. Twitter is not *the* preferred method, but it is certainly a popular way to share highlights from the stream and make connections beyond Twitch's Chat stream.

If you recall in Chapter 3, your console has been connected to Twitter, and sends out a tweet to let people know you are online. Streaming on OBS, you can still use Twitter to let people know you are going live. You can also drop in tweets of photos from the stream, quick highlights (10 seconds to 1 minute in length — keep it brief as this is Twitter), and even run polls on a wide variety of topics. Twitter offers streamers a wide range of options to connect and cultivate a community around your stream. Watch how other streamers manage it, and see what Twitter can do for you.

One of the most common tweets I have seen from streamer to streamer, along with a *"I am going live"* tweet is the *"thank you"* tweet. The anatomy of a good "thank you" tweet is easy to follow, even though the tweet itself can be robust:

>> Thank people for watching.

>> Tag with Twitter handles anyone you may have played alongside.

>> If you raided someone, tag them in the post as well.

>> If space allows, mention when you will be on again.

For extra flair, as shown in Figure 13-2, add an animated GIF from Giphy (`http://www.giphy.com`) that fits the sentiment of your message.

FIGURE 13-2: Dropping a "Thank you" tweet is a nice way to let people both in your community and in other communities how much you appreciate their watching.

Instagram

It should come as no surprise that Instagram is another place where Twitch streamers find a place to promote their stream. Between the visual nature of the platform, the ability to upload quick video clips there, and the additional option of Stories, Instagram offers plenty of opportunities for you to market yourself and your stream.

One tactic to be aware of when it comes to Instagram is how to get images or video from external sources — whether it is a photo from someone else's camera, gameplay or a cool highlight you happened to download from Twitch, like the one in Figure 13-3. Instagram is all about being in the moment, which is why it can be somewhat difficult to get other images or video onto your feed. The media has to be on your phone. That's the rule.

FIGURE 13-3: Getting gameplay from your Twitch stream onto your Instagram may seem a little complicated, but this workflow quickly becomes second nature after a few postings.

Okay, fine.

Edit Profile

1. **Launch Instagram on your smartphone and tap the *Profile* option to jump to your Instagram Profile. Tap the *Edit Profile* button.**

2. **In the Website field, put the URL to your Twitch channel there.**

   While links are active in Instagram cross-posts to Facebook and Tumblr, URLs outside of your Profile's link are not active. Take advantage of your Instagram URL and send people back to your Twitch Channel.

3. **Tap *Done* in the top-right corner of the Instagram app to accept changes and return to Instagram.**

4. **Go to the device that has the desired media saved and find it in whatever gallery it is saved.**

5. **From here, look for the *Sharing* feature, different for every device. This will be the option that will allow you to send the media either via:**

- Airplay / Wireless File Transfer
- SMS Text Messaging
- Dropbox
- Email

Find the best method and send the image to yourself this way.

6. **Once the image appears in your smartphone's gallery, go into Instagram and select it.**

7. **Create a post as you would for Instagram, but make sure to add in the following action item in your accompanying post:**

"Click on the URL in my Instagram profile to join the stream. Follow or sub today, and get notifications for when I go live!"

This workflow will feel a bit clunky at first, but the more you use it, the more second-nature it will become. Instagram is a popular and powerful platform for streamers, so make sure to take advantage of it and work it into your promotional machine.

WARNING

Hashtags — keywords used to help increase your visibility and discoverability in searches and feeds — have become something of a source of contention in social media. When there are more hashtags than actual content in a post, the keywords become something like SPAM Nouveau and junks up the whole look of the post. It may also land you false hits of bots programed to like your post or people liking your post but uninterested in actually supporting your content. If you are in it for the analytics, then have a go, but Instagram has been talking about cracking down on spamming hashtags. Best to practice quality over quality.

TIP

With Instagram, you have the ability to cross-post to other platforms like Facebook and Tumblr. Do so. This is a great way to keep your signal strong. Or if you want to take advantage of Facebook, do so. Make sure your YouTube Channel features a highlight reel that points back to your Twitch Channel. The wider a net you cast, the more visibility you have for your stream. Granted, more platforms means more work for you, so make sure you can easily manage the promotional pushing.

And remember, Twitch is supposed to be fun. Don't ever forget that.

Who Is "The Fam" and Why Do They Matter?

They go by many names. The Fam. Street Team. Chat. Some streamers give their own unique names for them. The Pit. Legendaries. Photobombers. Adorabullets. The Monsters. No matter what you call them or how you address them, they are there in your stream, fixtures to your Twitch like Cliff and Norm at the *Cheers* pub in Boston. This is your *Community* (yes, with a capital "C"), and these are the people and the atmosphere you build around your Channel to let people know what kind of stream this is, what people can expect from the host, and what in store on this Channel for the next few hours.

To grow a Twitch Channel, you are going to want to grow your Community. This means multitasking and connecting with your Chat. Easy, right?

Well . . .

Oh, hai, Mark: Talking to Chat

It is an art form, if not a superpower of some kind, how some streamers are able to work on costume fixtures, play video games, or maintain a train of thought while talking to Chat.

However, that is one way I judge the value of a stream.

Of course, the ability for some streamers to talk to their Chat while in-game depends greatly on the game being played, the amount of viewers in the stream, and the multitasking talents of the stream's host. It will be a lot harder for TheTrueVanguard (http://twitch.tv/thetruevanguard) to acknowledge you when he has hundreds on hundreds viewers versus PodsOfWar (http://twitch.tv/podsofwar) who has a modest 40 viewers in her stream. And while Pods has fewer people watching, she's playing *Fortnite,* which requires a lot of attention and focus in-game. Attempt to multitask, and you may find yourself in the crosshairs of a purple sniper rifle.

There are times and places, even in the most involved games, where you can reach out to your Chat and let them know you see them, and we cover them in Chapter 10. The more you stream and the more familiar you get with a game, the easier it will be for you to interact with Chat as well as riff off what is happening on screen. Streamers achieve this feat with lots and lots *and lots* of practice. They make inter-action look easy.

So it is equally important to pay attention to what's happening on stream. Read the signs of when it's a good time to engage and when it isn't.

Kinda busy right now: When not to engage

It doesn't matter if you are the host of a Channel or visiting a Channel, there are going to be those times in-game where you really cannot expect engagement. While admirable to want to talk to everyone that comes to your Chat, games are meant to grab your attention and demand 100% of it.

A few places where it isn't a good time to talk to your Chat would be . . .

>> **During story mode or cut scenes.** Whether first-time playthrough or during a second or third go-round, cut scenes are usually breaks in the action that allow you to catch your breath, but they may also be offering clues and important facts needed for upcoming challenges. Also, if the audience is as wrapped up in the story as the Channel host, calling out for attention may come across as a bit selfish. Watch the Channel host and take your cue from them about whether or not now is a good time to engage.

>> **During first playthrough.** Speaking of *first playthroughs,* which is when a host is tackling a game fresh out-of-the-box and going in with no prior knowledge of it, some hosts may get focused on the game and trying to master it. Always check the title or the Chat to see if this is, in fact, a first playthrough. Cut the host a break and let them discover this new world with few interruptions. Wise-cracking, however, is strongly encouraged.

WARNING

You might notice in the Chat Rules or on the Channel Page a "No Spoilers" clause. This doesn't just apply for favorite television shows (like that the Litch King resurrects and recruits one of Daenerys' dragons) or for recent movies (Spider-Man, Black Panther, Dr. Strange, and all of the Guardians of the Galaxy are eliminated by Thanos' snap), but it also applies to games as well. Like how in *Detroit: Become Human*, you can make Connor . . . oh no, I'm not going to reveal that. (Only a real twerp would do that.) Especially during first play-throughs, keep a lid on spoilers. Don't be *that* guy.

>> **During intense battle sequences or intricate designs.** Whether you are playing PVP of *Battlefield V,* executing a raid in *Destiny,* or facing off a boss in *Bloodborne,* you are expecting a lot from a host if you are posting *"Why don't you say 'hi' to me?!"* over and over again in Chat. As a host, you are expecting a lot more from yourself when you choose to engage at this point. Same goes for when you are on the Creative stream and working with power tools. Cool as it would be to see someone take off a finger with a Dremel, it is the fastest way to end a stream. Let the host tend to what they need to do, and again, read the host to see if they are engaging with Chat.

>> **When the host is working with others.** Group activities like *Dungeons & Dragons*, MMOs, or interviews and panels can be hard to acknowledge and interact with Chat. If you have a team leader calling out commands, a dungeon master setting a stage, or a moderator taking questions from Chat, you don't want a random *"Hey, QuirkyBacon77, welcome to the stream!"* disrupting the flow of things. Watch Chat for textual responses, if possible, but with group activities, it is no longer a single host's stream. Keep that in mind.

Many of these settings rely on the host and their own comfort level in multitasking. Trust your mods in making sure that your Chat is still moving forward and can speak for you when you can't. If you are visiting another Channel, watch the host to see if there is interaction or not. Constantly posting the same message to grab someone's attention doesn't really work, and if you do get the host's attention, it may not be the attention you want. Always take a moment to see what's happening in Chat and in-game. See if the time is right.

The Fam includes other streamers too

Competition between streams is omnipresent always. Let's be honest, and I mean brutally honest, if I am online at the same time as JamesWerk, Tessachka, Ashnichrist, or DrLupo, I am competing for viewers. Viewers have to choose where their attention will go, and sometimes I win. Sometimes, I don't. Heck, probably most times in a scenario like the one I created above, I *never* win. That is just the nature of streaming entertainment.

This competition, while always there in the background, is not fierce, at least, in the circles I've travelled in. To the contrary, other streamers are part of that Community you're building.

In the time I have started streaming on a regular basis, other streamers like Aura, ZG Photo, OneActual, and JSniperton have all taken an active role in my Channel. It could have been in a raid. It could have been paying a visit and saying "hello" in Chat. It could have been talking about my stream on their stream, offering constructive feedback or kudos for a fun time. The "competition" can be an important part of your Community, provided you are also taking on a positive role in their communities. It's a pretty amazing experience to see people you look up to in the Twitch Community take a part in your Channel. This participation comes from a sincere wish to participate in the fun, to be a part of what is happening on your Channel. That is a great feeling to engender and cultivate.

So when a streamer swings by your Channel and hangs out, make sure to say "Hi" and have a shout-out at the ready. They are there because they *want* to be there, and this time *they* are cheering *you* on.

Take my word for it: That's a pretty cool thing to have happen.

Remembering your roots

Success on Twitch can be a real roller coaster, and when I mean roller coaster, I'm not talking about the classic wooden roller coaster of Coney Island. No, I'm talking about *The Intimidator 305* of King's Dominion where you are dropping straight down, struggling to catch your breath as you plummet 300 feet and reach speeds up to 90 miles per hour and you are white-knuckled while pulling 5Gs during the longest three minutes of your life. *That* kind of roller coaster.

The Community Board: Discord

As you have been watching others stream, and as you have heard mentioned since Chapter 6, *Discord* is a preferred platform by some Twitch hosts, using the app for their game Chat as it offers better connections and better audio quality. It is another app that you should have on your phone . . . and on your tablet . . . and pretty much everything that you got that an app can run on.

But what exactly *is* Discord?

Discord provides a one-stop shop for gamers, streamers, and many others. You can post URLs into *channels,* which are topic-specific Chat streams. You can set up private audio channels and host open Chat, gaming sessions, or interviews for podcasts and streams. You also can set up certain Discord channels to be subscriber-only (another perk in being a subscriber), and you can even use Twitch emotes in Discord, provided you are a subscriber.

Back in Chapter 6, we set up Discord to serve as our audio Chat client on when you went live. Then we turned to Discord again in Chapter 7 for enabling Notifications. Now let's go into what it was made for: connecting with people.

1. **Launch Discord.**

2. **In the left-hand side of the Discord window, find the icon you created for your Server and single-click it. Here you will find in your server your text and voice *channels*. Under *Text Channels*, click on the *Add Channel* option (a large + sign located to the right of the Text Channels label) to create a new channel.**

   Channels are dedicated topics that you want to share with your followers and subscribers. Here are a few ideas for what you could have for channels:

   - Food

   - Highlight Reel

- Movies

- Sports

- Books

This is one of the best attributes of Discord. It offers you the ability to sort and organize your interests.

3. **In the Create Text Channel window, go on and label your new channel a topic relevant to your interests, and make sure the Channel Type is *Text Channel*. Leave the Private Channel option turned off.**

4. **Single-click the *Create Channel* button.**

5. **Repeat Steps 2–4 to create other channels of interest.**

6. **Right-click on the *TEXT CHANNELS* header and select the *Edit Category* option.**

7. **Give the Text Channels category the new title of *Main Channels* in the Category Name field. Single-click the green *Save* button.**

8. **Click-and-drag the channels of your Discord Server into their appropriate categories (see Figure 13-4).**

FIGURE 13-4: Categories help organize your Discord Server, assisting visitors in finding quickly what they want to talk about.

Your Discord is now live with channels available to everyone, a hub where followers, subscribers, and people who are completely new to you and your stream can take part of the conversation. All anyone needs to join your Discord is to have a URL and their own app.

Share with the class: Talking to your Chat

Now what about making a post? Let's say you have a wicked good clip you want to share on my #greatest-hits channel. How would we go about doing this?

1. **Go to** http://youtube.com **and look for a clip you exported recently of a "play of the game" you want to share.**

For a quick review on sending clips from Twitch to YouTube, check out Chapter 4.

2. **At the YouTube link, single-click the** *Share* **option. From the window, single-click the** *Copy* **option. Look for a notification at the bottom-left of the browser window.**

3. **Return to the Discord app and single-click on a Server's icon. Find the channel where you want to make a post.**

The various Servers you subscribe to will appear in a smaller window running along the left-hand side of the app.

TIP

Take a closer look at Figures 13-4 and 13-5. You will see small alerts by the Servers' icons. Those are the number of new messages waiting for you to review in those Servers.

4. **Single-click the channel you want to post in, and in the "Message [#name-of-channel]" field, enter in an accompanying message followed by the copied YouTube link.**

5. **Hit the** *Enter* **key.**

Pictured in Figure 13-5, your message and accompanying URL are posted in the channel. A preview is rendered of the link, and you can either watch the clip in Discord or click on a provided link to go to YouTube. Discord supports several kinds of media:

>> URLs

>> JPG and PNG images

>> Animated GIFs

>> MP3 files

>> M4V and MP4 files

>> Emojis and Emotes

WARNING

Discord will not upload any media files larger than 8MB in size.

One-on-one: Direct messages in Discord

Looking at your list of Servers again, you might notice the "Home" icon (the Discord logo) at the very top. If you single-click on this icon, you will see three additional sections of Discord:

>> **Activity:** News concerning favorite games of friends in your Discord network appears here. You can follow these alerts and announcements to other servers that could be of interest to you, or bring you up to speed on the latest development in your favorite games.

>> **Friends:** On Discord, you have the option to make even more direct connections between yourself and your Twitch regulars. You can still send open messages to people in your Server without being "friends," but with this distinction, you can host audio or video calls, or send private messages between one another.

>> **Direct messages:** Earlier, I showed you how to make a post on a Discord channel. Those channels are public unless you deem otherwise. You can make a *private channel* where you can limit who sees content there. But for direct conversation with one person, you use direct messages to swap media and messages, as well as audio and video calls, between one another.

Sending direct messages between friends is pretty straight-forward on Discord. (All the hard stuff is in your rear view mirror.)

1. **Where you see the *field Find or Start a Conversation* at the top left of the Discord app, enter in the name of someone you know in Discord; or go to your *Friends* list and right-click on any of your connections and select the *Message* icon.**

2. **At the bottom of the app where you see *"Message @[Discord Name]"* in the field, type your message out and then hit the *Enter* key.**

3. **Hold your conversation.**

You can always click on the friend appearing in the Direct Messages section to reference previous private conversations. Everything in this section happens between you and your connection. Sometimes, depending on the subject you want to talk about, privacy is needed.

There is a lot you can do with Discord, and it is a great place to build on your Twitch Community. You are free of the game or creative project, and here, it is more about getting to know those folks coming by your stream. The interaction ramps up on Discord, and it is important that you reach out and make time for numerous opportunities to turn your Twitch Community into something stronger.

Chapter **14**

Twitch Etiquette

My intent with this book is to be way more than just a *"Hey, here's how we stream on Twitch . . ."* book. As another friend from the platform, Chavez (http://twitch.tv/bachavez), put it, *"This would be my book on Twitch — Hit the Share button, hit Broadcast Gameplay, and you're streaming!"*

That would be a short book. Even with a lot of pictures.

Sure, it's not hard to stream, but there is a *lot* to Twitch. Beyond sharing what you love, this platform is about people and about managing people. That may sound a little cold as I have met some truly wonderful people here. Yet when you are hosting your own stream and trying to keep control of those who are watching and those who are taking part in it, you the host are in charge. This is your Channel, your show. You need to take care of it.

And it's always good to practice to other streamers how you yourself would like to be treated in your stream.

That's part of my intent with this book: This is a guide to being not only a solid streamer but a welcomed presence in other streams.

Don't Let the Door Hit You on the Way Out: Bad Behavior on Twitch

If I were to tell you, *"Everyone on Twitch is just overflowing with awesome . . ."* then I should also add that all of us on Twitch ride unicorns to work and barf rainbows. It's a nice fantasy to think we exist in a perfect world on Twitch, but let's be honest: There are some really nasty people out in the world and online. Sooner or later, these people will find you and your stream.

Many of the bad people you will come across on Twitch, fortunately, are easily categorized. The way you deal with them can sometimes be tricky, though, or creative, depending on your approach. The most frustrating thing about what people do to find themselves no longer welcomed to a Twitch Channel is that many of these infractions can be easily avoided. In some instances, it can just be a matter of common sense.

Other times, you just have to buckle up and brace for impact.

"Yo, check out my stream . . ."

In the previous chapter, I cover every conceivable way of promoting your stream. Except one. This approach to someone else's stream completely befuddles me, but it happens. Every. Single. Day. And I wish I knew where these idiots got this "tip" as a "great way to promote your stream and gain followers" so I could go up to that wellspring of misinformation and punch them in the throat.

I'm ranting — sorry, talking — about the ill-conceived approach of promoting your stream in someone else's Chat.

> *"Hey, TheTeeMonster, go on and follow my stream at http://twitch.tv/ arandogaming and I'll follow you back!"*

The message may be worded differently, or it may just be the link all by itself, but there is no reason whatsoever to do this on anyone's stream.

REMEMBER

The difference between blatant self-promotion and a shout-out is the shout-out comes from the host, either encouraged by the host directly or by the interaction and involvement of the streamer with the host.

Unwarranted, unwelcome self-promotion doesn't work. Never has. Never will. Many streamers attempting this usually are running down a directory, simply dropping the same message or link and moving on to the next unsuspecting streamer. This doesn't count as networking or a promotion, but it does count as a short cut to getting banned from a Channel.

WARNING

Sometimes, something as innocent as asking another streamer visiting another's Channel, *"How was your stream?"* could be misconstrued as promoting another's stream without consent. Sure, you may not mean any harm by it, but the host or their mods have no idea if you are two random visitors working as a "street team" for another streamer. To avoid any miscommunication or misunderstanding, keep talk of other streams out of Chat unless the host instigates.

They see me trollin' and hatin' . . .

No, it doesn't make a lot of sense when people pop into a stream about *Destiny, Fortnite, Overwatch,* or some other game, and they say something like *"People still play this game?"* Well, if you're in a specific Game Directory, yes, people are still playing this game. Nice hook there, Marty. Thanks for stopping by.

Or maybe you're playing a game, having a good day based on your own skillset, until god-players seem to creep out of the woodwork and make comments like *"You're trash at this game . . ."* which is easy to claim when you are *watching* and not *playing* said game. But hey, everyone needs an armchair quarterback, especially when they are busy hanging out on Twitch. Appreciate the critique, Sparky.

Then you have those even-more charming individuals who think saying the same thing over and over AND OVER AGAIN . . . and one more time for good measure . . . are making a contribution of some degree to your stream. Either that or they are trying to get your attention as if the fate of the free world may depend on it. Meanwhile, the free world can see you are neck deep in Vex as you are attempting to finish a Prestige Eater of Worlds. Still, this individual wants to talk to you. NOW.

Ah, yes, welcome to the wonderful world of Internet trolls.

The mission of a troll is a simple one: Rattle the host, derail the flow, and yank the rug out from under you. It's your mission — should you choose to accept it — to succeed in scoring what trolls hate the most in losing: the last word. There are several ways you can do this:

1. **Go to your Chat window and enter in the following command:**

```
/timeout ((username))
```

This command will silence the offending troll for ten minutes. Your mods also have this ability to time out offensive visitors to your Chat. If you wish to make the offense less severe, add [seconds] to the command to make the offense last one second, or ten seconds, just as a warning.

The timeout command can also be activated by single-clicking on the clock icon, seen in Figure 14-1 to the left of the username in your Chat window.

2. **If the offensive chatter returns, go to your Chat window and enter in the following command:**

`/ban ((username))`

While a time out gives people a second chance, the ban permanently prevents the offender from being able to Chat in your Channel (but they can still view). To restore membership to a channel, the host or mods must lift the ban. As shown in Figure 14-1, you can also ban a user with a single click of the ban icon (if available) to the left of the offender's username.

Some trolls may establish a new user profile under a different name and return to your channel to pick up where they left off.

FIGURE 14-1:
Twitch's Chat windows allows hosts to ban or timeout anyone in Chat if they are making you or your Community uncomfortable.

3. **If you wish to send a message to Twitch about the offender, click on the offender's name. Click on the Options menu (the three vertical dots) and select the *Report ((Username))* option. Then click on the icon of the minus sign inside a speech bubble and block the user.**

The important thing to remember about trolls is that *you* are to get in the last word, not vice versa. As you have heard repeatedly throughout the book, this is *your* stream. No matter how nasty a troll's intent is, your mods are watching out for you. If you are able to manage the Chat, you can easily shut things down. Don't hesitate to do so.

TIDDLY'S ADOPT-A-TROLL

While I am a big proponent of zero tolerance for trolls, one streamer has taken the game of one-upmanship to a whole new level.

Tiddly (http://twitch.tv/tiddly) makes it a point to focus on the fun in streaming. Make no mistake: She's an excellent gamer, running with some of the best players out there, but her stream is less about the hardcore strats and more about the ridiculous fun one can have playing video games. Her laugh, her smile, and her overall positive attitude are infectious. She is an absolute delight . . . which makes her a prime target for trolls. When these folks stray into her Chat and try to throw her off, Tiddly turns the tables on them and unleashes her Chat — whom she has dubbed the "Adorabullets" — and she asks her Chat if, based on the creativity of the troll's insults, the troll is a keeper or if they are banned from Chat. If the insults devolve into something base and crude (as it happens most of the time), Tiddly "doth smite them verily with her ban hammer, Mew-Mew." But on occasion, trolls are "adopted" into the Chat. "I have made a few friends in Chat this way, some of them still popping into Chat to say 'Hi' and hang out. It's easy to drop the ban hammer, but sometimes a little kindness can go a long way. It might even turn things around for a troll."

Your mileage may vary in handling trolls in such a fashion. I'd recommend swinging by Tiddly's stream and watch her handle trolls in real time. Try and see if you can master the magic that she has down to an art form. But fair warning: After visiting Tiddly's stream, your face might hurt from all the smiling she evokes out of you.

Hate speech

Beyond the trolls described in the preceding section are another group of haters that say things they would never be brave enough to say to you in public. Behind a keyboard and monitor, there is a lot of swagger and swearing, and even though you have it clear in your rules that you really don't want that sort of talk in your stream, these Chatters somehow think of themselves exempt of the rules.

"Ugh, this game is AIDS." (Um, no, it's not. It's just a bad game.)

"I hope you get cancer." (Considering how many friends I have lost to cancer, you really want to rethink that insult, me boy-o.)

"What are you? Some kind of fa—" (Okay, I think game time is done for you, Mr. Congeniality.)

This kind of toxic talk will wind up in your stream, and there is no real standard trigger for it. Sometimes, people think they are being clever. Other times, people might be quoting movies, thinking they are being clever, when out of context, the quote is just wrong. Sometimes, people are looking to start something. Hate speech is up to you to manage. Preferably, the best way to manage these corrosive personalities is towards the nearest exit.

This is why we have the rules of Chat, which I discuss back in Chapter 3. These rules are to make sure that people new to your Channel know boundaries. Other streamers may be more liberal when it comes to what they do and don't allow, and that is their business. It doesn't have to be yours. What happens on your stream falls under your standards. Make sure to stick by them and adhere to them.

Making a Music Bed for Your Channel

Something I have always found really, really, cool about Twitch is the soundtrack behind the streamers, and how each channel sets its own atmosphere. Some people offer up their stream to viewers for song requests, but many just fire up Spotify and let the tunes flow. Some streamers play a variety of songs, a few gems that maybe you forgot about from your college days. Other streamers will also play some electronica or the latest from a new artist that you might want to pick up after the stream is over and done. Yeah, sometimes the music these streamers are gaming to is slick. Pretty cool how they have permission to do that.

Oh wait, my technical editor is whispering something in my ear. Wait, what do you mean by *"Streamers don't have permission to play any of that music off Spotify?"*

I have been involved in music for a good portion of my life, and I appreciate and respect the power of music. Of course, if you've got some sweet trance playing in the background or some chill jazz as your bed music when hosting non-gaming stream, it adds a new dimension to things.

However, I also appreciate the law.

WARNING

I want to make this clear as polished crystal: I am *not* a lawyer. I'm a creator of original and (hopefully) entertaining content. Based on my history in podcasting and social media, I am familiar with the law on certain matters so that I understand what I'm talking about, but being familiar with certain laws does not make me a lawyer. I can tell you about the law and can give a few simple definitions of it, but I am *not* giving out legal advice. If you need legal counsel on a matter concerning your stream — whether it concerns the First Amendment, copyright issues, or slander — please consult an actual lawyer versed in the matters that you need dealt with.

The Big Three of content management

The government still regards the Internet even today as a digital Wild West, an unknown territory that's avoided regulation for many years, granting those who use it a true, self-governed entity where ideas, cultures, and concepts can be expressed without any filtering or editing, unless it comes from the users themselves. With the repeal of net neutrality, though, the Internet is now very much a hot bed of contention. The idea of *"Hey, we're online and we can do whatever we want!"* is no longer applicable.

The following organizations all have influence on the destiny of online content creation, and it's only going to benefit you as a streamer to understand how their legislation, activities, and actions are going to affect you.

The Federal Communications Commission (FCC)

The Federal Communications Commission, or FCC (www.fcc.gov), is the watchdog of anything and everything that gets out to the public via mass communications. The FCC keeps an eye on technology development, monopolies in the telecommunications industry, and regulating standards for telecommunications in the United States and its territories. They are most commonly known for enforcing decency laws on television and AM/FM radio.

The FCC can't regulate what is said online (yet) because it doesn't consider the Internet a major broadcasting medium. With the growing popularity of Twitch among mainstream personalities, the emergence of eSports, and the rising profile of popular streamers, it may not be long before the law catches up with technology.

The Recording Industry Association of America (RIAA)

Some Internet history for you: Sean Fanning was a clever guy who came up with a cool platform called Napster, originally designed to share files but became a haven for music being uploaded and downloaded without regulation. Fanning lost his battle against the Recording Industry Association of America (or the RIAA, found at www.riaa.com) after contesting that his file-sharing application in no way infringed on copyright laws and not promoting music piracy. The RIAA continues to protect property rights of its members — as well as review new and pending laws, regulations, and policies at the state and federal level.

The RIAA have a definite say as to why you cannot use Spotify for your stream: It's not your music. Sure, you purchased that album from iTunes, but the music you listen to is under the condition that you use it *for listening purposes only*. This is the "grey area" where streamers tend to reside in this issue as they are just listening to the music . . . but when previous streams are archived or highlight reels are created — unless you're granted licenses and you pay fees to the record labels and artists — you're in copyright violation when playing music without permission.

Creative Commons (CC)

One workaround is to work with independent musicians (and there are *plenty* who stream on Twitch) that might offer up to you their music to use on your stream. It's okay to use their music as their music is being released under a *Creative Commons* license. Founded in 2001, Creative Commons (http://creativecommons.org) is a nonprofit corporation dedicated to helping the artist, the copyrighted material, and the individual who wants to use copyrighted material in a constructive manner.

This complications within the digital copyright and the desire to exchange original creations (music, art, photography, audio drama, etc.) online brought about Creative Commons, shown in Figure 14-2. It's dedicated to drafting and implementing via the Internet licenses granting fair use of copyrighted material.

Creative Commons licenses are made up of permission fields:

>> **Attribution:** Grants permission for copying, distribution, display, and performance of the original work and derivative works inspired from it, provided credit to the artist(s) is given.

>> **Noncommercial:** Grants permission for copying, distribution, display, and performance of the original work and derivative works inspired from it *for noncommercial purposes only.*

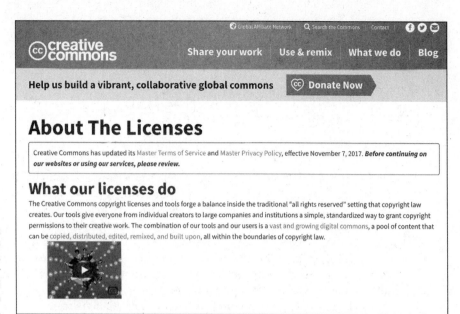

FIGURE 14-2:
Creative Commons offers free licenses for use of original content in podcasting.

>> **No Derivative Works:** Grants permission for copying, distribution, display, and performance of the original work only. No derivative works are covered in this license category.

>> **Share Alike:** Grants reproduction of the original work and also allows derivative works *if* they are also released under a similar Creative Commons license.

Creative Commons offers up details, examples, and an FAQ page that answers questions concerning the granting of licenses for use of protected content. Just on the off-chance you don't find your answer there, contact information for its representatives is also provided. This is a good group to be familiar with and can open opportunities for you with new and innovative ideas and works in your stream.

The grey area: Twitch, Spotify, and the Compromise

With an understanding of how copyrights work and the people who enforce them or offer you options, that doesn't change the fact that Twitch streams are letting Spotify set the tone for their stream. How are they getting away with this?

The wiggle room where Twitch, Spotify, the RIAA, and artists (on a whole, not all, mind you) agree on is that the gamers are simply listening to their own music instead of the soundtrack provided by the game (which Twitch and streamers are allowed to play as it is part of the game featured). That's fine, provided . . .

>> The music is played softly, strictly as background music.

>> The host is talking over the music.

>> The music is not the focus of the discussion.

Even if there are lapses in this casual agreement or understanding, depending on how you look at it, you can play your Spotify mix — even share the tracks you're listening to through specific *widgets* that Twitch and various overlay templates from Streamlabs — without any fear of repercussions. It is when you offer up your freshly-made content as a rerun or a *VOD* (video-on-demand) where Twitch steps in with algorithms that looks for protected pieces and drops the audio out. Twitch even flags the video with a tag saying there is "muted audio" in the clip, and on replaying the stream or clip, the muted audio is highlighted in red, as shown in Figure 14-3. Once the protected song ends, audio is restored. This is how Twitch and the music industry work together to allow streamers to listen to what they like while honoring copyright laws.

FIGURE 14-3:
When copyrighted audio is clearly audible in the background, Twitch mutes your recorded stream for the length of that particular song, give or take a few minutes.

Keep in mind that when Twitch drops the audio from your archived stream, it's all the audio, including whatever you are talking about. So take note about what you're talking about in that segment in case you want to repeat what it is you are talking about in that moment.

If you are comfortable with the compromise, you can stream under these conditions, but as I discovered when streaming with Spotify in the background, the protected music — at the time of writing this book — seems somewhat random. My D&D stream went through a "muting period" for one track while my two-and-a-half hour talk show experienced no violations whatsoever. It's a roll of the dice — pun completely and unashamedly intended — when and for how long your Twitch stream will go muted, but as this occurs, maybe you're not too concerned about VODs or repeats. And while you walk this line with the RIAA, artists can always hold broadcasters accountable under the DMCA, the Digital Millennium Copyright Act. If this happens, Twitch will carry out a minor punishment for the first offense, going into more stringent penalties for more offenses. Still, it's good to be aware of how the relationship between Twitch, the music industry, and artists stands at the writing of this book.

This relationship could change. At any time.

I'll Take the First: Free Speech versus Slander

Words carry weight. Sometimes, those toxic souls on Twitch, sometimes in Chat and sometimes on camera, either forget this or simply disregard the power behind what they say and do. When working live, words spoken in the heat of the moment or off the cuff can (potentially, at least) get you into a world of trouble and unwanted attention. Again, I'm not a lawyer, but let's review the legal definition of *slander: a verbal form of defamation, or spoken words that falsely and negatively reflect on one's reputation.*

So where does Twitch fit into all this? Twitch, like any platform on the Internet, be it podcasting, blogging, or any other social media, is a make and manner of a public space. Think about it: Before you open your mouth and begin a slam-fest on someone you don't like or go on a personal attack of someone you work alongside, remember that your little rant is reaching a *worldwide* audience. Don't ever assume that "nobody's watching," as your numbers can change in the blink of an eye. It doesn't take but a moment *before* you open your mouth to speak to really think about what's on the tip of your forked tongue. The best hard rule about trash talking of any kind — whether it is about a streamer or someone appearing in mainstream media — is to keep others names out of your mouth unless you are talking about these people in a positive light. Trashing others may attract attention, sure, but it's the kind of attention you will not want. The possibility of long term success coming from toxic chatter doesn't happen.

Keep it positive. If it isn't, keep it to yourself.

Family Matters

The discussion of Twitch etiquette includes a serious matter that should be at the top of your list of considerations before you stream, before you set a schedule, and before you *add* to that schedule. A stream is hard work if you are just starting off. You're trying to keep that Twitch time of yours so hard that people can set their smartwatches of choice by it. But hey, you know what, this is *your* time. Whether after work or first thing in the morning, your time in game, on your creative passion, or otherwise, you have no one to answer to but to yourself. . . .

That is, unless, you have a family. Not the "Twitch Fam" but your sharing-the-same-roof family. Don't kid yourself: They have a say in how your Twitch stream will run.

The significant other

I'm going to wager your significant other is going to be the one threatening to pull the router out of the wall if you don't shut things down and take out the recycling. If you feel like you're having difficulty explaining to that life partner exactly why Twitch matters, here are a few pointers:

>> If your partner tells you your child has a concert on the night you stream, you go to the concert. (Have a lighter ready for when they rock their triangle solo.)

>> If the kitchen needs to be cleaned as company is coming the next night, you're going to have that kitchen prepped for surgery.

>> If your significant other wants to watch *Thor: Ragnarök* for the tenth time because Taika Waititi is BAE, then start popping some popcorn.

>> If that important somebody had a bad day at the office and wants to talk to you about it, call it a night with Twitch. Your significant other needs to talk.

See where I'm going with this?

Even my own wife has sat down with me and had serious conversations about Twitch. Sure, she supports me in this passion of mine, but she reminds me of what matters: mainly, our relationship.

"I don't have a problem with streaming, and I don't have a problem with Tee gaming," Philippa "Pip" Ballantine, the aforementioned wife told me. "If I did have a concern, it is with that life balance. I'm okay with Tee streaming because he obviously enjoys it. There's a real community around it, and he is fostering friendships within it."

That doesn't mean Pip completely lets me stream without some policing. She calls herself the "bad cop," but to be fair, "I worry that Tee burns the candle at both ends. He's a writer. His job has its own high-end demands. He's a podcaster. And he makes time for exercise. There's only so many hours in the day."

So when the discussion of a schedule comes up, Pip asks for flexibility. "When you are a twenty-something single gamer, Twitch can be easy. When you are a father or a mother, husband or wife, it's different. You need to be able to have some flexibility when life kicks in." She agrees that without an open channel between me and her, streaming would be harder. "You need to have communication so you know what the expectations and concerns are."

Communication is key, not just with Philippa, but with significant others everywhere. "When I first saw Zac getting involved with Twitch, I immediately thought, 'Oh, here we go, *one more thing* with video games.' However, watching him grow on this journey, I knew this was something very special," admits Molly or "MsZGphoto" as she is known on ZGphoto's stream. "This is more than video games. This is a community, a community that Zac has built. That's amazing."

If Molly finds any frustration in her place within ZG's Twitch routine, it's how the two of them define success. "In the early days, I get it. It's about the numbers. Thing is, I see Zac bringing people together, building a second family. That is his real success. It's not about the numbers. Not anymore. Bringing people together is where he thrives, and I'm really proud of him for that."

What about when Twitch is a full-time occupation? How do the dynamics change in a relationship? With Samantha, a.k.a. MrsDrLupo (http://twitch.tv/mrsdrlupo), pictured in Figure 14-4, it's all about supporting your teammates. "I've always been into gaming, and DrLupo's also been into gaming, so Twitch made a lot of sense to me." Her own journey into Twitch was part of hers and DrLupo's courtship. "I'm a photographer, so Lupo took a class in photography to know what it was like to be me. So I launched a Twitch Channel to know what it was like to be him. I had a lot of fun, and now I stream twice a week, including a D&D stream with him." When the Lupos share the stream, it's a very different person people see. "Whether it's *Fortnite, Warcraft,* or D&D, our stream together is a fun, honest look at us."

"We are a team," Samantha states, "and that's why my proudest moment for Ben was when he went full-time with Twitch. He made a lot of sacrifices for me when I wanted to fulfil my dream of running my own business. When I saw a passion in him with Twitch, I knew this was a dream for him that needed to be realized. The day I sent him off to work — downstairs, in our basement — I knew he had done just that. I was so proud of him, and I am thrilled being a part of it."

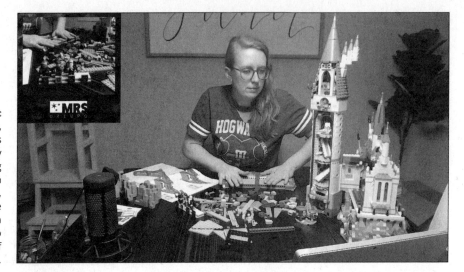

FIGURE 14-4:
DrLupo's wife,
Samantha, offers
a wide variety
of programming
on her Twitch
Channel,
including Creative
streams such
as this Lego
construction of
Hogwarts.

The constant thread between Pip, Molly, and Samantha, is open communication. Talk with your family about your stream; let them know what you are planning; and when you can, make sure they are part of the stream. There is nothing wrong with bringing them into the fun, provided they want to be a part of the show. Speaking of that . . .

When your kids want to stream

Twitch is all about video games, so naturally there are young people who want to stream. Maybe you are one of those young teens with the vicious reflexes, the killer aim, and the savage KDR (and if you don't know what I'm talking about, that's okay, you're young at heart . . .), and you have decided to take on the challenge of being the "next big thing" on Twitch.

Straight from the Terms of Service, here are the rules when it comes to age:

Use of Twitch by Minors and Blocked Persons

The Twitch Services are not available to persons under the age of 13. If you are between the ages of 13 and 18 (or between 13 and the age of legal majority in your jurisdiction of residence), you may only use the Twitch Services under the supervision of a parent or legal guardian who agrees to be bound by these Terms of Service.

The Twitch Services are also not available to any users previously removed from the Twitch Services by Twitch. Finally, the Twitch Services are not available to any persons barred from receiving them under the laws of the United States (such as its export and re-export restrictions and regulations) or applicable laws in any other jurisdiction.

BY DOWNLOADING, INSTALLING, OR OTHERWISE USING THE TWITCH SERVICES, YOU REPRESENT THAT YOU ARE AT LEAST 13 YEARS OF AGE, THAT YOUR PARENT OR LEGAL GUARDIAN AGREES TO BE BOUND BY THESE TERMS OF SERVICE IF YOU ARE BETWEEN 13 AND THE AGE OF LEGAL MAJORITY IN YOUR JURISDICTION OF RESIDENCE, AND THAT YOU HAVE NOT BEEN PREVIOUSLY REMOVED FROM OR PROHIBITED FROM RECEIVING THE TWITCH SERVICES.

According to the Terms of Service, everyone who is on Twitch at present is older than 18, and if anyone between 13 and 18 who are using Twitch are doing so in the presence of an adult. If you know Twitch, you know this is not just a lie, it is a right joke. There are a good amount of tweens and teenagers on Twitch, and guaranteed anyone on the younger end of this spectrum is probably not streaming with a legal adult in the room.

So why not let your kid stream? Simply put, if there is a problem, both your child *and legal guardian* are held accountable. If you think they can handle the workload, be there as a support crew. Ask how their stream went. Ask what they think they could do to improve or build upon it. If they suggest the latest model of gaming equipment from Cyber PC or Origin PC, this could be an opportune moment to talk about picking up a part-time job. . . .

And no, *"But Twitch could be a part-time job . . ."* is not an acceptable answer.

WARNING

While trusting your son or daughter with the responsibility of Twitch, there is always that possibility that you discover your offspring is turning into a troll. It could be with people in game. It could be with other streamers. And the level of trolling can go from being repetitive and obnoxious to bomb threats. Some minors have made statements threatening bodily harm, which led to local police being notified. And in the end, as stated earlier, both you and your child are held accountable. If you do find that your son or daughter is testing the limitations of Twitch's TOS or that they are testing limits of *your home's* TOS, step up and shut Twitch down for them. With streaming comes a degree of responsibility, and should be respected as such.

Burnout: The Specter of Twitch

You've read about "the grind" in video games, but a similar grind exists in Twitch, where the stream can be long and grueling. Ten to 14 hours a day, five days a week. Maybe six if you work in a Saturday or Sunday. They payout for this grind? Burnout.

"There are 168 hours in each week. As a full-time Twitch streamer, I'm expected to be live for as many of them as possible," streamer Professor Broman (http://twitch.tv/professorbroman) told Polygon in a 2017 op-ed on the potential problems of streaming (www.polygon.com/2017/1/16/14240224/twitch-irl-risks-dangers). "Growing my channel at the start involved a mind-crushing 12–16 hours of streaming every day, seven days a week, all year, for two years. This was the only way I could maintain growth," he recalled. "Many, including myself, absolutely overworked ourselves to make it happen. I destroyed every relationship I had with my family and friends for 'the dream.' I'm currently working to fix all the damage from it."

PowerGPU (http://twitch.tv/powergpu) remembered his own time grinding away on Twitch. "I was coming in at the right time, and I was playing alongside some exceptionally good players. My numbers were solid, but I was clocking in the hours," he told me in an interview. "Then I remember a new raid on *Destiny* going live, being invited to be part of a for 'World's First' run, and making arrangements in order to do it. Twelve hours later, I took a step back — me, my wife, and my two kids, 2 and 4 years old respectively — and I realized this was not good. From any perspective. So, I cut Twitch cold turkey. It was an emotional stream, but I had to do this not just for me, but for my family as well."

Burnout is a very real threat, especially to new streamers. At the core of the stream is you, and you can't stream at your optimum best without your wits about you. Take care of yourself, first and foremost, and take care of the people most important in your life. Without that support team, you may find yourself adrift. That is never a good place to be.

Whether it is talking to your kids or talking to your significant others, it helps to be able to interact with the outside world before heading into your innerspace of Twitch. I love interacting with regulars that visit my stream on a regular platform. I am deeply humbled by people subbing to my channel as it is their way of saying *"Yes, I want to support this channel."* Something else I love is enjoying a well-rounded, full-on life. Getting away from the stream, meeting people, and indulging in outside pursuits does have worth. It also impacts your stream in unexpected and (most of the time) positive ways. Don't miss out. Talk to those closest to you, and make sure opportunities are not passing you by.

Chapter **15**

Game Over: Twitch Outside of Gaming

We've been spending a good portion of this book talking about Twitch and video games. We have made the odd references throughout of other applications of Twitch, but the gaming aspect of Twitch predominates this book without question. This should come as no surprise. Twitch was founded on video games and is well-known for being the platform that brings star players to your laptops, desktops, and portable devices.

Here in Chapter 15 is where I drop some hard, fresh for the Stephen Colbert Bakery, truthiness on you: *Twitch isn't just video games.*

Over the years of Twitch offering hours on hours of content, and with more creative minds looking beyond Twitch's video game roots. This platform presents opportunities, including streaming Talk Shows and Podcasts, streaming Music, and streaming Creative projects.

Let's put down the controller, unplug the console, and explore.

Game On: The Rise of eSports

If you were to say "eSports" or "professional video game teams" in mixed company, especially in a sports bar, you might get laughed at because *"Video games aren't real sports."* What is truly sad about this all-too-common opinion of professional video gaming is that it is not a fad. Not even close. This is a real thing.

Here are just a few stats to consider:

>> In March 2018, the Luxor in Las Vegas, Nevada, opened their eSports Arena, pictured in Figure 15-1 and found on Twitch at `www.twitch.tv/esport sarena`. The stadium is a 30,000 square foot multi-level arena featuring a competition stage, a 50-foot LED video wall, gaming stations open to visitors through various access passes, and a network tv-quality production studio. (`http://esportsarenavagas.com`)

>> Paris is considering adding eSports to the 2024 Olympics. The strategy is to win over younger viewers, getting them hooked on the Olympic Games as a whole. (`https://atomicnetwork.io/2018/06/29/the-rise-of-esports/`)

>> The High School eSports League, an online league that allows club teams to participate in tournaments, have registered as of May 2018 15,000 students representing 800 schools nationwide. (`www.edweek.org/ew/articles/2018/05/24/gamers-are-the-new-high-school-athletes.html`)

FIGURE 15-1: The Luxor opened in March 2018 the eSports Arena, a massive 30,000 square foot stadium dedicated to professional video game competition.

>> In October 2018, *ESPN Magazine* released "The Gaming Issue" featuring Tyler "Ninja" Blevins on the cover, hailing him as the Biggest Gamer in the World. The articles all centered around eSports.

eSports events are very different from usual gaming on Twitch. Instead of watching one player and one point-of-view, you are watching video games from multiple points-of-view with color commentary provided by a bevvy of hosts. It's no different from watching any sporting event on television, but this time, it's video games.

One downside with eSports on Twitch: the Chat window. Messages on these Channels happen at a bit of a blur, so it's better if you host an event on your Channel and interact with those watching alongside you. Some channels that regularly host eSports include:

>> FACEIT TV (www.twitch.tv/faceittv)

>> Heroes of the Storm (www.twitch.tv/blizzheroes)

>> Beyond the Summit (www.twitch.tv/beyondthesummit)

>> Pokémon (www.twitch.tv/pokemon)

>> Overwatch League (www.twitch.tv/overwatchleague)

Hosting eSports events can be like a virtual "Game Day" at your house, only in your Twitch Chat window while adding Discord lends itself to a voice channel option. You and a few select friends can "armchair quarterback" the pros while they play in Vegas. It's totally up to you how to interact.

Bungie TV: Going Live with the Latest

Bungie (www.bungie.net) are the creators of *Destiny*, my personal gateway into Twitch. As you have heard in my own adventures, I first got into Twitch through Bungie's numerous reveal streams from Bungie TV (www.twitch.tv/bungie). You might be thinking we are still in the world of video games on Twitch — and technically, we are — but now we're talking more about the *business* of video games.

Bungie TV leans less on game play and more about the hype, their channel dedicated to product reveal and rollout through a talk show format. Hosted by Community Manager David "Deej" Dague, Bungie TV interviews the creative minds behind the popular, award-winning video game. From writers to developers to directors, Deej asks about the goings-on in the game's upcoming releases.

Interspersed throughout the Q&A sessions are trailers, cut scenes, and glimpses at what players have got coming in new DLC's, as shown in Figure 15-2. Bungie TV's streams are meant to excite, meant to promote, and meant to reach game audiences old and new. And they do!

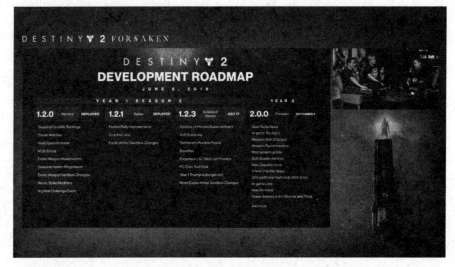

FIGURE 15-2:
Bungie TV is less about seeing the game in-play and more about getting people excited about what is coming next from the studio.

The excitement and the anticipation of "what's next" is part of what makes the Bungie stream such a successful platform. While their Channel is about selling video games, there is also a sincere effort on Bungie's stream to share a personal dive with those who make the game happen. From a business perspective, Bungie TV is a shining example of how rollouts and demos can be presented on a higher level, on a platform that offers you a unique way to connect with your base.

And the corporate world is taking notice.

How Can I Help You: ServiceNow

Chuck Tomasi hosts the NOWcommuity (`www.twitch.tv/nowcommunity`), shown in Figure 15-3, which he describes as an opportunity *"to get inside the head of some of ServiceNow's top talent"* with questions about ServiceNow, a cloud computing company headquartered in Santa Clara, California. The NOWcommunity work through questions and issues presented in their Chat. Along with offering an innovative approach to customer service, NOWcommunity also offers a look into the way ServiceNow's developers and IT associates work through various problems. Sometimes, getting a look at the troubleshooting process provides insight on how to solve an issue encountered.

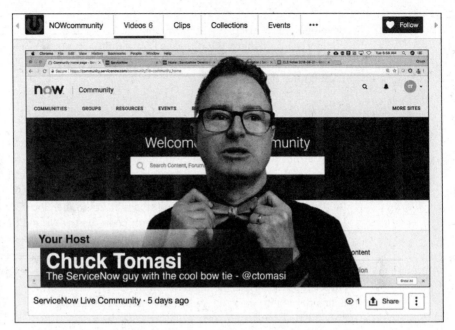

FIGURE 15-3:
Chuck Tomasi (and his amazing collection of bow ties) hosts NOWcommunity, a Twitch Channel that works as an extension of both Customer Service and Community Outreach.

"When I first started working with Twitch, I had to admit to a bit of skepticism," Chuck admits. "I know enough about Twitch to know its core audience wasn't our core audience. However, when word got out that we were on Twitch, our customers found us." Maybe the Chat is not as lively as you would find on an artist's stream or on Bungie TV, but once Chuck hits a stride, so does his audience. "I think, sometimes, people get nervous asking that first question; but once the first question is asked, I see it spark another, and another. This is a very interactive approach to what we do, and I'll admit, it's kinda fun."

In fact, NOWcommunity is so much fun that ServiceNow launched Live Coding Happy Hour (`www.twitch.tv/servicenowdevprogram`), a place where developers gather to swap ideas and approaches to making ServiceNow a better product.

Wait. Coding? On Twitch? Would people really watch someone on Twitch *code*? For *hours?*

Yes, there's an audience for coders.

Coding at the Speed of Chill: SKFroi

Froilán "Froi" Irizarry is a backend engineer at Code.gov, an aggregator for federal government projects that are eventually released to the public as Open Source. To keep his skills sharp and bring his own approach to coding online, Froi took his development projects to Twitch (www.twitch.tv/skfroi) and shared it with audiences everywhere. What makes Froi's approach, shown in Figure 15-4, different from others is in his preferred language. Not Python. Not Ruby. Not even JavaScript.

Spanish.

"I've been very much dedicated to creating quality content," Froi states. "It was at PyCaribbean when a friend of mine put me on the spot and said, 'You got a following in this community. You should stream in Spanish,' and so I took on the challenge." Twitch, he found out, was something of a calling. "My brain codes in English, but I speak in Spanish; and this matters to me. Showing the world that a Latino can code, can code well, and can code for the United States government really does send a message. This is not just possible, it is happening. There is a real demand for quality content *en Español*. The different between other coding streams is that a majority of these stream are teaching code in a tried, tested, and clinical approach. I make mistakes in my code. I work on expressions on the fly. I consider what I do as a real-world approach to coding."

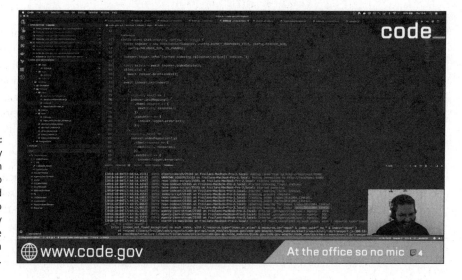

FIGURE 15-4: Froi Irizarry brings his passion for coding to Twitch, and remains true to his heritage by hosting the channel in Spanish.

Froi's stream is a real testament for how new streamers can quickly make an impact. While struggling to find regulars due to his content and his language, Froi found himself attracting attention from Latin America and Spain, one being JuanCarlosPaco (www.twitch.tv/juancarlospaco), another Twitch streamer from Argentina.

Juan, a developer specializing in a programming language called NIM, started asking about Code.gov. "I remember Juan very excitedly asked me, *'Wait, do you mean to tell me that the US government has an API that lets us search for projects and code that we can use? Can I make a client for it?'* What we do is Open Source, so of course, it's open to everyone.

"The next day I received a message from Juan saying that he had finished an API (Application Program Interface) client — a library or series of libraries that make interaction with an API easier — for Code.gov. He even made the documentation and code available, both of which were impeccable."

This was not only a real accomplishment for Code.gov, but for Froi. Without his Twitch stream, this exchange would have never happened. "Having an open source contribution like this coming from *outside* the USA is incredibly exciting."

A Twitch Worth a Thousand Words: Dawn McTeigue

If you know your comic book artists, then you know Dawn McTeigue, pictured in Figure 15-5 and found at `http://twitch.tv/dawnmcteigue`. If you do not know McTeigue by name, but you enjoy comic books and graphic novels, then you know Dawn McTeigue's work:

>> *Batman*

>> *Harley Quinn & Her Gang of Harleys*

>> *Lady Mechanika*

>> *Lady Death*

>> *Zenescope Magazine*

When you see Dawn's work, it's hard to resist. Her depictions of superheroes and supervillains are amazing, and when you sift through her portfolio, you have to wonder how does she make all this happen?

Dawn answers that question by bringing her work to Twitch.

She makes her stream look effortless but Dawn still considers herself a newcomer. "I started streaming back in January of 2018, and my colleagues told me *'Well, you need to move on over to Twitch.'* I said *'Twitch is for gamers,'* but quickly I discovered there were other creative types streaming there, so I made that jump in June." The jump did include a few more accessories and upgrades in her studio, but for Dawn this was a "levelling up" in streaming. "There was a lot of technical limitations on the platform I first originally started streaming on, but Twitch's Support and the community on a whole helped me make this transition, and now I'm working without constraints."

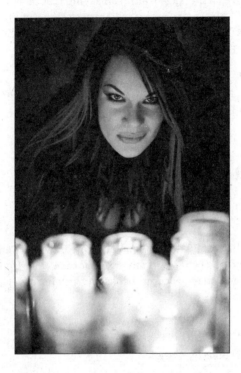

While many artists are known for working in solitude, Dawn draws inspiration from the outside world joining her in her comic book sanctum. "Twitch turns my art projects into a shared experience, and I get to share my elation in seeing the final project in print with my Chat. I accept ideas and suggestions, and they get a kick out of seeing their suggestions applied and in print. They think, '*I helped make this happen*,' and that's a great feeling."

Her Community also inspires her to *"Art Harder!"* as she discovered at a recent Launch Party. "Part of this stream included raffles for 15-minute sketch sessions because my own backlog for schedules for commissions is ridiculous. I used Moobot to pick winners for a fully sketched, inked, colored shaded, 4 x 6 cards of original artwork. I was so exhilarated, like this was a workout. Power drawing, if you will."

Whether coding or comic book art is your passion, the idea of creation with the world watching serves as quite the appeal for some creatives, including musicians.

Harping on a Passion: Meadow Fox

Musicians are no stranger to Twitch. For years artists of all levels, including headliners like Imagine Dragons and Deadmau5, have staked their claim on Twitch, either to build a following or cultivate a fanbase. Much in the same manner as Dawn McTeigue, musicians are inviting their audiences into jam sessions to see how music is made. From rehearsals to full-on performances, musicians are discovering an intersection of creativity and commerce previously unexplored.

Twitch also serves as a platform for some musicians who are looking to just entertain. They are not looking to land a recording contract (although they wouldn't say 'no' if one came along), but they are looking to bring their love of music to a global audience.

That's how Meadow Fox (`www.twitch.tv/meadowfox`) approaches her stream. "I consider myself a Creative-Variety streamer, but harp music is the most popular content I create, especially when I was going for the Partner push. I enjoy mixing up my content because it is good for my brain, but playing the harp is what I am known for." Meadow started streaming in March of 2017, reaching the rant of Partner in September 2018, and while she occasionally would break out the odd video game on her stream, she always felt more at ease with non-gaming pursuits. "With a Creative stream, you're sharing something more personal out into Twitch. Gamers do share themselves in their own way when gaming, but they are following someone else's story or strategy. Music is a very different entity. It's a more personal, more intimate experience."

While some artists would consider Twitch a distraction from their art, it was a motivator for Meadow. "Yes, it is all well and good to practice music in the solitude of your home, but art — whether it is music or drawing — is meant to be shared, and Twitch provides me with a platform where I can share my music with anyone who wants to listen. I can perform on my schedule from the comfort of my own home, and through my music I have made some wonderful friendships, something I did not even think about when I started this whole Twitch adventure."

The Twitch adventure for Meadow, she feels, has been not only fun but a new challenge on what she can accomplish with Twitch. On Halloween, for example, Meadow tapped into her love for costuming and cosplay, turning herself into a ghost, shown in Figure 15-6. With the magic of green screen and OBS, she took her ghost to the next level with a simple translucent effect. "Twitch has made me a better performer. I want to be the performer, where people can come by, relax, and have a little fun. That's where my love of costuming and cosplay comes in, and my music streams become full-on productions."

GEM1908
3D_VAMPIR
FINCH_O
FINCH_O
FINCH_O

RESUB X
FOLLOW
RESUB X12
RESUB X12
RESUB X12

FIGURE 15-6: Meadow Fox loves making music on Twitch and enjoys making her streams memorable, such as turning herself into a ghost (complete with special effects) for her Halloween streams.

Gaming for Good: Charity Streams

You've heard me talk about *charity streams* before. These are the streams where it's all about the numbers. Streamers rally their Communities around a cause, and those causes are wide and varied. Aura hosts Gaming4Pits, benefitting the Villalobos Rescue Center. GuardianCon and many other streamers on Twitch game for St. Jude Children's Research Hospital, raising millions of dollars for them. TheBigMarvinski worked with SHELTER in his corner of the UK to raise money and awareness. And then, in response to the August 2018 shooting at a *Madden 19* tournament that claimed the lives of gamers Elijah "trueboy" Clayton and Taylor "SpotMePlzzz" Robertson, EA Games hosted the Jacksonville Tribute Stream (pictured in Figure 15-7), raising over a million dollars for the Jacksonville Tribute Fund to support the victims.

TIP

When hosting charity streams, it's a good idea to try out your effort solo before recruiting others to your cause. Why? Coordinating a charity stream can be difficult, and trying to figure out how things are going to go while managing a team a volunteers might appear overwhelming. Go on and fly solo your first time out. Then, after an idea of how a charity stream goes, take some time to reach out to others and see if they want to help.

FIGURE 15-7: Following the tragic events of the *Madden 19* tournament in Jacksonville, Florida, EA Games hosted the Jacksonville Tribute Stream to raise money and promote solidarity through video games.

There are so many good reasons to host a charity stream. Obviously, it feels *really* good. That's a given. Regardless if you are playing games or just getting on camera and talking to your Chat about the why's behind this charity, it's a lot of fun to host. Then there are the end results. Doesn't matter if you have raised $1 or $10,000 — your contribution makes a difference.

Doing a little prep before you get started

Before you close this book and say, *"I'm going to host a charity stream . . ."* I have to ask that you take a moment. Just going for it, while passionate and inspiring, might not be the best course of action. You are going to want to do a little bit of prep work beforehand.

>> **Set a *realistic* financial goal:** Sure, we want to shoot for the moon, but consider your audience, consider your stream time(s), and consider the cause. It could be a very niche cause. It could be a cause with mass appeal. Whatever the case, think modestly.

>> **Set a stretch goal:** So I set for my own charity stream a goal of $1,000, but my *stretch* goal — the over-the-top, dream goal for this charity stream — I set at $10,000. If I landed somewhere in-between that, it would be a double win.

>> **Contact the charity/nonprofit:** Maybe they won't know Twitch but what is important is that they know you and they know what you are doing and when. The charity may even offer you some logistic support. Whether it is in official photos or even a little bit of additional support on a promotional level, it's good to let your charity know you are streaming for them.

>> **Incentives:** For certain levels of donation, your audience should get something in return. What will it be? And what if you get a HUGE donation? Within reason, what would you do? Whatever the incentive you give for people to donate big, keep it within reason.

Setting up the collection jar

Once you plan your charity, you then need to find a third party to collect funds on your behalf. Here are some options:

>> **Tiltify** (http://tiltify.com)

>> **GoFundMe** (www.gofundme.com)

>> **JustGiving** (http://justgiving.com)

It's very important that you find a third party that will collect the funds on your behalf. Some services will collect funds and charge a fee before sending the funds to your charity. Others may not take any charge, provided the organization you are raising funds and awareness for are set up with the service. For example, Big Cat Rescue (www.bigcatrescue.org) is set up with GoFundMe, so once I was done with my own charity stream, I could tell BCR to pay GoFundMe a visit. What matters is that your charity is recognized by the third party, their reputation is reliable, and money never touches your hands. Do a little research before talking up your future fundraiser, and then, when everything is set, start talking it up.

And good luck. You're doing the right thing. You really are.

WARNING

If you are doing a charity stream simply because you want an opportunity to grow your channel, your audience will catch on. Very quickly. Hosting a charity stream without really caring about the organization or believing in the cause, simply for your own recognition, will assuredly backfire on you. If you don't believe in the charity, don't attempt false sincerity.

And with all this, I have only just touched on a few of talented people on Twitch streaming amazing, non-gaming content. There's only so much space I have in this one book that I can't share with you what Alkali Layke (www.twitch.tv/alkalilayke) is creating on her cosplay stream, or showcase TD0013 (www.twitch.tv/td0013), who recreates iconic props from various video games. I would need another page or two to tell you about how Reverend Matt Souza (www.twitch.tv/GodSquadChurch) has turned his Twitch Channel into a church for gamers, where even the snarkiest of life's questions is seriously addressed and tied into a message of faith. And how about Babs Who Takes Pictures (`www.twitch.tv/iambabs`)? I would be remiss if I didn't mention how she streams various tips and techniques in making beautiful photographs absolutely stunning.

Maybe I can't feature all these terrific people, but I can drop you their URLs. (See what I did there?) And from here, you can see where "Recommended Channels" takes you next.

To simply pigeon-hole the platform to be by gamers, for gamers, about gamers, limits the reach of those who go beyond the offerings of a PS4, Xbox, or other gaming device. With a dash of imagination, and a lot of passion and drive, Twitch can open a door of possibilities and opportunities for you.

Are you ready to go exploring? Your next big discovery is only a stream away.

5

The Part of Tens

Meet ten Twitch streamers that influenced the author.

Learn ten (or more) life lessons that Twitch streamers have learned from their time online.

Chapter **16**

Ten Twitch Streamers Who Influenced the Author

When putting together the *Podcasting For Dummies* "Part of Tens" chapter covering podcasters you should know and podcasts you should be listening to, Chuck Tomasi and I undertook a Herculean labor in narrowing down a multitude of podcasts and podcast personalities down to a humble ten to feature. And this was for the 2nd edition. On the 3rd edition, we attempted to broaden that scope with "Ten *Types* of Podcast to Listen To," which granted us a little more wiggle room in who we featured and what we could offer to the reader. But to narrow down all of Twitch down to ten streamers? Sure, I could have written "Ten Twitch Influencers," but based on who? Influence on the platform as a whole, or on me as a new streamer in his first year?

When talking to individual streamers, you may get a Rogue's Gallery of gamers, cosplayers, artists, and other streamers, all leaving their mark on that individual channel. So while narrowing down Twitch to a single list of ten streamers may be short of impossible, I could take a look at my own list of streamers who have made some sort of impression on my own stream.

These are the streamers who have, willingly or unbeknownst to them, gave me perspective, challenged me to improve my stream, and offered insight on how I could take what I did to unwind and turn it into an interactive pocket of time with the world. Many of these streamers have already appeared in this book either in interviews or in shout-outs, but this is a deep dive into why I turn to these ten for guidance. Check these folks about because they might inspire you the way they inspire me.

ItsOrd (Matthew J Drake)

Matthew J Drake, or ItsOrd (`http://twitch.tv/itsord`), hasn't streamed for years. I'm hoping that will change as it was Matthew J Drake who first told me about Twitch.

When he was streaming, Matt commentated *StarCraft* tournaments. He also gamed with his creative-partner-in-crime, Piper J Drake. (And if you happen to be a reader of romantic suspense, yes, *that* Piper J Drake.) He was an early adopter of Twitch, attending TwitchCon in its early incarnations, and each stream involving him was a delight to watch as you could hear the joy in his voice.

And Matt, every time he would pay me a visit, would ask *"So, when are you getting on Twitch, Tee?"*

Many conversations and beers over my firepit would go into what Twitch was, what the platform could do, how it was different from early efforts into streaming media, and the like. I remember the almost-Christmas-morning-like glee he showed when I told him, *"Okay, Matt, I've set up a Twitch account."* And this was before I set up any info panels or even hit "Broadcast Gameplay" on my PS4. Since my first step, Matt has been there, offering feedback on how to interact better with my Chat, what I could do to attract more viewers, and how to find a groove that would evolve into a schedule. Matt even provided me with a webcam so I could introduce myself visually as well as aurally. Whenever I would find myself perplexed on something in Twitch, I turned to Matt for an answer, or at least a lead to an answer. And even though he no longer streams, I still turn to him for that insight.

Will my great enabler ever return to Twitch? I can't speak for either ItsOrd or Matt Drake, but anything is possible. Stay tuned.

OneActual

You never forget your first.

What I considered my first real introduction to Twitch came from one of Bungie's streams. On Deej's sign off, my eyes strayed to the Recommended Channels section of Twitch, and the name OneActual (`http://twitch.tv/OneActual`) topped my list, and OneActual was playing *Destiny*. So I gave the name a click and got my first impression of the *Destiny* Community on Twitch.

Maybe I was expecting something toxic. Maybe I was thinking OneActual would be similar to the Chat I caught glimpses of when I was watching Bungie. What I got instead was a West Coast gamer who appeared very much at piece with *Destiny*, with his community, and with his world on a whole. So I stuck around, watched his Community, and dropped a quick hello.

Imagine the surprise when he responded back with *"Yo, what up, TeeMonster?"* With such an active Chat, and his Chat was extremely active, I was really impressed. And so I stuck around longer.

OneActual was the first streamer I made laugh. He was the first streamer I ever followed. And he was my first sub. Even before subscribing to his stream, he continued to invite me to mentor me through Trials, *Destiny's* very intensive PVP Competitive showdown. I wasn't quite ready to take him up on the offer, but still stuck around because OneActual always made me feel welcome. That was, I think, my first lesson in Twitch: Make everyone feel welcome. And I try to do that.

Playing *Destiny* as chill as he does? Well, that's a whole different goal to shoot for altogether.

ZGPhoto

Once again, under Recommended Channels, ZGPhoto (`http://twitch.tv/zgphoto`) appeared, also playing my game of choice. I was anxious to pick up tips from these streamers, and while OneActual specialized in PVP, Zac (or ZG, take your pick) was more focused on *raids*, missions involving a team of six that would end with a massive boss battle. Wanting to get over a personal hang-up with raids, I hoped to watch and learn from a gamer who possessed the sharp skills, all the right moves, and a keen eye that never . . .

Mmmmmmmmmmmmm.

Wait. What was that?!

ZG call for "Mmm's" in Chat literally stopped me in the middle of my office deliverable as he suddenly got close to his mic and softly went *"Mmmmm."* Chat immediately filled with emotes and messages all expressing the same message: *Mmm.* So now I *had* to know what this was all about.

ZG's stream, Mmm's and all, is highly entertaining, highly irreverent, and always a great place to hang out. Much like OneActual, ZG's stream of "Photobombers" welcomes you into the fold as if you are one of the gang. What amazed me about ZG as a streamer then, and still does now, is his seemingly unending patience. I remember testing its limits when, after months of following him, I went on and threw my name into his Raid Raffle. On hearing my name chosen, I jumped into a raid with him and the team he had assembled . . . and discovered that I did not understand the jump mechanics of *Destiny*. As we were deep into the raid by this point, I waited for the inevitable boot from the fireteam, or at the very least being asked politely by ZG to step out in order to give a more skilled player a chance.

Instead, he and his fireteam stuck it out with me; and even after the game shut down on account of scheduled maintenance, I was invited to come back and finish it. ZG even went so far as to offer other streamer to watch for advice on character class mechanics and such. This won me over so much that I stuck around with ZGPhoto's stream, eventually struck up a friendship with him that lead to our meeting at GuardianCon (http://twitch.tv/guardiancon) in the summer of 2018. Watching him also inspired me to stream, and as I do, I try to practice patience with those who visit and join in to play. And with that patience, I also try to encourage my fireteam to challenge themselves and grow. It's how we improve, both as gamers and as streamers.

iLulu

High-energy, whip-smart, and so much fun to watch in-game, iLulu (http://twitch.tv/ilulu) always has a smile for her "Legendaries" and solid gaming advice for anyone in her Chat. Lulu is always open to new games and new experiences, but her heart belongs to *Destiny*. In particular, Lulu loves to raid. Her fireteam trusts her calls without question. She knows where to go, what to do, and how to keep cool when some strategies seem not to be working. (No surprise there as she is part of a group called the Game Guides, which includes JamesWerk, GCX Clyde, ZGPhoto, BlacKoreaNate, and many other talented streamers.) Part of this coolness can be contributed to her love of gaming on a whole. "Coming from a family of triplets," she recalls, "I have always been competitive." That competitive streak in Lulu, though, has never hindered her ability to welcome others into her fireteam and make them feel essential and important to the team's success. That feeling of being essential carries over in her Discord community, as well, where the conversation is still ongoing and invitations to run in a variety of games are exchanged frequently.

With Lulu, I take a lot of notes in not only how she plays but also in how she develops her community, especially outside of Twitch. It always amazes me how able Lulu is in opening herself up to her audience, but manages to keep a few things private. True, Twitch is about openness, about sharing, and about connection between the host and the audience; but Lulu also stresses an importance in keeping some things for yourself. It can be gaming off-stream, time out with family, or just some down time in Westeros. (She's a *Game of Thrones* fan.) The lesson Lulu offered me is balance. Finding that balance makes for a better stream, and Lulu personifies that.

Aura

Out in the grand arena of Twitch streamers, you have gamers that possess incredible — nay, superhuman — skills behind a mouse-and-keyboard or console controller. Laser focus. Fantastic strategy. Relentless intensity. All the while, remaining cool and calm under mind-boggling pressure. And then there's Aura.

When I first found Aura (http://twitch.tv/aura), he was known as 3vil_Aura; but honestly, I think the only think evil about Aura was his wicked wit. Blazing through the Crucible or Salty Springs, Aura will eliminate an opponent with a quick *"Hi, my name is Aura..."* salutation or proclaim *"Got 'em, Coach!"* for his Chat, affectionately referred to as The Pit. His snarky sense-of-humor and unabashed love for his rescue pit bull Layla, all set to a backdrop of high-octane rock, makes Aura's feed a great place to hang out, play games, and enjoy some time with one of the straightest of straight talkers on Twitch.

His stream, however, is not just limited to gameplay peppered with tongue-and-cheek banter. Aura also covers the business side of streaming. On occasion, his stream hosts a talk show about what happens behind the scenes and in-between streams, presenting his perspective on how to take your stream to a higher level or in a different direction. It is a very different side to Aura that The Pit is used to, but a side they respect. His is a voice of experience, analysis, critique, and conclusions, and you can learn a lot about streaming, not only while watching him play but by asking him direct questions about what to do with a stream and how to make it better.

That's one of many reasons why I asked Aura to serve as Technical Editor for this title. Yeah, I think I know lot about starting off with Twitch . . . but it never hurts have someone smarter than you watching over your shoulder.

And there is the takeaway for me from Aura: trust. You want your stream to trust you. A lot of things can be accomplished on Twitch when your Chat trusts you.

That Token Guy

One morning, while working from home, I looked up who was online. On the Twitch app, the iPad informed me that a streamer called That Token Guy (`http://twitch.tv/thattokenguy`) was online and hosted by multiple streamers that I followed as well. Always with an eye open to new streamers, I jumped to That Token Guy's stream and immediately discovered why so many in my Twitch network were hosting this streamer.

What really impressed me about That Token Guy was not his gaming strategies (not to say that he isn't good at whatever game he's streaming because, yeah, he is) but his overall contentment. "When I first got on to Twitch," he said that morning, again my first morning visiting his stream, "I was determined to be the next Ninja. Get those followers, get those subscribers, stream long hours . . . but I realized I was no longer me. I was becoming something that just wasn't me. So, I am streaming for the love of it, and I'm working to be the best streamer I can be. That makes all the difference."

While I've heard other streamers talk about avoiding numbers, focusing on the quality of their content, working to make a stream a good place for their Chat, That Token Guy was the first streamer I had watched that opened up with some heavy honesty. There are many new streamers that jump into Twitch with the intent of being "the next big name" in gaming and streaming. Then they discover what that entails, and some never make it to Affiliate level. And then even some new Affiliates disappear after a few weeks. That Token Guy not only acknowledged that but also found that there's a difference between streaming for success versus streaming for the love of it. It reminds me of when aspiring authors tell me *I want to be the next Stephen King . . .*" when it comes to their writing. That always makes me cringe, as it shouldn't be about writing like someone else but creating the best work that you can create. Streaming is no different.

That Token Guy taught me perspective. Keep your wits about you and stream because you love it. Trying to stream "like someone else" rarely works out.

Tiddly

I've already mentioned Tiddly (`http://twitch.tv/tiddly`), but honestly, a sidebar is not enough ink for this force of nature on Twitch. I first met Tiddly through Lulu's Channel, the raid dropping me into a stream featuring a lot of laughs, even more irreverence, and oh yeah, are we playing a game here? That was one of the first things I noticed about Tiddly's stream. The game did matter, sure, but if there was something more important or something more fun to focus on, she would not hesitate to bring it front-and-center. Of all the strange and delightful distractions from *Fortnite, Overwatch,* and *Destiny,* she hosts *Death by Song,* a game show where Chat submit song requests, and submissions are judged by those listening as to whether or not the song is worthwhile. The submissions range from old favorites of rock to deep tracks from the Monty Python library. There's a lot of reactions from Chat when certain songs hit the rotation, but regardless of who wins and who loses in *Death by Song,* everyone — host included — is having a good time. It's a win-win on stream.

The lesson, and the influence, Tiddly has on my stream is remembering that no matter the content, no matter the intent, make sure your stream is having fun. As I've stated repeatedly in this book, if you aren't having fun, your Chat is not having fun. Without whimsy, a stream can feel a bit cold and unpleasant. Keep control of your stream, but have fun above all else.

RealMunchle (read as "RealMunchie")

I have a lot of goals in Twitch. One of them is to be like my buddy, Munch.

RealMunchle (`http://twitch.tv/realmunchle`) is best described as one of Twitch's most valuable resource. I remember when Munch first popped up into my feed. He was my first sub. He introduced me to Nightbot. If I were struggling with anything Twitch related, Munch would be there, pointing me in the right direction.

Now, if you were to talk to Munch, he would say he did the same thing with me in *Destiny.* And *Fortnite.* And *Tomb Raider.* And . . .

Anytime Munch would appear in my stream, I knew I was in for a fun ride. We would challenge one another to see who would break first. If I could make this Brit laugh while on stream, I would consider that a Platinum Level trophy achievement. Whenever he would impart his knowledge, it would never come across as Munch showing off what he knows but more about helping out a streamer and a friend who is looking to "git gud" at this whole Twitch thing. He embodies all the best qualities of Twitch; and if I'm not learning something new from him, I'm enjoying the time spent with a friend.

Munch taught me one of the most important lessons of Twitch: Good people are out there. When you meet them, return the love. In most cases, the good people you meet on Twitch are some of the best people. Period.

Thanks, Munch.

Danfinity

It was the above streamer, Munch, who introduced me to Danfinity (http://twitch.tv/danfinity), and it was Danfinity who introduced me to one of the most basic of aspects with Twitch.

Danfinity welcomed me into the fold when I joined him and his clanmates from Current Meta on a raid. The best way to describe running with Current Meta would be *"Brace yourself!"* as the back-and-forth banter, the trending jokes, and the good-natured hump-busting comes at you fast and furious, all while you are running one of *Destiny's* action-packed raids. Every time I wrap up an evening with Danfinity, I am more than ready for bed as I am exhausted. Usually from laughing. A lot.

Dan's stream is a fun corner of Twitch, similar to the shenanigans you would find on Tiddly's stream: a lot of laughter, a lot of great plays, and a lot of Community. Dan is a staunch believer in the importance and power of Community.

And his clan, Current Meta, believe in this wholeheartedly.

In a spirit of giving back to the *Destiny* community, Dan formed a fireteam (which included me) with the sole purpose to join a "Guided Games" raid, a special mode where a fireteam forms but leaves a slot open for one random Guardian looking to accomplish a raid, Nightfall, or some particularly difficult challenge. The Guardian joining us on this particular night caught on to the playful ribbing of Current Meta, and that night the attention was turned on me. All was fun . . . at first. My own playing was a bit off that night, and our guest Guardian started turning toxic on account of it. As we were in the final phase of the raid, and knowing Bungie's penalties on teams that quit a raid on a whole, we stuck it out. Afterward, Dan and I talked in depth about Guided Games, about improving gameplay, and about handling toxic players. Obviously, I didn't stop playing on account of this one malevolent gamer, but this was Dan's influence on me as a streamer. It's just a game, but the people playing it are what matter. When it stops being fun, there's very little reason to go on.

And protect your family. Make sure everything's good. That's paramount.

DrLupo

There are some amazing players on Twitch. Just in the *Destiny* community alone, there is TheTrueVanguard (`http://twitch.tv/thetruevanguard`), the B0nj (`http://twitch.tv/theb0nj`), Burnbxx (`http://twitch.tv/burnbxx`), Ninja with No L (`http://twitch.tv/ninja_with_no_l`), and SchviftyFive (`http://twitch.tv/schviftyfive`), just to name a few. Their skills are unparalleled and their Communities are vast. This is a higher level of gameplay, and it can be a little intimidating watching these gamers work both their current games of choice and their lively Chat feeds.

And then there is DrLupo (`http://twitch.tv/drlupo`), one of the rock stars of Twitch. I heard him mentioned by Aura on his stream during Aura's run with *Fortnite.* Not knowing anything about who Lupo was or what his stream was all about, I followed the link provided to Lupo's channel. Within seconds, I knew I had just entered into was a higher level of both Twitch and gaming. I felt a little over my head as I watched him build structures, quick snipe opponents, and rack up "Victory Royale" after "Victory Royale" on his Channel. As for his Chat — large enough to be a "Subscribers Only" feature — it was impressive to watch when Lupo would address the odd question here and there, and read off new subs, resubs, tips, and the like. Without question, Lupo's Channel was in a class by itself, and I could not see then how it would have an impact on me.

Where Ben Lupo made his mark on me was in the final day of GuardianCon when he agreed to sit down with me for an interview.

I was sitting with one of Twitch's and *Fortnite's* rock stars, and what impressed me the most was his laser focus on me. It wasn't like he had just come off a five-and-a-half hour signing alongside Ninja (which, yes, he had just done that), but it was as if we were the only people there at the convention center for that pocket of time. Alongside that intensity of attention, I was awestruck at the humility of this gaming and streaming dynamo. I had watched him crank out victory on victory, take quick defeats in stride, manage his Chat, and touch base with his son, all on stream, never missing a beat. And yet for DrLupo, he attributes his success to one lucky play. "I got incredibly lucky," he told me. "I managed to land the perfect shot on the perfect day. I said on stream, 'Wouldn't it be funny if Ninja and I ran doubles?' and next thing I know, Ninja and I are talking. We run doubles. We have a lot of fun. We became friends. And now, here I am. Want to know how I got here? I got lucky."

DrLupo's influence on me as a streamer: Take nothing for granted. Just game and see what happens. There are no guarantees, no promises, no sure-fire formulas of success. Appreciate every moment. Tomorrow's a whole new game.

Thanks, Ben.

Chapter **17**

Ten (or More) Life Lessons from Twitch

O n the writing of this book, I hit my first anniversary as a streamer. My first stream was actually in May of 2017, but that was more of an impulse stream. I knew there was this thing called Twitch and that "Broadcast Gameplay" was an option on my PS4, but as far as setting schedules, raids, Chat interaction, and all that, I was oblivious. (I would say, *"If there had only been a book that could have clued me in . . ."* but had there been, I would not be here, now would I?) On the day *Destiny* 2 dropped — Tuesday, September 6, 2017 — I hosted a marathon stream, and with my drive to play more, I found the best time to play, which also became my best time to stream.

A year later, still gaming, still streaming.

There have been, along the way, a good amount of lessons I have banked, and I would dare say I have shared all of them here in this book. But I only have a year to pull from. I've got a few names in this final chapter that bring a lot more of experience, time in front of the camera, and time away from the platform in order to build up a community. All of these amazing creatives — gamers, cosplayers, artists, and so on — appear on Twitch feeds not because they have to, but because they want to. They have something to share. They have something to celebrate.

And in their regularly scheduled programming, they manage to learn a thing or two along the way. In their own words, here are just a few of those life lessons they have discovered between the follows, the subs, and the raids.

Twitch Continuously Makes Me Strive to Be Better

"Twitch holds a magnifying glass on my negative qualities, but on my positive qualities at the same time. If you're having a bad day and you're streaming, people know it straight away. It's so transparent, and it's hard to laugh it off. If you are having a rough go and you are streaming, it's hard to keep that contained. When things go wrong at work, eh, *c'est la vie*. Something goes wrong with my stream, and I am fit to rage. When things are going well though, it is the exact opposite exponentially. Your mood's pulled up, you come off your stream feeling amazing, elated. But even if you think you've had a bad stream, you take a moment — maybe half and hour — and you ask yourself what went wrong, how can you improve. I suppose that's the life lesson there. I've got something I care about so passionately, that I want to continue to improve on it."

— The Big Marvinski (http://twitch.tv/thebigmarvinski)

Twitch Opened the World to Me

"I have been able to diversify myself around other people. Because of Twitch, I have been able to meet people from all over the world. I live in a small town in Indiana, I'm an introvert, and this is the first online multiplayer game I have ever played. I've met people from *everywhere*. It's very humbling and a little over-whelming. My life is richer, my view of the world is much broader, thanks to Twitch."

— iLulu (http://twitch.tv/ilulu)

Success Is Waiting for You If You Are Ready to Work for It

"The advice I would give anyone starting out in Twitch, in Mixer, in any platform, whether you see a friend you have seen streaming less time than you or someone seeming to come out of nowhere and get partnered, success doesn't happen overnight. Let your stream happen. If you are motivated, keep doing it. Success is there for the taking if you want it. You just have to be willing enough to work for it. It's not easy. You can succeed on Twitch, but it's not going to just happen. You got to work for it.

— ZGphoto (http://twitch.tv/zgphoto)

Insults Can Sometimes Be the Highest Form of Flattery

"Don't take anything seriously. Oh, man, the number of things I've heard coming out of people's mouths. I'm not even talking about the rude stuff. Just the amount of things that people have said — you can't take it seriously. You can't take it personally. You can't let it affect you, no matter if it is good, or bad, or whatever it is. Over these three years, I've heard all sorts of stuff, dude. Every time I've hit a new growth plateau, I've had people tell me *'I hate the channel because it's changed . . .'* but hey, I can't do anything about growth. People are going to scrutinize you. If people are saying negative things about how you look, they are just projecting on themselves. That is the number one thing you have got to remember. Someone will come in and say, *'Wow, your nose is huge!'* You must really not like yourself if the only thing you have got to say about me, over something genetic, over something I have no control over, over how I look? If that is all you got, I'm doing *great!* Because you can't scrutinize anything that matters, so you're going after how I look? Realizing that changed my self-confidence big time. If all you got is *'You're ugly!'* then great, sub to me because that means I'm doing great, everything on the channel is looking great, and the game is going the best it has ever been. I mean, you should be criticizing my gameplay, which is the other 95 percent of my screen, but you're not so then I must be doing wonderful!"

— DrLupo (http://twitch.tv/drlupo)

No Matter the Time, No Matter the Place, You Always Have Someone Watching Your Back

"It feels really good to help others; it feels really good to have people to talk to, to vent to, to have an outlet . . . where you can be yourself, be accepted for yourself. But most importantly, it feels really good to give a place for people to escape whatever it is they have going on in their lives, if for only 2 minutes, and have a laugh and community. Sometimes, the important thing is just being there. One of my closest friends lost a family member, and he had been doing everything he could — as is his nature — for the rest of the family. Just giving, giving, and giving. Then one night, I get this ping online. It's him, and he said he needed to go running. Strike, raid, it didn't matter, so long as I was there, on the comms. I had to be there to help. You see, he would have done the same for me. Without question. That's family. You don't see that too many places online, but you do see it on Twitch."

— JamesWerk (http://twitch.tv/jameswerk)

When You Doubt Is the Time to Work Harder

"If you love something, if you have a passion for something, sometimes that passion diminishes, sometimes you have moments, you doubt, and you might think, *'I don't think I can do this.'* When you feel that dip is when you need to keep pushing, regardless of what other people are saying, regardless of what you think you can't do, regardless of other people holding you back. All these things I will never let anyone — including myself — do to me ever again. Twitch has inspired me to reach higher than I ever thought possible. I now believe when you reach ridiculously high for what look like impossible goals, you become stronger. Twitch has taught me to be tenacious for what I want out of life."

— Ashnichrist (http://twitch.tv/ashnichrist)

Don't Love the Game. Love the Player

The hardest thing for a Twitch streamer to understand and accept is that they themselves are enough. And that is *huge*. I learned this from my *Hearthstone* sensei, Asmodai (http://twitch.tv/asmodaitv). He's raided me, dropping 4,000 followers on my stream and leaving me to keep on streaming while hyperventilating. And talk about great timing. I was at a rough point — moving everything over to Twitch, wondering what I'll do when I age out of cosplay, what will happen when the fad dies down, all that. Well, when Asmodai raided me, I said, *'If you have any tips for me, I would love to hear them . . .'* and that was what he told me: People will like you for you. And that's not just for Twitch, but for life in general. Once you accept that your viewers are there because of you. Not for the game. Not for what you are doing. Once you accept that, then you'll grow and succeed on Twitch."

— Alkali Layke (http://twitch.tv/alkalilayke)

It's a Glimpse of How Good We Can Be

"It genuinely astounds me when people sub to my channel, send me bits, and all that. When someone drops $20 in my stream and I ask *'Really?'* and the response is *'Because you're a nice bloke and I enjoy watching you.'* Twitch is a lot like going on a blind date. There's that great unknown. You don't know what's around the corner; but on a larger scale, this whole Twitch Community is a giant selfless act. There's a lot of giving, there's a lot of generosity. Sure, there are nasty types on Twitch, too, but you know, mods will sort them out. It's the generosity of others that makes Twitch what it is and the people on Twitch — the hosts and the audience — who they are. Look at what happened with St. Jude and Twitch. Playing video games and people *watching* people play video games. And they raised all that money? That's amazing, and that's hopeful. There's so many positive people out there."

— Munch (http://twitch.tv/realmunchle)

To Thine Own Self Be True

"When people say *'Be yourself'* there is so much more to that than I ever realized. When I started to be more of myself on stream, my stream blew up. The more I was every part of myself — the nerdy stuff, the anger, the depression, everything — it brought more people that had those same feelings and interests. Being yourself to the full degree, especially when there are so many different opportunities for so many people to see you being yourself when you are broadcasting every day, it brings meaningful connections to your life based on those commonalities. The less I am afraid of hiding all I like about life, about myself, about the things I am really fascinated by, the more I connect with the people I meet and talk to because we can nerd out on stuff together. Whatever you are into, guaranteed someone else is into it, too; and the more open you are, the more likely you are to meet that person, make a true friend, and grow a solid, tight-knit community."

— SheSnaps (http://twitch.tv/shesnaps)

No, Really . . . Just Be Yourself

"No matter what, in person or online, just be yourself. I've seen a lot of people who try to fake it or create an over-the-top persona and it never works out. People want to see who you truly are. Trust who you are deep down and just be yourself."

— Power GPU (http://twitch.tv/powergpu)

Speak from the Head as Well as the Heart

"I will say it has changed the way I approach development because I am no longer talking to myself. I'm talking to an audience. They are people who want to be there. For me and my code. So I am a bit more cautious. I've had people that have asked me professional advice, about where to take their career, so I tend to put a little more thought behind my words before I speak my mind."

— Froilán Irizarry (http://twitch.tv/skfroi)

There Are a Lot of Good People Out in the World. Connect with Them

"Twitch and streaming on a whole has served as a way of meeting people that I would never think of connecting with. You can walk down the street and think, *'I am alone with so many people around me, and I would never connect with these people.'* But I have discovered so many people with so much in common. Different ages. Different backgrounds. Different careers. These are people from all over the world I would never expect to connect with. My compassion, my empathy, for others has grown, and that's an amazing thing to experience through Twitch. Sure, you have to be careful online because *The Internet*, but it can also be a beautiful place to share."

— Meadow Fox (http://twitch.tv/meadowfox)

It's Not the Tech That Matters. It's You

"Obviously you need a camera that will focus on you, a microphone that will pick up your voice clearly, a device to broadcast your stream; and once you have all those things, you are going to make your Twitch Channel succeed. Not the tech. *You.* The success or failure of your Channel is on you. Not the game you're playing. Not the prop you're making. Not even your cat walking in front of your camera — that helps, actually. Bonus points for your stream if you get them to lick themselves on stream and you are unaware of it happening behind you. Seriously though, you can be successful on Twitch but you have to *want* to do it. Schedule is everything, and you have to keep it."

— Kevin O'Connor (http://twitch.tv/td0013)

Once through the Looking Glass, What New Possibilities Await?

"There are always possibilities. There are possibilities in where Twitch can go from here, and where social media can go from here. I have never even heard of Twitch until this year, never thought of it as something that would serve as a platform for my art or for creatives; and yet here it is. So what is there going to be years from now? There is this concept of being willing to ever move and change with the times. It's so easy for me as an artist to say, *'I sit down in my quiet room and I either listen to metal music or watch my TV shows and that is as much as I want to interact with the outside world,'* but Twitch has shown me that it *is* possible to multitask. You can show people the creation process, and improve as an artist, and encourage people in their own craft while progressing in my own. There's just so many ways that so much more can be done as an artist than there ever was, and it is easy to think, *'This is as far as it's going, nothing's going to change.'* But Twitch has shown me there is possibility for everyone. It's the best time to be alive to be an artist!"

— Dawn McTigue (http://twitch.tv/dawnmctigue)

A Few Final Words from a TeeMonster . . .

What about me? What about the guy who has been managing all these words in between DLC launches, side quests, and hours of shenanigans on his stream? With all that I've shared, are there any life lessons from me that I can share in wrapping up this book?

For myself, it comes back to exploring new frontiers, even when being told you can't. When I first let people know I was streaming in the early mornings, I had a work associate come up to me one afternoon and say to me, *"Do you know why you will never get those crazy numbers on Twitch that others do?"*

REMEMBER

When someone offers you an unsolicited answer to a question you didn't ask and probably would never ask to begin with, you are going to get that answer whether you want it or not. Now, back to my story . . .

Keep in mind that while this associate of mine gamed now and then, and didn't stream, but he proceeded to tell me, *"See, you have a family, and a job, and you will never clock in the amount of hours that they do. You aren't at the skill level, and never will be, because you will never have that time investment that they do. So, yeah, harsh reality."*

My response to this was to wake up the next morning and stream.

Maybe "extended streams" will always be a special thing for me. Maybe I will never have the lightening reflexes of a Lupo, a Werk, or a Lulu. (I've always been a late bloomer, so who knows?) Maybe I will remain out of the spotlight and at the feet of Twitch gods and goddesses. That might be. That doesn't mean I stop streaming. Nor does it mean I stream with an attitude of *"It doesn't get any better than this."* And no, I don't stream thinking I can't improve. I stream because I can. I stream because I want to. I stream because I love it. When I started podcasting a decade ago, I stumbled into an incredible community and an incredible platform of creativity, expression, and passion. Now, I'm doing it all over again, this time with Twitch. The lights are up, the mic is hot, the camera's live. *Let's gooooooo!*

My life lesson from Twitch: You're never too old to get your game on.

Index

videos. *See also* video editing
  deleted, 185–186
  expired, 185–186
  importing, 189–190, 195–196
  settings for, 18–20
  templates, 137
violence, extreme, 78–79
virtual assistants. *See also* Nightbot
  add-ons, 210
  commands, 41–43
  Deepbot, 20
  Discord server and, 42
  managing Twitch stream, 41–43
  Moobot, 262
  overview, 41
  social media and, 42–43
  spam protection, 42
  Streamlabs, 41
  timers, 42
visibility, 71, 229
visitors, regular, 138
VOD (video-on-demand), 185
voice chat, 112

W

wall adornments, 153
Warning icon, 3
warranties, 97
webcams, 38
Whispers, 21
White, Alex, 177
widescreen resolution, 154
widgets, 104, 248
Wikipedia, 173
wives, prioritizing relationship with, 250–252

working blue, 78
writers, interviewing, 170

X

Xbox Kinect webcam, 38
Xbox Live accounts, 36, 37
Xbox One console
  Apps for Gamers, 54
  capture cards, 100
  hacking, 219
  overview, 93
  setting up, 34–37, 54–57, 101
  streaming from, 54–57
Xbox One X console, 34–37, 126
xMinks (user handle), 201
XSplit, 103

Y

YouTube
  channels, 148, 186–188
  clips, sharing on Discord, 235
  streams, uploading to, 69–72

Z

ZGphoto (user handle)
  achieving success, 283
  emotes from, 205, 206
  green screen, retiring, 155
  link to, 80
  multitasking and, 166
  quote from, 114
  raids with, 273–274
  titles from, 123
Zomei 18-inch LED Ring Lighting Kit, 154

About the Author

Tee Morris began his writing career with his 2002 historical epic fantasy, *MOREVI The Chronicles of Rafe & Askana*. Tee then released in 2004 *The Case of The Singing Sword: A Billibub Baddings Mystery*. It was in 2005 when his idea — podcasting a novel — established him as a pioneer in the Social Media movement, becoming the first author to podcast a book in its entirety. That experience led to the founding of Podiobooks.com (with Evo Terra and Chris Miller), and writing with Evo *Podcasting For Dummies* (with later editions featuring Chuck Tomasi). He has penned and contributed to other nonfiction titles including BenBella Books' *Farscape Forever: Sex, Drugs, and Killer Muppets* and *So Say We All: Collected Thoughts and Opinions of BATTLESTAR GALACTICA*.

In 2011, Tee Morris returned to his first love — fiction — alongside his wife, Pip Ballantine, with *Phoenix Rising: A Ministry of Peculiar Occurrences Novel* (Harper Voyager). This title went on to win the 2011 Airship Award for Best Steampunk Literature and was a finalist (the only steampunk to make the final round in any category) for Goodreads' Choice Awards under Best Science Fiction of 2011. The six-book series won the Steampunk Chronicle's Readers Choice of 2012 for Best Steampunk Literature and RT's 2015 Best Steampunk of the Year; and its companion podcast *Tales from the Archives* received the 2013 Parsec Award for Best Podcast Anthology.

In between titles, Tee plays a variety of video games including *Destiny, Detroit: Become Human*, the *Tomb Raider* series, and *Overwatch*. He established a regular Twitch schedule on September 6, 2017 and continues to develop his stream to include live podcast recordings, charity streams, and special in-studio guests. Tee can also be heard podcasting short with *The Shared Desk, Tales from the Archives*, and *Happy Hour from the Tower: A Destiny Podcast*.

Twitch For Dummies is his third title with Wiley Publishing.

Find out more about Tee Morris at www.teemorris.com.

Author's Acknowledgments

Since my first mention of the writing *Twitch For Dummies*, the outpouring of support and enthusiasm has been truly overwhelming. It would take a small book just to mention everyone who has gotten me through the ups and downs during this title's creative process. To everyone traveling in my circles on Twitch, you have made an impression on this book. A part of you is within these pages. Thank you for being there.

Still, there are three people I need to single out for making this book happen:

Matthew J Drake, mentioned a few times in this book, was the first person to tell me about Twitch. He seemed convinced it was a good fit for me. I honestly had no idea what I was getting into, but he did. I'm more than convinced he knew what journey he was setting me on. So, yeah, that. Thanks, Matt. I owe you.

Aura, there was a reason I reached out to you as my Technical Editor. I followed the stream to your Channel and first saw a gamer that I could relate to. He demanded better of himself, and it was because he believed in the game that much. Later on, I saw a streamer that demanded the same. Of course, you had to be the Technical Editor on this title. No question.

Finally, a special nod to Munch. I went from a streamer who was trying to moderate his own channel to finding out about Nightbot. Then I set up a Streamlabs hack. Every time Munch dropped into the stream, it seemed I would learn something new. Here we are, a year later, and I'm still learning new tricks from this bloke. One of the best blokes I know. He's freed me up enough so I can now work on my aim. That's another challenge for us to tackle, right?

Publisher's Acknowledgments

Acquisitions Editor: Steven Hayes

Project Editor: Tim Gallan

Production Editor: Vasanth Koilraj

Technical Editor: Aura

Cover Image: © gorodenkoff/Getty Images